First
Corinthians

First Corinthians

PHEME PERKINS

Baker Academic
a division of Baker Publishing Group
Grand Rapids, Michigan

© 2012 by Pheme Perkins

Published by Baker Academic
a division of Baker Publishing Group
PO Box 6287, Grand Rapids, MI 49516-6287
www.bakeracademic.com

Printed in the United States of America

Library of Congress Cataloging-in-Publication Data
Perkins, Pheme.
    First Corinthians / Pheme Perkins.
        p.   cm. — (Paideia: commentaries on the New Testament)
    Includes bibliographical references and index.
    ISBN 978-0-8010-3390-2 (pbk.)
    1. Bible. N.T. Corinthians, 1st—Commentaries. I. Title.
BS2675.53.P44 2012
227′.207—dc23   2011043242

12   13   14   15   16   17   18   7   6   5   4   3   2   1

Contents

Figures and Tables

Foreword

Paideia: Commentaries on the New Testament is a series that sets out to comment on the final form of the New Testament text in a way that pays due attention both to the cultural, literary, and theological settings in which the text took form and to the interests of the contemporary readers to whom the commentaries are addressed. This series is aimed squarely at students—including MA students in religious and theological studies programs, seminarians, and upper-division undergraduates—who have theological interests in the biblical text. Thus, the didactic aim of the series is to enable students to understand each book of the New Testament as a literary whole rooted in a particular ancient setting and related to its context within the New Testament.

The name "Paideia" (Greek for "education") reflects (1) the instructional aim of the series—giving contemporary students a basic grounding in academic New Testament studies by guiding their engagement with New Testament texts; (2) the fact that the New Testament texts as literary unities are shaped by the educational categories and ideas (rhetorical, narratological, etc.) of their ancient writers and readers; and (3) the pedagogical aims of the texts themselves—their central aim being not simply to impart information but to form the theological convictions and moral habits of their readers.

Each commentary deals with the text in terms of larger rhetorical units; these are not verse-by-verse commentaries. This series thus stands within the stream of recent commentaries that attend to the final form of the text. Such reader-centered literary approaches are inherently more accessible to liberal arts students without extensive linguistic and historical-critical preparation than older exegetical approaches, but within the reader-centered world the sanest practitioners have paid careful attention to the extratext of the original readers, including not only these readers' knowledge of the geography, history, and other contextual elements reflected in the text but also their ability to respond correctly to the literary and rhetorical conventions used in the text. Paideia commentaries pay deliberate attention to this extratextual repertoire in order to highlight the ways in which the text is designed to persuade and move its readers. Each rhetorical unit is explored from three angles: (1) introductory matters; (2) tracing the train of thought or narrative or rhetorical flow of the argument; and (3) theological issues raised by the text that are of interest to the contemporary Christian. Thus, the primary focus remains on the text and not its historical context or its interpretation in the secondary literature.

Our authors represent a variety of confessional points of view: Protestant, Catholic, and Orthodox. What they share, beyond being New Testament scholars of national and international repute, is a commitment to reading the biblical text as theological documents within their ancient contexts. Working within the broad parameters described here, each author brings his or her own considerable exegetical talents and deep theological commitments to the task of laying bare the interpretation of Scripture for the faith and practice of God's people everywhere.

Mikeal C. Parsons
Charles H. Talbert

Preface

Lay readers often complain that they cannot understand what Paul is saying in the passage assigned for a given Sunday. A brief explanation before the service enables them to present his message intelligibly. The emphasis on laying out the biblical author's train of thought, which the editors of the Paideia series have set as the goal of these commentaries, should answer many such questions.

Working through all of 1 Corinthians under that mandate brings to light the subtlety of Paul's approach to highly charged issues in the life of the church. At the end of the day, some passages remain ambiguous. The reader must make choices about Paul's tone: harsh or conciliatory, humorous or sarcastic, siding with one group or another. One must also imagine how his words might have been received by the very diverse audience in first-century Corinth. I have explained the rationale for my choices on these issues as they emerge in the course of commenting on the letter. Different sets of assumptions produce very different images of the apostle's relationship to the church in Corinth.

Much of what I know about Paul and the Corinthians is thanks to conversations over the years with Fr. Jerome Murphy-O'Connor, OP; Fr. Joseph A. Fitzmyer, SJ; and Fr. Raymond Collins. My debts to their written work are reflected in what follows. However, my biggest debt in reading Paul is owed to my first academic encounter with New Testament studies, when the late Krister Stendahl, former dean of Harvard Divinity School and Bishop of Stockholm, gave a nineteen-year-old a reading list. But more important for this project were three basic lessons Krister repeated over many years: the NT never quite means what you (or the pious) think it does, all the little details of language matter, and the Bible is the church's book. Its best interpretation nourishes and expands faith by pruning the tree.

August 8, 2011
Feast of St. Dominic

Abbreviations

General

AT	author's translation	OT	Old Testament
ca.	*circa*, approximately	trans.	translator/translated by
cf.	compare	vol(s).	volume(s)
e.g.	*exempli gratia*, for example	x	following a numeral indicates
i.e.	*id est*, that is		times, number of occurrences
NT	New Testament		

Bible Texts and Versions

LXX	Septuagint
NA²⁷	*Novum Testamentum Graece*. Edited by [E. and E. Nestle and] B. Aland et al. 27th rev. ed. Stuttgart: Deutsche Bibelgesellschaft, 1993.
NETS	*A New English Translation of the Septuagint*. Edited by A. Pietersma and B. G. Wright. New York: Oxford University Press, 2007.
NRSV	New Revised Standard Version

Ancient Corpora

OLD TESTAMENT

		Deut.	Deuteronomy
Gen.	Genesis	Josh.	Joshua
Exod.	Exodus	Judg.	Judges
Lev.	Leviticus	Ruth	Ruth
Num.	Numbers	1–2 Sam.	1–2 Samuel

1–2 Kings	1–2 Kings	Sir.	Sirach
1–2 Chron.	1–2 Chronicles	Wis.	Wisdom of Solomon
Ezra	Ezra		
Neh.	Nehemiah	**NEW TESTAMENT**	
Esther	Esther	Matt.	Matthew
Job	Job	Mark	Mark
Ps./Pss.	Psalm/Psalms	Luke	Luke
Prov.	Proverbs	John	John
Eccles.	Ecclesiastes	Acts	Acts
Song	Song of Songs	Rom.	Romans
Isa.	Isaiah	1–2 Cor.	1–2 Corinthians
Jer.	Jeremiah	Gal.	Galatians
Lam.	Lamentations	Eph.	Ephesians
Ezek.	Ezekiel	Phil.	Philippians
Dan.	Daniel	Col.	Colossians
Hosea	Hosea	1–2 Thess.	1–2 Thessalonians
Joel	Joel	1–2 Tim.	1–2 Timothy
Amos	Amos	Titus	Titus
Obad.	Obadiah	Philem.	Philemon
Jon.	Jonah	Heb.	Hebrews
Mic.	Micah	James	James
Nah.	Nahum	1–2 Pet.	1–2 Peter
Hab.	Habakkuk	1–3 John	1–3 John
Zeph.	Zephaniah	Jude	Jude
Hag.	Haggai	Rev.	Revelation
Zech.	Zechariah		
Mal.	Malachi	**DEAD SEA SCROLLS**	
		1QH	*Thanksgiving Hymns*
DEUTEROCANONICAL BOOKS		1QM	*War Scroll*
1–2 Esd.	1–2 Esdras	1QpHab	*Pesher on Habakkuk*
1–4 Macc.	1–4 Maccabees	1QS	*Community Rule*
		1QSa	*Community Rule, Appendix A*

Reference Works, Series, and Collections

BDAG	*A Greek-English Lexicon of the New Testament and Other Early Christian Literature.* By W. Bauer. Rev. and ed. F. W. Danker, W. F. Arndt, and F. W. Gingrich. 3rd ed. Chicago: University of Chicago Press, 2000.
CIL	*Corpus inscriptionum latinarum*
LCL	Loeb Classical Library
OTP	*Old Testament Pseudepigrapha.* Edited by James H. Charlesworth. 2 vols. Garden City, NY: Doubleday, 1983–85.

First
Corinthians

Introduction

Christianity in an Urban Setting

Much of Jesus's ministry took place in the small villages and towns of rural Galilee. The movement he founded established itself in cities (Furnish 1988). Peter and the other disciples had moved to Jerusalem before Paul's conversion from foe to apostle in about AD 34 (Gal. 1:13–17). By that time believers could be found in the Jewish communities of Damascus and Antioch in Syria. Several years later disturbances over a certain "Chrestus" in the synagogues of Rome led Emperor Claudius (41–54) to expel those responsible from the city. Some scholars associate the expulsion with the emperor's attempt to pacify the Jewish community during the first year of his reign. If so, the gospel had reached Rome by 41 (Murphy-O'Connor 1996). Most scholars credit a tradition found in later church historians that places the expulsion in 49 (Lampe 2003). The statement in Acts 18:2 that Claudius banned *all Jews* from Rome is hardly credible. Banishing persons held responsible for civic disturbances was routine practice.

Consequently Aquila and Prisca must have been preaching the gospel in Roman synagogues to have been exiled from the city. Like Paul, they were *skēnopoioi* ("tent

> ### Claudius Takes Action
>
> *"He expelled from Rome Jews who were rioting repeatedly at the instigation of Chrestus."* (Suetonius, *Claudius* 25.4 AT)
>
> *"... a certain Jew named Aquila of Pontus and his wife Priscilla, who had recently arrived from Italy on account of Claudius's order to expel all the Jews from Rome."* (Acts 18:2 AT)

or awning makers"), and had transported their trade to Corinth (Acts 18:3). Some scholars assume that one should consider them to have been leatherworkers, making anything from tents to harnesses to sandal thongs, but there is no reason not to employ the traditional meaning of the Greek word. Inscriptions provide evidence for an association of tent makers (*collegium tabernaclariorum*) in Rome (Barrett 1998, 863). In addition to the routine use of tents or awnings for shade and shelter in theaters and arenas and by travelers, the biannual Isthmian Games, which took place outside Corinth, provided plenty of opportunity for such artisans.

Workshops excavated along the north market area of Corinth are only eight to thirteen feet wide. Stone stairs and a ladder lead up to a loft, where an unglazed window with wood shutters provided the only light except what came in through the doorway. As their lodger, Paul would have had to sleep among the shop tools on the ground floor (Murphy-O'Connor 1996, 263). Apostolic hardships such as relentless toil, sleepless nights, cold, hunger, and lack of sufficient clothing (2 Cor. 11:27) represent daily life for workers. Men and women, free persons and slaves often toiled side by side. Women are mentioned in trades associated with textiles and food shops or as lessees of inherited pottery shops, vineyards, or other agricultural facilities (Rowlandson 1998, 218–79). Though the educated elite considered the slave-like conditions of laborers demeaning, tombstone inscriptions refer to an artisan's trade with pride (Thomas 2005). Prisca would have worked alongside her husband and Paul making and repairing the tents and awnings out of coarsely woven cloth or leather.

This social setting is the urban equivalent to that of Jesus's original followers—a movement that took hold among those who worked at trades. Scholars use such slender hints about occupation, travel, and background to assess the economic and social position of the earliest Christians (Horrell 2006). Had they drawn from the most destitute rural or urban poor, Christians would not have had the means to carry their message between cities and to engage in the network of communication between churches that is so evident in the Pauline letters (M. Thompson 1998). One should not, however, imagine that these first believers belonged to a comfortable middle class, assured of sufficient food, some leisure, and future well-being. At best some 3–4 percent of the total population comprised the wealthy elite classes, the imperial household, senatorial families, regional kings, members of the equestrian class, and provincial and municipal elite families. Some freedmen, wealthy merchants, and retired military commanders might have joined their ranks. An additional 7 percent—merchants, veterans, those able to employ others in larger workshops—could be considered comfortable, that is, able to provide their families with more than the basic needs for food and shelter. If the destitute comprised about 28 percent

The Social Standing of Artisans

"While we delight in the work, we despise the workman . . . for it does not of necessity follow that, if the work delights you with its graces, the one who wrought it is worthy of your esteem." (Plutarch, *Pericles* 1.4–2.2, trans. LCL)

"Their trades, however, were petty, laborious, and barely able to provide them with just enough." (Lucian, *Fugitivi* 12, trans. LCL)

of the population, that leaves the remaining 65 percent at or near subsistence level. Such folk comprised the overwhelming majority in Pauline churches. The few individuals who had sufficient wealth to be patrons of the apostle or the community as a whole belonged either to the 7 percent just below the elite or to a higher end of the "above subsistence" group (Friesen 2005).

Paul's participation in the manual labor at local workshops created a bond of solidarity with believers in Thessalonica (1 Thess. 2:9). Like a loving father, the apostle had their interests at heart (Ascough 2003; Bartchy 2003). But such labor drew persistently harsh criticism from some Christians in Corinth (1 Cor. 4:10–12; 9:8–18; 2 Cor. 11:7; Marshall 1987). Apparently the apostle could have been supported by wealthier Christians in Corinth. There was no need for him to engage in such socially demeaning activities. Paul even agrees with the status judgments behind this criticism. His labors put him among the masses who are considered beneath notice by the 10–15 percent of the population considered elite or at least well off. Many of the problems he faces in Corinth involve the clash between such human criteria and God's perspective revealed on the cross (Theissen 1982; Marcus 2006). He must persuade his audience that those who live in Christ no longer live by the routine standards of their culture.

Why is the situation much more divisive in Corinth than in the less prosperous churches of Macedonia (2 Cor. 8:1–6)? Paul's sarcastic description of their pretensions (1 Cor. 4:6–13; Du Toit 1994) suggests that the Corinthians identify with the values of the civic elite even though few could claim membership in the upper classes by either birth or wealth (1:26–31). Scholars attribute this impulse to the economic and social dynamism of first-century AD Corinth.

Figure 1. The Diolkos at Corinth. This track for hauling cargo across the isthmus from Cenchreae to Lechaion made it possible to transport wares from the Aegean Sea to the Adriatic without circumnavigating the Peloponnesus.

After lying in near ruin for almost a century, the city had been refounded by Julius Caesar in 44 BC. Veterans and other colonists from Rome settled there. Some new inhabitants may have been from Rome's Jewish population, descendants of those brought to Rome as slaves by Roman armies. Others may have arrived when Emperor Tiberius expelled Jews and Egyptians from Rome (Tacitus, *Annales* 2.45.4; Josephus, *Antiquitates judaicae* 18.65–84). Prisca and Aquila might have known Jewish immigrants in Corinth. With harbors on both the eastern (Cenchreae) and western (Lechaion) side of the isthmus, Corinth served as a transit point for goods being shipped across the Mediterranean. It was safer to haul a ship's cargo on the track between the two ports, the Diolkos, than risk a sea voyage around the Peloponnesus. By the first century AD the city was a major economic hub in the eastern Mediterranean, owing its considerable wealth to the goods and services it supplied to merchants and other visitors (Engels 1990). It served as the capital of the Roman province of Achaia.

A city that was rebuilding and expanding had room for ambitious merchants and artisans to push forward into that 7 percent of comfortable means. Since

Figure 2. Erastus Inscription. A paved limestone area east of the theater at Corinth included this inscription: "Erastus paved this at his own expense in return for the aedileship."

Corinth did not have a long-established group of aristocratic families as its "first citizens," some recent arrivals might even aspire to join the ranks of the "municipal elite" with the help of newly acquired wealth and marriage into a prominent family. History preserves a tantalizing bit of evidence that one such individual could have belonged to the church. Paul sends greetings to those in Rome from a certain Erastus, a steward or financial officer (*oikonomos*) of Corinth (Rom. 16:23). East of the theater, an area of paved limestone included an inscription identifying its donor, Erastus, as an aedile. The aediles were responsible for supervising the city's markets and other commercial functions. If this Erastus is the same man, he has moved up to a higher civil office. Several factors favor the identification. Erastus is not a common name. Since no formal patronymic is given, the person in question was probably a wealthy freedman. Some scholars wonder how a Christian could serve in a public office that required participation in civic religious activities (Bookidis 2005; Turcan 2000). But some believers had few scruples in that regard (1 Cor. 10). Therefore it is quite likely that the Erastus of Rom. 16:23 became an aedile in Corinth (Jewett 2007, 980–83).

The workshop setting provides more than clues about the socioeconomic demography of Pauline churches. Evangelization probably occurred in that context as well (Hock 1980). Jewish synagogues provided instruction in the law and ancestral traditions. Roman inscriptions refer to individuals as "teacher of the law" (*nomodidaskalos*), "teacher and student of the law" (*didaskalos kai nomomathētēs*), and "student of wise men" (*mathētēs sophōn*). Philo notes that the "ancestral philosophy" (*patrios philosophia*) was taught in Rome's synagogues (*Legatio ad Gaium* 156; Lampe 2003, 78). Pious gentiles associated with local synagogues, which provided Christians with the first non-Jewish believers. But measures taken against Jews in Rome under Claudius either severely restricted or terminated Christian recruiting in the synagogues (Lampe 2003, 14–15, 69–70). Acts 18:4–8 imagines a similar forced separation between Christian sympathizers and other Jews at Corinth. Although Paul shifted his preaching to the nearby home of a gentile god-fearer, Titus Justus, tensions with the local synagogue persisted. After some eighteen months

---

Dream Visions of Asclepius

"Arata, a Spartan, suffering from dropsy. On her behalf her mother slept in the sanctuary while she stayed in Sparta. It seemed to her that the god cut off her daughter's head and hung her body with the neck downwards. After a considerable amount of water had flowed out, he released the body and put the head back on her neck. After she saw this dream she returned to Sparta and found that her daughter had recovered and seen the same dream."

"An anonymous woman from Troezen, for children. She fell asleep and saw a dream. The god seemed to say that she would bear children and asked her whether she wanted a boy or a girl. She said that she wanted a boy and after that within a year a son was born to her."

(Lefkowitz and Fant 2005, 286–87)

---

during which Paul established the nucleus of the Corinthian church, the apostle was charged before a disinterested Roman proconsul and left the city (18:9–17), taking Prisca and Aquila along and leaving them in Ephesus (18:18–19).

The story as Luke tells it has been shaped by the assumptions of a more elite audience. Christian preaching does not pose any threat of civic discord. A dispute over teaching causes Paul to shift to the household of a private individual, often the context for itinerant philosophers in the Roman world. The Roman proconsul refuses to intervene in an argument about Jewish matters. In short, the social stigma of a fractious movement among the city's artisan class has been omitted from the story. Though Acts has not forgotten Paul's trade, the workshop plays no role in spreading the gospel. In addition, its version of the story enhances the significance of moving from synagogue to private home with a dream vision. This divine oracle strengthens the apostle and demonstrates that his ministry is unfolding according to God's plan (18:9–10). Both residents and visitors would have been familiar with dream oracles at the sanctuary of the healing god, Asclepius. The complex was located outside the city four hundred yards north of the theater, near the spring of Lerna (Fotopoulos 2006). Mass-produced, terra-cotta body parts were dedicated by those who had been successfully cured. Local artisans must have supplied these items as well as other services required by visitors to the sanctuary.

Urban Pleasures

Corinth, which overlooked the entire isthmus from its acropolis, dominated land traffic between central Greece and the Peloponnesus, just as its two ports

Figure 3. Fountain of Peirene. This fountain provided a gathering spot for lounging and talking.

linked by the Diolkos controlled east-west sea trade. Two natural features enhanced the pleasure a traveler might feel upon arriving in Corinth: its fertile agricultural plain and its abundant water. Natural springs, Roman baths, and public fountains made good use of the water supply. The Fountain of Peirene, a gathering spot since classical times (Euripides, *Medea* 68–69), was rebuilt in the Roman period to provide a square, arched courtyard for lounging and talking. In the early second century, the wealthy family of a Corinthian orator, Antonius Sospes, paid for the impressive white marble veneer (Pausanias, *Graeciae descriptio* 2.3.3; Mee and Spawforth 2001, 154–55). The waters of the fountain were thought to flow from a spring on the acropolis, which always had clear, potable water (Strabo, *Geographica* 8.6). Legend had it that Bellerophon captured Pegasus as the winged horse drank from the spring.

Today nothing remains of the temple to the goddess Aphrodite, which stood near the spring on the Acropolis. Sailors passing through the city's ports allegedly flocked there for less noble pleasures, including its many prostitutes. There is no evidence of temple prostitutes in Roman times. The women frequented by some of Paul's addressees (1 Cor. 6:12–20) plied their trade elsewhere in the city, such as in public baths and bars. Selling both female and male prostitutes was a regular part of the commercial slave trade in any ancient city.

Corinth was prone to earthquakes because its gulf lies between fault lines. A temple to the god Poseidon stood in Isthmia from the sixth century BC into Roman times. Herodes Atticus, a second-century AD Athenian orator, endowed the Roman temple with a colossal ivory and gold sculpture of Poseidon and Amphitrite in a four-horse chariot to replace the earlier marble sculpture of the same theme. The biannual Isthmian Games, whose victors received a celery wreath, began in the sixth century BC. After the Romans destroyed the classical city, the games were moved to neighboring Sikyon (146 BC), whose inhabitants also continued to farm the Corinthian plain. Emperor Nero returned the games to the traditional site for his own performances in the musical, heraldic, and acting competitions as well as chariot racing (AD 66; Champlin 2003, 54–58). Paul's audience would have associated his athletic metaphors with the local contests. The "perishable crown" (1 Cor. 9:25) of these athletes was not our Olympic gold, but celery or pine.

The city possessed facilities for various other entertainments. Its ancient theater was rebuilt for stage performances in the first century AD. Reconstruc-

Figure 4. The Acrocorinth. The Acropolis in Corinth overlooked the entire isthmus, positioning Corinth to control northwest land traffic up and down the isthmus as well as cross-isthmus traffic on the Diolkos.

tions to accommodate such Roman spectacles as wild beast hunts and aquatic shows did not occur until the third century AD. Erastus may have supervised public theater expenses as part of his aedileship (Engels 1990, 18). A smaller, covered building nearby, the Odeion, provided musical and poetic recitations until it was converted to an arena in the third century. Thus some of the characteristically Roman entertainments associated with the arena may not have been a routine part of civic life in first-century Corinth as in the second and third centuries (Apuleius, *Metamorphoses* 10.28–35; L. White 2005). Many exegetes doubt that Paul's remark about "fighting with beasts in Ephesus" (1 Cor. 15:32) refers to an encounter in the arena.

> ## Aphrodite's Prostitutes
>
> *"The sanctuary of Aphrodite was so wealthy that it possessed as temple-slaves more than a thousand prostitutes who were dedicated to the goddess both by men and by women. And so, by reason of them, the city was thronged and enriched; for the sailors spent their money easily, and on that account the proverb says, 'Not for every man is the voyage to Corinth.'"* (Strabo, *Geographica* 8.6.21, trans. Mee and Spawforth 2001, 158–59)

Competitions in singing and tragic acting kept the poetry and myth of the classical world alive in the eyes and ears of Roman audiences. Roman theater developed popular comic forms of mime in which such lowly born characters as slaves, idiots, the useless philosopher, adulterers, disobedient sons, and assorted rogues take advantage of their betters. Such performances were not confined to the theater or homes of the wealthy elite. Traveling mime troops might set up a temporary wooden stage in the marketplace (Welborn 2005, 7–9). Paul might have manipulated some of the familiar characters and plots of the comic stage in confronting Corinthian pride with a fool's persona. Is he the anxious parent annoyed with the delinquent son whose lack of progress is abetted by the slave pedagogue in 1 Cor. 4:14–21, perhaps (Welborn 2005, 86–87)?

Rhetorical competition not only served to advance the public career of those who could afford such training but also provided entertainment. Paul's Corinthian audience appears to have been enamored of such verbal virtuosity ("wisdom of words"; 1 Cor. 1:20–21; 2:1–5; Betz 2004). A young man who had been away studying with a famous orator in Athens, Alexandria, or Antioch would be expected to put on a display for his fellow citizens upon returning to his hometown. Afraid of failure, some pupils of the famous fourth-century rhetorician Libanius even delayed their return home (Cribiore 2007, 84–91). Of course, the teacher had as much to gain or lose with the young man's performance in the theatrical display piece. A star would bring others from that town's elite to his school. A failure meant dishonor for even the most famous teacher. For those who had endured such rites of passage, Paul's

Nero's Acting Parts

"Among his performances were Canace in Childbirth, Orestes the Matricide, Oedipus Blinded, and Distraught Hercules. There is a story that a young recruit on guard recognized him in the rags and fetters demanded by the part of Hercules and dashed forward to his assistance." (Suetonius, *Nero* 21 AT)

remark that he came preaching "in weakness, fear, and much trembling" (2:3) would have suggested a first performance that crashed under pressure. Paul's weaknesses as a public orator continued to be a bone of contention with some in Corinth (2 Cor. 10:1–2). Of course, as the previous demographic discussion indicates, neither Paul nor his audience belonged to the elite for whom such training was an option. They gained their knowledge of its requirements as audiences for such public displays of oratory.

Religious Activities in the City

Corinth's religious monuments, temple buildings, altars, precincts, statuary, and sacred places—the Asclepeion, temple to Aphrodite, temple of Poseidon in Isthmia, and a sacred spring—were as important to the ancient city as its other public buildings. First-century visitors to the forum in Corinth would have found other sites from the classical period that had been restored or rebuilt by the Roman-period settlers as well as new temples that reflected their Roman heritage. One temple was dedicated to Apollo, another to the oracle of Apollo at Claros in Asia Minor. Next to the latter one could find a temple dedicated to Venus as the ancestress of Julius Caesar and his descendants. A sanctuary

Congratulating a Successful Student

"To Julianus.

It is because I predicted this that I urged you to return to your fatherland. You were an excellent orator but a coward. . . . I think yours is a city of good men who honor you like a god. Many other cities are not aware of the virtue of their citizens or . . . resent it; this one, however, recognized your talents, rejoiced, celebrated, and adorned you with honors in the theater. . . . The joy that these events brought you is the same as the joy the things written in your letter brought me. But besides the facts themselves, the length of the letter and its charm was showing that I am the father of a good child. Your letter is a greater gift to me than if you had sold most of your land and sent me the money." (Libanius, F1130; trans. Cribiore 2007, 287–88) dedicated to Demeter and Kore was located on the Acrocorinth (Pausanias, *Graeciae descriptio* 2.4.7). Activity at the site dedicated to the oldest of the Greek mysteries picked up in the mid-first century AD. A much larger temple was dedicated to either Augustus's sister Octavia or Jupiter Capitolinus (Mee and Spawforth 2001, 150–54). In addition to appearing in temples, statues of gods and goddesses such as Apollo, Athena, and Aphrodite could be found in public areas.

Excavators found a broken inscription in Greek, "synagogue of the Hebrews," from a much later period (fourth century AD). With earthquakes, looting, and the common practice of reusing marble for other purposes, finding a late inscription along the Lechaion road does not help locate the first-century AD synagogue. Other bits of marble decoration, seven-branched candlesticks, palm branches, and citron belong to the fifth century AD.

The Egyptian goddess Isis, popular with sailors, had a temple complex in Cenchreae.

Figure 5. The Egyptian God Sarapis. This life-size marble head, found in the South Stoa at Corinth, dates to the first century AD.

Her temple at Pompeii dates from the second century AD, and that on the Campus Martius from 43 BC, despite imperial suspicions of foreign cults. A famous fresco from Herculaneum depicts priests of Isis performing religious ceremonies. Her cult at Corinth was immortalized in the *Golden Ass*, a novel by the second-century AD orator Apuleius. The novel's hero has been turned into an ass thanks to a misadventure with a love potion. After a series of treacherous adventures, this "human" ass prays to the "Queen of Heaven," whichever form the goddess takes. Isis appears in his dream, claiming to be the divine power behind the universe and all the goddesses. She instructs him to seek the procession of Isis worshipers the next day. The celebrations mark the beginning of the season when it is safe for ships to put to sea. There, instructed by the goddess in a dream, the main priest gives the ass his rose garland to eat and so restores Lucius to his human form. Further initiations into the mysteries of Isis follow. The goddess promises initiates who have descended to Hades and returned a blessed afterlife and freedom from fate in this life (Apuleius, *Metamorphoses* 11).

Her male priests are represented with shaved heads and are clad in white linen. A final sign of Lucius's complete devotion in the novel was a willingness to resume his rhetorical practice in Rome's law courts with a shaved head (*Metamorphoses* 11.30). Priestesses wore long hair and a fringed mantle tied

Erich Lessing/Art Resource, NY

Figure 6. The Rites of Isis. A wall painting at Herculaneum depicts priests of Isis performing religious ceremonies.

in a characteristic knot, often carrying the characteristic sistrum rattle and the situla vessel holding a libation of milk or water. Participation in mysteries or other rituals might require such preliminaries as washing in a river, sacred stream, or sanctuary pool and abstaining from sexual relations for a short period. Paul's advice to married couples includes the latter element (1 Cor. 7:5; Oster 1992; Wimbush 1987).

Though initiation into the mystery cults was secret and, according to Apuleius, expensive even for someone at the lower end of the elite scale, the elaborate public processions staged by devotees could be witnessed by outsiders. Various artistic representations from classical to Roman times depict the processions in which an animal was conducted to the altar of sacrifice. They might include women carrying holy things on their heads, a man or boy leading the animal, instrument players, persons carrying wreaths or lustral branches, and a jug containing the wine for the libation (Connelly 2007, 168–70).

What happened to the cow, ox, or sheep being led off to a sacrificial altar? Much of the animal remained to be consumed by those participating or was sold in the market. Both options raised questions for Corinthian believers. Apparently "sacrificial meat" was so designated when sold in the market. Perhaps the "blemish free" and "no stress reaction" required for such animals made their meat desirable. Could believers buy such meat or consume it if it

Satirical Account of Isis Devotees

"In winter she'll break the ice, enter the river, be immersed three times in the morning Tiber... then she'll crawl, naked and trembling across the whole field of the proud king [Campus Martius]. If white Io so orders, she'll go to the ends of Egypt and bring back the required water... so that she can sprinkle it in the shrine of Isis which stands next to the ancient sheep pens. For she believes, she is instructed by the voice of the mistress <i.e., Isis> herself—being no doubt just the sort of person, in soul and mind, to whom gods would speak in the night! That is why the one who deserves the special, highest honors is Anubis, since he runs about jeering amongst the linen-clad, bald crew of people lamenting <the death of Osiris>. And it's he <Anubis> who begs forgiveness for a wife, whenever she fails to abstain from sex on the forbidden sacred days and incurs the great penalty for wrong-doing between the sheets, and whenever the silver snake is seen to move his head. His tears and practised mutterings do the trick: Osiris does not refuse forgiveness for her guilt—bribed, of course, by a fat goose and a fine sacrificial cake." (Juvenal, *Satirae* 6.522–41, trans. Beard, North, and Price 1998, 2:302)

was served at a private dinner? What about the banquets associated with the sacrifice at a temple itself? Some Christians had no problem with eating such meat or attending the banquets (1 Cor. 8; 10; P. W. Gooch 1987; Phua 2005). For Jewish believers, the issue would never arise, since the meat in question was not kosher. In fact, most people rarely had meat in their diet. Sacrificial meat distributed on a special civic or private occasion might be the only form meat-eating ever took (Theissen 1982). The religious diversity of Roman Corinth becomes even more complex when social and economic differences enter the picture.

First Corinthians 8:10 and 10:19–22 assume that the sacrificial banquet occurred within the temple complex of the god or goddess to whom the animal had been sacrificed. Literary references to such meals are common, though visual depictions are infrequent. Terse invitations to banquets have been discovered. Archeologists have been hard put to find the "temple dining rooms" referred to in 1 Corinthians (Fotopoulos 2006). Sometimes storage rooms have been taken as such. The Asclepeion complex does include a building with dining rooms at a level lower than that of the temple courtyard itself. Blackened stones suggest that cooking occurred in the center of the rooms. The colonnaded courtyard outside the rooms provided shade and a place for guests to stroll. With that setup it would be easy for others not invited to the feast to observe who was present, as 1 Cor. 8:10 suggests. This setting was much less public than the processions and sacrifices that took place in the city center or at one of the harbors. Some scholars imagine that the Asclepeion functioned

Figure 7. Animals for Sacrifice. This procession with animals being led to sacrifice appears on a small frieze from the inner altar of the Ara Pacis.

as more of a "local country club" for the wealthy elite than a public facility (Fant and Reddish 2003, 60–61). If so, those to whom Paul's words are directed comprise a tiny minority of the church as a whole.

Gallio as Proconsul

Paul's letters lack indications of a date, such as references to Roman rulers or to the civic calendar. Even piecing together a relative chronology based on the travel plans of Paul and his associates mentioned in the letters leaves so many gaps that scholars come up with very different solutions to dating. The account of Paul's initial visit to Corinth in Acts 18 provides some historical clues. Luke assumes that Paul arrived in Corinth from an unsuccessful mission in Athens (also mentioned in 1 Thess. 3:1), shortly after Prisca and Aquila were exiled from Rome by Claudius (Acts 18:2). Despite the efforts of some scholars to push that edict back to 41, the generally accepted date of 49 stands (Fitzmyer 2008, 37–39). Therefore Paul's mission in Corinth began in about 50.

Paul had been evangelizing for some time before Jews opposed to his message dragged him before the Roman proconsul, Lucius Junius Gallio Annaeus (Acts 18:12–13). Luke depicts Gallio as disinterested. It is more likely that he followed the policy of Claudius and simply banished troublemakers from the city. Roman proconsuls were dispatched to govern a province for a year. Knowing when Gallio served would provide a date for Paul's expulsion from the city. Fragments of an inscription at Delphi open up the possibility of assigning dates to Gallio's term of office. The inscription records an edict in a letter from Emperor Claudius to the city's leaders. As governor of the region, Gallio had informed Claudius that Delphi was losing population among the local elite, who were needed to manage the affairs of a city.

The formulaic language of imperial edicts makes the reconstruction of this badly broken text almost certain. How long it took Claudius to respond and

Claudius's Edit

"Tiber[ius Claudius Caes]ar A[ugust]us G[ermanicus, invested with tribunician po]wer [for the 12th time, acclaimed imperator for t]he 26th time, F[ather of the Fa]ther[land . . . sends greetings to . . .]. For a l[ong time I have been not onl]y [well disposed toward t]he ci[ty] of Delph[i, but also solicitous for its pros]perity, and I have always sup[ported th]e cul[t of Pythian] Apol[lo. But] now [since] it is said to be desti[tu]te of [citi]zens, as [L. Jun]ius Gallio, my fri[end] an[d procon]sul, [recently reported to me, and being desirous that Delphi] should continue to retain [inta]ct its for[mer rank, I] or[der you (plural) to in]vite [well-born people also from ot]her cities [to Delphi as new inhabitants and to] all[ow] them [and their children to have all the] privi[leges of Del]phi as being citi[zens on equal and like (basis)." (trans. Fitzmyer 2008, 41)

whether Gallio was still proconsul when this edict arrived in Delphi, we do not know. Claudius's twelfth regnal year began in January 52. A proconsul would head from Rome for his province as soon as the spring sailing season permitted travel, likely in April. After a year's service, he would have to return no later than September/October to avoid dangerous travel. How far into the year 52 was this edict composed? The acclamation "emperor" did not occur at any specific interval. It was often associated with an event that could be construed as a victory. Other inscriptions help scholars date the acclamations during the reign of Claudius. The twenty-sixth acclamation mentioned here must have occurred before August 52.

Those clues narrow down the possibilities for Gallio's term as proconsul. He arrived either in June 51 to serve until fall 52 or in June 52 and reported

www.HolyLandPhotos.org

Figure 8. Gallio Inscription. This fragmentary Greek inscription from the temple of Apollo at Delphi mentions Gallio in connection with datable historical circumstances, enabling us to date his proconsulship to AD 52.

about Delphi shortly thereafter. Gallio did not complete his term as governor of Achaia. His younger brother was Seneca, the famous Stoic philosopher and tutor to a young Nero. Seneca notes that his brother cut his term short and hurried home to Italy after catching a fever that he attributed to the unhealthy climate (*Epistulae morales* 104.2). Therefore Gallio actually served only a few months as proconsul. Assuming that Claudius sent the edict concerning Delphi while Gallio was still in office narrows the date for Paul's appearance before Gallio to summer or early fall 52 (Fitzmyer 2008, 40–42). Paul may have left Corinth for Asia Minor from its eastern port at about the same time that Gallio decided to sail back to Rome from the western one. Gallio was suffect consul at Rome in 55 or 56. Shortly after Paul was martyred there under Nero (64?), suspicions that Seneca had been involved in a failed plot to assassinate Nero led both brothers to commit suicide (65).

Dating 1 Corinthians

After Paul's departure from Corinth, Ephesus becomes the center of his activities (Acts 18:23). Paul makes his final journey through Asia Minor and Macedonia back to Corinth in about 57–58. The travel plans in Rom. 15:14–33 indicate that Paul considers his mission in Asia Minor and Greece accomplished. After taking the collection from his gentile converts to believers in Jerusalem (spring 58?), he intends to visit Rome en route to a new effort in Spain. Assigning plausible dates to the letters, visits by Paul or his associates, and other communications that went back and forth between Paul and Corinth in those years is a complicated puzzle. The accuracy of Luke's information about Paul's journeys continues to be disputed, since it fits awkwardly with clues in Paul's own letters. At least two letters that Paul sent to Corinth were not preserved. One written prior to our 1 Corinthians had been misunderstood by the recipients (5:9). The other, a "letter of tears," was fired off after a brief, disastrous visit to Corinth during which Paul was humiliated by a member of the community (2 Cor. 2:1; 12:14, 21; 13:1–2). In addition, our canonical 2 Corinthians may have been the composite of several shorter letters Paul sent to Corinth.

Paul tells us that he is writing 1 Corinthians from Ephesus, where he intends to stay until Pentecost (1 Cor. 16:8). Perhaps the phrase "Christ our Passover has been sacrificed" (5:7) also points to the time at which Paul writes. If one allows for the travel back to Judea and Antioch mentioned in Acts 18, along with the earlier exchange of letters and a visit by Timothy overland through Macedonia, then early spring 55 or 56 is a plausible date for the composition of 1 Corinthians. Scholars who discount Acts or push the appearance before Gallio back a year opt for an earlier date (ca. 54; Murphy-O'Connor 1996, 184). In any event, Paul would have spent much of the spring and summer of the year in question preoccupied with problems in Corinth.

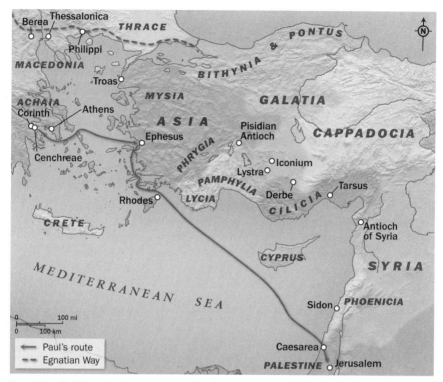

Figure 9. Map of Paul's Journey East from Corinth, according to Acts 18:18–19:1.

Communicating by Letter

With the advent of global electronic communication, the expression "snail mail" is used for a communication between two parties dispatched on paper or a comparable medium. For the ancient world the speed and reliability of "snail mail" would have been quite astonishing. Though kings and emperors had systems of couriers to convey official documents across their empires, private letters had to wait until there were travelers headed in the desired direction. Wealthy individuals might dispatch slaves to convey a letter and return with the reply. Official diplomatic correspondence between rulers or between a ruler and subjects existed for centuries before private individuals began exchanging letters in the mid-fourth century BC (Trapp 2003, 6). After the papyrus sheet had been folded and sealed or rolled and tied, an address for delivery had to be written on the outside. Some letters include additional information to help the courier find the recipients (Trapp 2003, 8).

Letters might be written on media other than papyri. Brief practical notes, instructions, and even legal documents have turned up on clay potsherds. A major find of postcard-sized wooden documents and letters details the life of

---

Brief Private Letters

Outside address: *"Take to the earthenware pottery and give to Nausias or Thraskyles or his son."*

Letter: *"Mnesiergos sends to the people at home to rejoice and be healthy, and says it is so with him. Dispatch a covering, if you please, sheepskins or goatskins, the cheapest possible and not shaped into cloaks, and shoe soles; I will make a return when I get the chance."* (fourth century BC, trans. Klauck 2006, 19)

Outside summary: *"To Zenon. About fleeces. Nikon, about 2 fleeces if they should be given to Bia. Year 29, Daisios 11."*

Letter: *"Nikon to Zenon, greeting. Bia is asking for the two rams' fleeces which you left behind for spinning yarn. Write to us therefore whether they should be given to her. For she said that she is in need of woollen yarn and because of this is behind schedule. I have written to you previously about these matters. Farewell. Year 29, Pharmouthi 25."* (third century BC, trans. Rowlandson 1998, #200)

Roman soldiers stationed along Hadrian's Wall in Britain during the early second century AD. The elite had well-trained secretaries, usually slaves, to write letters, copy books, and the like. Others had to employ a local scribe or letter writer when they had to send a letter. It is easy to distinguish the practiced hand of a secretary or the cramped cursive of an everyday scribe from the few awkward words or sender's signature at the end of a letter. Paul added the final verses of 1 Corinthians in his own hand (1 Cor. 16:21–24). The scribe Paul employed to write Romans adds greetings in his own name, Tertius, to the letter's conclusion (Rom. 16:22). Tertius ("Third") is a slave name. The unusual personal greeting suggests that he was known to believers in Rome. He may even have learned the rapid system of shorthand prevalent in first-century AD Rome there (Jewett 2007, 978–79).

Once a letter reached its recipient, someone had to read it. Anyone who has struggled through actual letters or other documents from the first century knows how tough the task can be. These are not scribes trained to write the fine book hand one sees in the great fourth- and fifth-century AD biblical codices. Routine legal documents such as leases, marriage contracts, or wills have enough stock formulas that picking out a few letters can identify a string of words. Personal letters are more difficult. Additional problems emerge for an individual writing home in Greek to female relatives who do not understand that language. Someone on the other end has to both read the letter and translate the message into their native tongue (Rowlandson 1998, 311–12, #246).

When the letter carrier was the secretary or an agent of the sender, he might be charged with reading the letter, filling in details the sender omitted, or even negotiating tricky details on the sender's behalf (for the latter, see Mitchell 1992). Timothy and Titus acted as envoys on Paul's behalf in dealing with assorted problems at Corinth (1 Cor. 16:10–11; 2 Cor. 2:13; 7:6–7; 8:16–17).

Some of the ancient letters discovered by archeologists come from collections belonging to an individual. They may have been addressed to a local official or been an individual's personal archive of letters. For example, a collection of legal documents traces the business dealings of a second-century BC Egyptian woman, Nahomsesis. She herself could not read or write Greek (Rowlandson 1998, 250–51, #184). Such private letters are important to students of ancient history for the direct insights they provide about the daily lives of ordinary people, family demographics, economic arrangements, and even the type of Greek they spoke.

These private letters with their brevity and matter-of-fact communication about matters at hand and future plans resemble briefer letters in the NT like Philemon, parts of Philippians (e.g., 1:12–30; 4:2–3, 10–20), or 2–3 John. The longer letters like 1–2 Corinthians and Romans are more like essays than personal letters (Reed 1996). They belong to a second broad category of letters, those that were literary objects. Though not as extensive as the correspondence of Cicero or Pliny, Paul's letters were copied and circulated and formed a collection (Klauck 2006, 330–33). Some scholars think that copies the apostle had kept formed the basis for an early group consisting of Romans, 1–2 Corinthians, and Galatians (Trobisch 1994). Study of other ancient letter collections shows that such "published" letters differ from ordinary papyrus letters. Perhaps the literary polish is indicative of socioeconomic distinctions. The educated elite were familiar with literary poetry and prose, oral rhetoric, and written media generally (Trapp 2003, 11).

Such evidence continues to fuel debates about the Pauline letter collection. The earliest manuscripts show that our familiar canonical order was not the only one in use (Klauck 2006, 332–33). Editing letters for incorporation into a collection could produce composites that actually combine several letters to a particular addressee. Repeated copying by scribes provides the opportunity for marginal comments or editorial clarifications to find their way into the text of a letter. Theories about the editing of Paul's letters can be quite complex. Most scholars, however, agree that 1 Corinthians was composed as a single work, though Paul may have added to an initial letter as further information became available. Some scholars think that two passages might fall into the category of later additions: 11:2–16 and 14:33b–36. These passages take contradictory positions on women prophesying in the church.

Even in letters from a philosopher to a student, the teaching is more limited in scope than what we find in Paul's longer letters (Engberg-Pedersen 1995; Sampley 2003). Detailed explanation of doctrine associated with the interpretation of authoritative texts belongs to the genre of a philosophical treatise or dialogue. What appears to be a collection of fictitious letters to his friend Lucilius in about AD 64 allowed the philosopher Seneca to provide instruction in Stoic philosophy for general readers, for example (Klauck 2006, 166–73). Perhaps as he neared the end of his life, Seneca felt that the more informal and intimate discourse in letters between friends offered a better form of moral instruction than the longer essays and dialogues he had published previously. Unlike the rhetorician's speech or the tightly reasoned philosophical treatise, the letter's author can adopt a gentler tone. Seneca's friend Lucilius does not need the philosophical pedagogy presented in these letters. But the lessons presented in them may take root in the souls of readers who pick up the collection.

Like published collections of philosophical letters, Paul's letters intend to promote the moral progress of their readers (Meeks 2002). A fourth-century Christian even composed a collection of fictitious letters between Seneca and Paul (Elliott 1993, 547–53). Though Paul uses popular maxims and arguments of philosophy (Engberg-Pedersen 2000), his vision of the moral life is shaped by the gospel. Unlike letters of advice and encouragement exchanged between friends or between a teacher and former pupil, Paul's letters are addressed to

Letter as Informal Conversation

"Seneca to his dear Lucilius, greetings.

You are right to demand that we should make this exchange of letters of ours more frequent. Informal conversation does the greatest good because it slips into the mind gradually; lectures prepared in advance and spouted in front of a mass audience are noisier but less intimate. Philosophy is good advice, and no one gives advice at the top of their voice. One does sometimes have to make use of harangues like that, if I may so call them, in cases where a doubter has to be spurred on; but where the aim is to get someone to actually learn, rather than to want to learn, one needs to resort to more softly spoken words like these. They sink in a ledge more easily, because what is required is effective words, not a mass of them. They should be scattered like seed. Small though it may be, when a seed lands on the right soil, it releases its strength and expands from the tiniest starting point into the most far-ranging growth. So it is with reason too: it doesn't spread broadly, to external appearance, but it grows as it works. What is said is little enough, but if a mind takes it in well, it gathers strength and swells up. Yes, teaching has the same quality as seed: both achieve great results, and yet are themselves tiny. Only, as I say, let the right mind receive it and assimilate it; in its turn it too will engender much and give back what it has received. Farewell."
(*Epistulae morales* 61, trans. Trapp 2003, 99–100)

the Christian assembly in a city or region (Aasgaard 2004). He often names others as cosenders (e.g., Sosthenes in 1 Cor. 1:1). And the exchange of greetings at the conclusion strengthens the personal relationships between those around the apostle and believers in the churches to which a letter is sent. Thus Paul's letters are instrumental in creating the bonds among Christian churches necessary to the survival of the movement (Fitzgerald 2003).

Letters to communities must be presented in a public context. If the letter comes from the emperor with directions to local officials, it might even be inscribed on stone in a public place, as Claudius's edict to Delphi was. Though Paul's letters are not formal, diplomatic correspondence, they would have been read to the Christian assembly. Elements of Christian liturgical speech appear in them, such as familiar formulas, benedictions, doxologies, sections of hymns, and the apostle's references to his own prayers. Paul also employs characteristics of formal rhetoric in his letters, though he was not a trained public orator. Critics pointed to the contrast between impressive letters and the apostle's weak personal appearance (2 Cor. 10:1–2). Perhaps those who read Paul's letters to the Corinthian assembly measured up to the performance standards of an orator better than Paul himself. By the time Paul writes 2 Cor. 10–13 he faces competition from traveling missionaries. He challenges the "superapostles" to display the marks of a true apostle, conformity to the suffering and humiliation of the cross (11:21b–33). Because Luke identifies Apollos as an Alexandrian Jew skilled in speech and interpretation of Scripture (Acts 18:24), some scholars think that Apollos was responsible for the negative assessments of Paul's "wisdom" evident in 1 Cor. 1:10–4:21 (Murphy-O'Connor 1996, 274–75).

The formal parts of ancient letters are easy to recognize. Of course, any given letter may omit or expand a given element. Sometimes comments about the exchange of letters or the process of writing, sending, and receiving (or not) letters occur near the beginning of a letter. The sender may react to news about the recipient either in a letter or from some other persons. An additional phrase or honorific might be attached to the name of the recipient in the greeting, such as "beloved" or "honored." Letters of condolence often replace the verb *chairein* and its overtones of "rejoice" with some other phrase, such as "do well" (Trapp 2003, 34–35).

Paul's letters follow this four-part structure. Their length, however, includes considerable expansion in the various sections. The complex description of the Corinthians in 1 Cor. 1:2a (opening) and 1:5–7 (thanksgiving/prayer) points ahead to topics addressed in the letter: the holiness of the church, and how to evaluate knowledge and spiritual gifts (Arzt 1994). Scholars who employ rhetorical categories to analyze Paul's letters treat the thanksgiving of 1 Corinthians as equivalent to the proem of a speech (Mitchell 1993, 184). The assertion that Paul employs formal conventions taught in rhetorical schools remains debatable (Fitzmyer 2008, 55; in favor, see Mitchell 1993). Analysis of the rules

---

Parts of an Ancient Letter

Opening of the letter: From X (sender) to Y (recipient), Greetings!

Health wish/prayer: Formulaic expression of hope that recipient is well, comment on the sender's situation, and/or formula (*proskynēma*) assuring recipient of sender's prayer to the gods.

Body of the letter: Actual reason for writing the letter, including reports of the sender's situation and requests or instructions to the recipients as well as future plans.

Closing of the letter: Additional greetings to or from various persons and good wishes. Farewell (Be healthy! or Be fortunate!).

(Klauck 2006, 17–27; Trapp 2003, 35–37)

---

for letter composition does not appear in theoretical works until late antiquity (Trapp 2003, 42–45; Klauck 2006, 206–11, 224–25). Even if the formal rules of rhetoric do not describe the overall structure of a Pauline letter, rhetorical devices shape smaller units within the letters. The apostle is not completely innocent of the arts of persuasive speech (Porter and Olbricht 1993). Paul employs rhetorical techniques in denying that he engages in such forms of persuasion (1 Cor. 1:10–17; R. Collins 1999, 75). Consequently studies of rhetoric contribute to understanding the flow of the argument in various sections of a Pauline letter (Vos 2002).

Scholars who employ the divisions of a rhetorical speech to describe the sections and argumentative structure of 1 Corinthians as a whole point out that Paul envisages the letter being read to the recipients. He refers to the process of writing, a feature common in letters (4:14; 5:11; 9:15; 14:37). But even more frequently, he uses verbs of speaking: "say," "speak," and "assert" (1:12; 6:5; 7:6, 8, 12, 35; 9:8; 10:15, 19; 15:12, 50; R. Collins 1999, 17–20). Assigning rhetorical labels to major divisions in 1 Corinthians has not contributed much to understanding the points Paul is making. This commentary considers 1 Corinthians to be an unusually long letter, not a "speech in the framework of a letter" (R. Collins 1999, 20). Both the conversational elements and the loose sequence of topics are appropriate in letters intended for public instruction. Paul may have expected his longer letters to be copied and circulated among churches in the region to which they are addressed. If so, then he writes with at least the possibility of a collection or publication in view. Whether the two missing letters to Corinth (the letter previous to 1 Corinthians and the "letter of tears") were lost, deliberately not included in the first collection of Paul's letters, or incorporated as sections of 1 and 2 Corinthians, we cannot know for certain.

The suggestion that Paul began a letter to Corinth based on information received from "Chloe's people" (1:11) or began with the questions from Corinth

Table 1
Paul's Rhetoric against Divisions at Corinth (1 Cor. 1:10–4:21)

	Valued categories	**Negative categories**
1:10–31	believers	nonbelievers
	"in the Lord Jesus" (baptized)	Jews and Greeks
	preaching the cross	human wisdom
2:1–16	Paul "the mature"	"rulers of this age"
	revealed wisdom	hidden from the rulers
	possess God's spirit	natural humans
3:1–4:14	mature Christians (spiritual persons)	infants (baby food)
	understand and imitate the apostle	lack of moral progress
	"foolish" according to God's wisdom	claim to be "wise, strong" in Christ but employ human wisdom
4:15	Paul the "father" of community/ children	pedagogue (slave) employed by the father to watch over and discipline young children
4:16–17	Timothy, a genuine "child" of the apostle, to visit and remind Corinthians of what Paul teaches	absence caused Corinthians to forget the pattern they were to imitate
	universality of what Paul teaches "in all the churches"	divisions within the community
4:18–21	the visit Paul hopes to make to Corinth soon; an exhibition of (transforming) power	visit delayed, or when he comes, there are persons inflated with self-importance; mere talk
	love and gentleness between Paul and the Corinthians (children)	an elementary schoolmaster's "rod," discipline

(7:1) and then reshaped the project as he received other reports about the situation allows for the checklist division of topics. If Paul had to wait for a suitable messenger to take his letter to Corinth, then he may have written the letter over some time (Sampley 2002).

Rhetorical analysis raises questions about 1 Corinthians. What sort of letter or speech is it? Clearly it is not the type of speech in praise of a city that the young orator returning home from years at school was expected to make. What tone would the audience take away from the letter? One might infer that Paul is laying out the rules, adopting the tone of a ruler toward subjects or of a parent/teacher addressing an immature youth. Or one might consider the ironic comments about the apparent immaturity of his audience (e.g., 3:1–2) as just a bit of rhetorical showmanship intended to get readers to take the problems Paul is foregrounding seriously. Much of the content of 1 Corinthians did not come from the letter that the Corinthians had sent to Paul.

An additional difficulty in getting the tone of this letter right attaches to the diversity of the community itself. A number of the topics that Paul

> ### The Major Divisions
> ### of 1 Corinthians
>
> **The letter opening (1:1–9)**
>
> **Against divisions: God's wisdom (1:10–2:16)**
>
> **Against divisions: Paul and Apollos as** *exempla* **(3:1–4:21)**
>
> **Reports about unholy conduct among believers (5:1–6:20)**
>
> **Questions in a letter from Corinth (7:1–11:1)**
>
> **Problems in the community assembled for worship (11:2–14:40)**
>
> **Reports that some deny the resurrection (15:1–58)**
>
> **The letter closing (16:1–24)**

addresses may have more relevance to the minority from the ranks of the elite than to the rest of the assembly. Although we think of letters as a conversation between two parties, the exchange is more complex in this case. Just as the orator or actor knows that a reaction by one group in the crowd can influence others, so Paul may have calculated that an enthusiastic reception by his informants will influence others to adopt his point of view on contentious issues (Mitchell 2005).

Emphasis on the dynamics of communication is transforming study of the NT letters. For example, use of opposing categories is elemental to structuring language that is easily remembered. It also figures in elegant verbal patterns that knit a speech together. If the oppositions are emotionally charged, the audience will be moved to favor or identify with one side over another (Martyn 2007). Finally, in a speech intended to get its audience to adopt policies favored by the speaker, a well-constructed set of oppositions may tip the balance for those unsure about which side to favor.

Paul's letters are replete with such antithetical constructions. Two other common rhetorical devices widely used in Paul's letters, the diatribe and *prosōpopoeia* ("speech in character"), contribute to their dynamic character. In the diatribe, the author posed a hypothetical question, to which the audience would give an immediate response. A series of rhetorical questions running through 1 Corinthians can shift the audience to Paul's side (1:13, 20; 3:4; 6:9, 15, 16, 19; 7:16; 15:29–32). *Prosōpopoeia* introduces the position being taken by a fictitious interlocutor, which the speaker then rebuts in a sharp exchange of verbal sparring (15:35–37). The imaginary person may frame objections based on experience. Neither the rhetorical questions nor the interlocutor represent actual opponents. They serve the rhetorical needs of a speaker at particular stages in the argument. Therefore it would be a serious mistake to treat such material as the theology or ideology of persons opposed to Paul in Corinth.

A skilled speaker can use opposing categories to criticize powerful persons or important patrons without taking them on directly. Paul does not name particular individuals at Corinth in connection with views that he rejects. Instead he operates with different configurations that set an elite minority (high status, educated, philosophically enlightened, wealthy, endowed with spiritual gifts) over against the masses (low status, uneducated, prone to superstition [lack of philosophical understanding], poor, without spiritual gifts that confer status in the group). Rhetorical criticism requires careful attention to the sequence of an argument as well as its categories. The initial section of 1 Corinthians, Paul's response to the report of factions in Corinth, moves the audience from the positive to negative side of the ledger and then concludes with the option for restored unity.

Commentators disagree over how to evaluate the tone of Paul's admonitions in 1 Corinthians. It appears most appropriate to consider 1 Corinthians within the broad category of letters exchanged between friends (Konstan 1997). Even though the letter opens on a critical note, the report of divisions within the community (1:10), Paul acknowledges that his audience has been enriched by God's grace (1:5). They have believed the message about the cross and been baptized, unlike most of those living in the busy city of Corinth. Paul's claim to a wisdom taught only to the "mature" (2:1–16) might seem to further divide the community. Paul does not employ the antithesis in that fashion. Instead, he presents the "rulers of this age" as those ignorant of God's wisdom. That move leaves all believers in the positive column.

The tone changes when Paul castigates his audience for remaining infants (3:1). They are not mature enough to be taught revealed wisdom. Given the lowly social status of most of the audience (1:25–31), it is possible that listeners would have been split by the references to "the mature" (*teleioi*) or "spiritual persons" (*pneumatikoi*). The majority might conclude that Paul's remarks are not addressed to them, but to an elite minority within the church. By using the rhetorical device of "covert allusion" Paul reprimands unnamed leaders responsible for the divisions (R. Collins 1999, 176). Once Paul shifts to the images of infants unable to eat solid food (3:1–3a) or schoolboys disciplined by slaves and schoolmasters (4:15–21), however, he appears to put the entire community on notice. The possibility that visits by Timothy and later by Paul will cure things is offered as the rhetorical conclusion. The father image in 4:15–21 offers the option of severe or gentle treatment (Malherbe 2000, 163).

Although the imagery of a father concerned about the child's progress belongs to a rhetoric of gentle persuasion in 1 Thessalonians, Malherbe (2000, 160) reads 1 Corinthians as a shift to harsh, authoritarian correction. Similarly Winter (2003, 300, 303) construes 4:21 as a threat, not a possibility for renewed affection. Since the letters preserve only part of the communications between Paul and the Corinthian Christians, interpreters must fill in the larger situation. Often the disastrous collapse of relationships between the apostle and that church evident in 2 Corinthians shapes the reading of tensions in 1 Corinthians. Scholars who adopt this strategy point to Paul's *apologia* as evidence for an apostle already on the defensive (Winter 2003, 301–2).

The rhetoric of 1 Corinthians, however, permits a milder interpretation. Mitchell treats the letter as deliberative oratory. The audience must be persuaded that Paul's recommendations are to their advantage. Any criticism leveled at Paul has not reached the hostility of 2 Cor. 10–13. The *apologia* in 1 Cor. 9 is not defensive. Rather, it provides an example of how members of the audience should conduct themselves (Mitchell 1993, 53–56; similarly R. Collins 1999, 167). Paul anticipates two visits that will provide the personal contact for which letters are only a pale substitute. Timothy's visit (4:17; 16:10) will be followed soon after by one from Paul himself. Timothy may be on his way to the city as Paul writes (Fitzmyer 2008, 223). It is possible that 1 Corinthians will arrive before Timothy does (16:10). Using both the letter and the personal avenues of communication, Paul anticipates improving conditions in Corinth. We know that his expectation was shattered. Paul's own visit to Corinth was a humiliating disaster (2 Cor. 2:1–11). Therefore 1 Corinthians seems to have failed at least in part (Fitzmyer 2008, 43).

Theological Themes in 1 Corinthians

Paul's letters would not have been edited and collected if that rejection was the end of the story. The apostle's ability to articulate the theological principles at stake in concrete situations makes his correspondence comparable to the letter collections of philosophers like Seneca. Paul answers a number of important theological questions in 1 Corinthians. How is the God who called these non-Jewish believers to be a holy people related to the many gods and goddesses in the city? How have the death and resurrection of the Lord Jesus secured the salvation of believers? How is God's Spirit active in the life and worship of the community? What are the ethical requirements for God's people? An image that Paul uses repeatedly to address problems that occurred in Corinth, the community as the body of Christ, continues to shape the way in which Christians speak about the church. Paul's reflections on apostleship and ministry warn readers not to adopt human measures of success in spreading the gospel. Big balance sheets, platinum records, and huge crowds do not prove that individuals are preaching and living the gospel of Christ crucified.

Paul concludes the sequence of diverse topics with eschatology, the end-time transformation of believers into the glory of the risen Christ. He insists that the risen body in which God's people experience eternal life is not just a rehabilitated physical body. It is God's new creation. As some scientists today hold out dreams of unlimited repairs to our physical body as the promise of immortality, Christians must reconsider what it means to believe in the resurrection (Segal 2004).

Turning Away from Idols to the True God

For the non-Jew turning away from the idols to God was not a simple choice like changing one's breakfast cereal. It implied rejecting the city's ancestral divine protectors (Aphrodite and Poseidon), other popular deities (like Ascle-

Pagan Views of Jewish Monotheism

"Then he [Apion] attributes to us an imaginary oath, and would have it appear that we swear by the God who made heaven and earth and sea to show no good-will to a single alien, above all to Greeks." (Josephus, *Contra Apionem* 2.121, trans. LCL)

"It is right, therefore, that the Jews throughout the whole world under our sway should also observe the customs of their fathers without let or hindrance. I enjoin upon them also by these presents to avail themselves of this kindness in a more reasonable spirit, and not to set at nought the beliefs about the gods held by other peoples but to keep their own laws." (Claudius's edict to Alexandrian Jews, in Josephus, *Antiquitates judaicae* 19.290, trans. LCL)

pius and Isis), and also divine honors accorded deceased members of the Roman imperial family. Such a radical change could involve a radical reconfiguration of familial and social relationships (Chester 2003). Some believers might be divorced by a spouse (1 Cor. 7:13–14).

Perhaps it was the desire to avoid such tensions that led some church members to participate in the social aspects of idol worship, meals that followed cult sacrifices (10:1–24). Visitors to a holy city in modern India with temples to many gods and goddesses get a sense of the religious pluralism in ancient Corinth. From an outsider's point of view, Jewish monotheism was offensive, not because it claimed that the one God created the world but because Jews insisted on worshiping only that God. Roman philosophers might agree that a single, all-powerful, divine spirit ordered the cosmos, but they still participated in the ceremonies that honored the city's gods (Barclay 1996, 430–32). The Jewish refusal to do likewise struck non-Jews as an irrational lack of civility.

Despite their conviction that there is only one true God, Diaspora Jews did not attempt to save their non-Jewish neighbors. They lived in cities filled with idols and used local coinage with representations of gods and deified emperors without complaint. Violence broke out, however, when pagan images were introduced into Jewish sacred space, such as Roman eagles in Jerusalem (Josephus, *Antiquitates judaicae* 17.149–63), or when Alexandrian crowds defiled local synagogues by setting up statues of Emperor Caligula in them (Barclay 1996, 53–55). Other outbursts of violence against Jewish communities may represent reactions to more explicit proselytizing activities on the part of some Jews (Feldman 1993, 288–382). Jews could appeal to their ancestral customs, but Christians—who sought to change their religious heritage—faced persistent hostility (e.g., 1 Thess. 2:14–16).

Scripture as the Word of God

When we want information, we read something, perhaps a book or information found online. Most people in Roman Corinth could not read. They depended on seeing, hearing, and remembering. As non-Jews, they had not grown up with the stories of God and Israel. They had to hear and learn about God. Greek translations of the Hebrew Scriptures, referred to as the Septuagint (LXX), circulated among Greek-speaking Jews. The LXX not only served as Scripture in Diaspora Jewish synagogues but also made it possible for non-Jewish sympathizers to learn about the God of Israel (Feldman 1993, 311–14). It may have been too expensive for small house-churches to own copies of every book in the Bible. But they must have heard readings from the Torah, Psalms, and Major Prophets.

The citations and allusions threaded through the argument in 1 Corinthians assume that its audience accepts the truth of Scripture as God's word. Knowledge of God is based on what is written there, not on philosophical speculation.

These references assume a knowledge of Torah, Prophets, and Psalms. Paul's own citations are not always accurate to the text as we have it. He may know a different Greek translation, be quoting from memory, mixing the Greek and Hebrew versions, or substituting a different word in a citation to match his argument. For example, the "in the law" formula for Isa. 28:11–12 in 1 Cor. 14:21 does not match either the original citation or its genre as a judgment oracle.

Scripture references are not evenly distributed throughout the letter. Paul resolves the practical issues in 1 Cor. 5–7 without appealing to the authority of Scripture (Ellis 2007). It is possible to determine how Christians should conduct themselves by appealing to images of what it means to be God's holy people. Paul decides important questions about sexuality, legal disputes, and marriage without creating a Christian version of the Torah interpretation that he knew as a Pharisee (Instone-Brewer 2001).

God's Plan of Salvation

The scriptural references confirm or develop the picture of Israel's God that emerges in this letter. As the only God and creator of all that exists (8:4–6), God shaped the honored and concealed parts of the human body (12:24) as well as the diverse kinds of material bodies found in the universe (15:38–41). God's plan of salvation began with the first Adam and will culminate when Christ returns the kingdom to the Father in the triumphant victory over death (15:24–28, 54b–55; Dunn 1996). There is no sense in which God is the Spirit guiding an evolutionary development in human consciousness, a model of religious development popular with modern authors (T. Martin 2006). In Paul's understanding, humanity remained in a static position with regard to

Table 2
Scripture Citations in 1 Corinthians

1 Corinthians	Citation formula	OT citation
1:19	"for it is written"	Isa. 29:14 LXX modified: "put aside" for LXX "hide"
1:31	"as it is written"	Jer. 9:23 LXX abbreviated
2:9	"as it is written"	not an identifiable citation; an oral formula based on Isa. 64:3 or a saying from an apocryphon
2:16	none	Isa. 40:13 LXX
3:19	"for it is written"	Job 5:13a LXX modified: "catch" for LXX "seize"; "in their cunning" for LXX "in their wisdom [*phronēsis*]"
3:20	"and again"	Ps. 93:11 LXX
8:4	none	allusion to Deut. 6:4
9:8b–9	"Does not the law also say this? For it is written in the law of Moses"	Deut. 25:4
9:10	"Does it actually speak for our sake? For it was written for our sake"	citation unclear; Sir. 6:19 or a later adage?
10:1–2	general reference	Exod. 14:19–22
10:3–4	general reference	Num. 11:6–9; 20:1–13; also Exod. 16:4–17:7
10:5–6	general reference	Num. 11:4–6, 34; 14:16; 26:65
10:7	"as it is written"	Exod. 32:6
10:8	general reference	Num. 25:1–2, 9 (for number of dead as 23,000 see 26:62)
10:9	general reference	Num. 21:5–6
10:10	general reference	Num. 14:2; "the destroyer" as avenging Lord in 14:15–16; also Exod. 16:3, 11–35
10:26	"for"	Ps. 24:1
11:12	indirect reference	Gen. 2:18–25
14:21	"in the law it is written"	Isa. 28:11–12, omitting 28:12a–b
15:22	indirect reference	Gen. 3:17–19
15:45	"thus it is written"	Gen. 2:7 LXX modified: addition of "first Adam"
15:47–48	general reference	Gen. 2:7
15:49	general reference	Gen. 5:3 (and 1:27)
15:54b–55	"the word that had been written"	Isa. 25:8; Hosea 13:14

sin and death from Adam until Christ. The death and resurrection of Christ made a new relationship with God possible (Dunn 1998, 317–19; Byrne 1997). Believers enjoy an imperfect view (13:12) of the final salvation, but they can rely on God's fidelity to promises (1:9).

Paul connects the present situation of believers with the story of Israel in Scripture on the principle that such events as the wilderness wandering and rebellions serve as warnings for Christians (10:18–22). The rebellion of Israel reminds readers of an aspect of God that would not have surprised ancient readers, Jewish or gentile, that God will punish the wicked (10:1–13). Paul warns the Corinthians against provoking a similar flare-up of divine jealousy. He invokes a familiar axiom concerning divine judgment in 11:30–32. Rather than defer punishment until the day of judgment, God disciplined a disobedient Israel so that it would not be condemned along with the world.

The most important phrases about God in 1 Corinthians express what God does for believers. Their faith itself is a response to the call of God (1:4; 7:17, 20–24). Both the existence of the church and the activities of the apostles that brought it into being are signs of God's power (2:5; 3:6–7). In addition, God's gifts to the faithful (1:5–6; 7:7; 12:6) represent the Spirit of God at work among them (2:10, 12; 6:19; 12:7, 11; 14:2). Thus God is more immediately present to those who love him than the so-called gods revered in Corinth are to those who worship them (8:3–6). Polemic against pagan idols in Jewish Scripture regularly highlighted the impotence of such human fabrications (e.g., Isa. 44:9–20; Wis. 13:10–14:8). By contrast, Israel's "God is living" (*theos zōn*; Dan. 5:23 LXX; also *Jubilees* 21.3–4). Consequently Jewish texts from the Second Temple period speak of converts turning to the "living God" just as Paul does in 1 Thess. 1:9 (Esther 8:12q LXX; *Joseph and Aseneth* 11.10–11; Dan. 6:27–28 LXX).

Acts 17:22–31 imagines the speech Paul might have given to explain God's sudden interest in non-Jews. In the past gentiles had been consigned to their own gods, since the Jewish nation was the repository of the ancestral tradition of worshiping the true God (Barclay 1996, 404–5, 430–32). The death and resurrection of Jesus changed the status quo. Now the gentiles are being summoned to a belief in God the Creator, which includes the Son as an agent in creation (1 Cor. 8:6; Hurtado 2003). The formula in 1 Thess. 1:9b–10 suggests, however, that creation was not the starting point of Paul's preaching. The starting point was eschatological. God would soon judge the world through the Son. Paul repeats that premise to support a diverse range of instructions in 1 Corinthians (1:7; 4:5; 5:5; 11:26, 32; 15:50–58).

Jesus Tradition in Paul

Paul puts his preaching of the cross in the foreground of 1:18–2:16. Neither Jews who seek "signs" nor Greeks who seek wisdom can be persuaded of its truth on their own terms (1:18–25). Nor did the powers responsible for condemning Jesus recognize that they were crucifying God's chosen one (2:7–8). What Paul had said about the cross when he presented the gospel to new converts is never spelled out. Paul says he conveyed to others two established traditions as they had been given to him: the formula concerning the bread and cup at the Lord's Supper (11:23–25) and the creedal formula (15:3–5). The latter refers to Jesus's death "for our sins according to the Scriptures." The former employs "for you" in regard to the bread and "new covenant in my blood" for the cup. So it is reasonable to assume that Paul also presented the death of Jesus as a sacrifice for a sinful humanity that made a new relationship with God possible. First Corinthians 5:7 refers to Christ as "our Passover." These passages assume that Paul's readers are familiar with a basic passion story that runs from the supper on the night before Jesus's death through resurrection appearances to his disciples.

Modern readers can be puzzled by Paul's emphasis on the death, resurrection, and final triumph at the judgment when the Son returns all things to the Father. What about the teachings of Jesus? Of course, the Gospels we know are still decades in the future. Paul had no extended written account of Jesus's ministry and teaching to deposit in every church he founded. There may have been brief collections of Jesus's sayings used by missionaries. References to a "saying" or "command" of the Lord in 1 Corinthians diverge, however, from the Gospel versions we know. It is difficult to tell whether Paul's audience recognized as Jesus's teaching only the passages he marked as such or if they were familiar with the wider range of sayings that a modern reader would connect with Jesus.

> ### Pagan Gods as Elements of the Universe
>
> *"A great delusion has taken hold of the larger part of mankind.... For some have deified the four elements, earth, water, air and fire, others the sun, moon, planets and fixed stars, others again the heaven by itself, others the whole world.... Different people give them different names: some call the earth Korē or Demeter or Pluto, and the sea Poseidon,... the morning-star Aphrodite.... Now to one who is determined to follow a genuine philosophy ... Moses gives this truly admirable and religious command that he should not suppose any of the parts of the universe to be the omnipotent God."* (Philo, *De decalogo* 52–58, trans. LCL)

Jesus's Teaching and 1 Corinthians

Cited as Jesus

- 1 Cor. 7:10: neither husband nor wife should seek a divorce (Mark 10:11–12)
- 1 Cor. 9:14: those who preach should be provided with means to live (Luke 10:7)
- 1 Cor. 11:23–25: words at the Last Supper (Luke 22:19–22)

Refers to a command of the Lord

- 1 Cor. 7:12, 25: Paul's opinion; he has no command of the Lord on these questions
- 1 Cor. 14:37: generic claim that those with spiritual gifts will recognize Paul's instructions as command of the Lord

Topical allusions

- 1 Cor. 5:4–5: excluding a member from the community (Matt. 18:15–17)
- 1 Cor. 6:5: settle disputes internally, not in court (Matt. 5:23–26)
- 1 Cor. 6:7: suffering injustice to be preferred (Matt. 5:38–40)
- 1 Cor. 13:2: without love "faith that moves mountains" is valueless (Matt. 17:20)
- 1 Cor. 13:3: without love, to "give away all my possessions" is valueless (Mark 10:21)

Kingdom sayings

- 1 Cor. 6:9–10: the unjust and others will not inherit the kingdom (Matt. 25:34)
- 1 Cor. 15:24: when he hands over the kingdom to God the Father (Matt. 26:29; Mark 9:1)
- 1 Cor. 15:50: flesh and blood does not inherit the kingdom (Mark 12:25–27)

Since there is so little verbal overlap between these examples and gospel versions of the sayings of Jesus, many scholars take a minimalist position. Paul has only a few sayings of the Lord in addition to the formulas singled out as tradition. It is not the teachings of Jesus but the example of the Son of God enduring humiliation and death on the cross to save humanity that is the heart of Paul's gospel.

Christian Life in the Spirit

Although the letter itself shifts from one set of problems to another without tracing each back to a single source, failure to understand how God's Spirit informs the community of faith turns up repeatedly. Knox (1950) takes 1 Corinthians as a preliminary example for the link between "enthusiasm" (claims to special endowments of the Holy Spirit) and sectarian divisions within Christianity. The cultural and social factors that contributed to the problems Paul faced in Corinth may explain why particular religious views took root there

(Tibbs 2008). But they should not obscure the unified theological perspective that Paul seeks to instill in his churches. God's plan contradicts human wisdom.

Paul speaks of baptism as participation in the saving death and resurrection of Jesus (Rom. 6:3–4; Col. 3:1–11). Reminding the Galatians of their conversion experience, Paul associates the depiction of Christ crucified in the gospel message with the Spirit of God that awakened faith in their hearts. Signs of power or miracles were evidence that the Spirit was working among them (Gal. 3:1–5; Martyn 1997, 279–85). Such experiences confirm that God's holy people now includes all humanity; divisions of ethnicity, status, or gender no longer matter (Gal. 3:26–28; 1 Cor. 12:13). The Spirit enables these new children of Abraham to call on God as "Abba, father" (Gal. 4:6; Rom. 8:15; Martyn 1997, 391–92). The Spirit of God is distinguishable from Father and Son (e.g., 1 Cor. 6:11; 12:3), and at the same time, for Paul, the Spirit is always that of the crucified and risen Lord (e.g., Gal. 4:6; Rom. 8:9–11; Dunn 1998, 407–8). The death and resurrection of Christ as the turning point in God's plan of salvation inaugurates the eschatological gift of the Spirit. At the same time, the Spirit that is the basis for participation in Christ is only a down payment on the final transformation of God's faithful (Rom. 8:18–30; 2 Cor. 1:22; 5:5).

Though Paul does not articulate his theology of the Spirit in a systematic fashion, misunderstandings about the Spirit as experienced in the lives of believers surface at every turn in 1 Corinthians. Factionalism rather than unity was associated with baptism (1:10–17). Competitiveness and self-promotion by those claiming a superior status based on their endowment with particular spiritual gifts contradicted the "one Spirit" that all believers receive in baptism (12:4–11; D. Martin 1991). Ethical lapses among the Corinthians contradict the Spirit of holiness that dwells in the community as God's temple (3:16; 6:19). Nor could the Spirit that animates the community as one body give rise to the conflicts over spiritual endowments so prevalent at Corinth (12:12–13). Paul employs the famous encomium on love to reorder Corinthian priorities. None of the dramatic signs of the Spirit—tongues, prophecy, miracles, or heroic physical sacrifice—count for anything in the absence of love (12:31b–14:1a).

Even though the "mystery" to which they refer could not be known in advance of Christ's death and resurrection, reading the Scriptures in light of those events provides examples to instruct believers (10:11–12). The God who has called believers in Christ and endows them with the Spirit is the God of Israel. Israel's ancient confession of faith, the Shema (Deut. 6:4), "Hear O Israel, the LORD our God is one," comes to Paul's lips immediately when he is confronted with the question of food sacrificed to idols (1 Cor. 8:4). Therefore the incipient trinitarianism evident in Paul's references to the Son and the Spirit (Fee 1999) does not negate Paul's conviction that the God of Israel had intended to call the nations to faith in Christ from the beginning.

Christ's Resurrection and Ours

The Corinthian fascination with spiritual gifts makes it unlikely that skepticism about surviving this life caused them to deny the resurrection (15:12). Paul's counterargument highlights the proper order of events yet to occur. The risen Christ is himself a "firstfruit" of what awaits God's faithful ones (15:20–28). The final triumph over death will return all things to God through the Son (15:28, 53–57). One spiritual gift, insight into God's preordained plan of salvation (or "mystery") expressed in Christ, has been given to the apostle (2:1–12). He invokes that revelation schema in support of resurrection (15:51–52). Paul still imagines that the eschatological transformation of all things is temporally near at hand. Some in his audience may experience resurrection transformation without having died (15:51). Earlier in the letter, his rationale for saying that remaining single is preferable to marrying depends on the short time remaining before the Lord comes in judgment (7:25–35). Thus the Corinthians appear to have difficulty understanding the distinctions between their present religious experiences and salvation as an end-time return of all things to God.

They may have misunderstood the spiritual gifts as evidence of an inner transformation that was already complete. Or like the Isis initiate granted a preliminary visit to the blessed afterlife, they may have thought that ecstatic spiritual experiences were expressions of eternal life. Paul needles their pretensions to spiritual insight (knowledge) and perfection. The Corinthians are not mature enough for the "mysteries"—God's salvation through the cross—that Paul could teach (2:6–16). Whatever insight or spiritual experiences occur in this life, they are poor reflections of our future with God (13:12).

Skepticism about Immortality

"For they [the ungodly] reasoned unsoundly, saying to themselves,
'Short and sorrowful is our life,
and there is no remedy when a life comes to its end,
and no one has been known to return from Hades.
For we were born by mere chance,
and hereafter we shall be as though we had never been,
for the breath in our nostrils is smoke,
and reason is a spark kindled by the beating of our hearts;
when it is extinguished, the body will turn to ashes,
and the spirit will dissolve like empty air.'"

(Wis. 2:1–3 NRSV)

A Believing Community

Believers baptized into the crucified and risen Christ receive the Spirit so that their lives will continue to exemplify that new pattern (Thiselton 2000, 40). The modern tendency to read the conversion language of Scripture as though it addressed individuals in their subjectivity misses the communal nature of ancient and traditional cultures. God's call creates a community whose life and worship is a witness to their Lord. Jewish Christians had their traditions, an ethical code based on Torah, and modes of worship to structure communal life as God's people. Gentile believers had to build an understanding of religious community from the ground up. Paul describes his role as the founding apostle in architectural terms. He is like the skilled architect who created the plan and laid the foundations (3:10). Confusion arose in every facet of the church's life in Corinth. Arguments between Christians led Paul to describe the church as a body that must work together inspired by the Spirit (12:12–27). In some instances, the Corinthians fail to see that the holiness of being in Christ requires behavior different from that accepted in the society around them (6:12–20; 8:10–13; 11:27–34). In others, Paul's own words or example have caused misunderstanding (5:9–10; 7:1–7).

> **Isis Promises Devotees a Blessed Afterlife**
>
> *"You shall live a blessed life, you shall live under my protection a life of glory, and when you have reached the end of your time and go down to the underworld, there too you will often worship me (who will be favorable to you) . . . seeing me shining in the darkness of Acheron and ruling in the Stygian depths, when you yourself are living in the Elysian fields. But if by diligent attention, devout service and continuing purity you will be worthy of our divine power, you will know that I alone can extend your life beyond the span laid down by fate."* (Apuleius, *Metamorphoses* 11.6, trans. Beard, North, and Price 1998, 2:299)

Although modern readers often react negatively to the points at which Paul terminates discussion by laying down rules (5:3–5; 11:16, 34; 14:33b–40), there is very little rule making in the letter. Paul hopes to persuade his audience to become God's holy people by responding to the Spirit in love. That means putting the needs and concerns of others ahead of one's own.

In many situations, Paul prefers an adaptability guided by the needs of those involved instead of a community rule book such as that employed by the Essene Jewish sect. Thus, as one reads through some of the more puzzling or controversial sections of 1 Corinthians, it is important to keep the apostle's context in mind. We are witnessing the birth of a Christian church with all the growing pains that that entailed. Paul's tone is one of a deeply concerned but loving parent. A rule book will not solve their problems. In part, rules would fail for a practical reason. There is no authority to enforce rules. The community must be persuaded to act as a whole, though Paul may be recommending the "household of Stephanas" as a local authority (16:15–16). But at a deeper level, Paul's vision of a Spirit-guided community formed by its vision of the Christ who "gave himself for us" cannot be created through a rule book. Love goes beyond the rules and sees the needs of others in a very

Rules for Behavior among the Essenes

"If one is found among them who has lied knowingly concerning possessions, he shall be excluded from the pure food of the Community for a year and they shall withhold a fourth of his bread. And whoever replies to his fellow with stubbornness, and speaks sharply . . . defying the authority of a member who ranks ahead of him, he has taken the law into his own hands. He shall be punished for a year." (1QS 6.24–27, trans. García Martínez and Tigchelaar 1997, 85 [modified])

different light. Paul offers himself as an example. The rules would allow him to demand payment from those among whom he preaches. To show his own desire to freely offer others the gospel, Paul waives that right and works at a trade (9:1–18). Christians can adopt in today's churches the spirit that Paul brings to solving the complex problems of an urban church in Corinth.

Outline of 1 Corinthians

The letter opening (1:1–9)

Formal greeting and introduction (1:1–3)

Thanksgiving for gifts received from God (1:4–9)

Against divisions: God's wisdom (1:10–2:16)

Against valuing one apostle over another (1:10–17)

Preaching Christ crucified against human wisdom (1:18–25)

The weakness of believers (1:26–31)

Preaching the gospel against rhetoric (2:1–5)

The wisdom of mature believers (2:6–16)

Against divisions: Paul and Apollos as *exempla* (3:1–4:21)

Factions as signs of immaturity (3:1–4)

The role of apostles, planting and building (3:5–23)

Responsibility of apostle servants to the Lord (4:1–5)

Apostles as "fools for Christ" (4:6–13)

Paul's concern for the community and travel plans (4:14–21)

Reports about unholy conduct among believers (5:1–6:20)

An incestuous marriage (5:1–8)

Misunderstanding of a previous letter (5:9–13)

Lawsuits between believers (6:1–11)

Sexual relations with prostitutes (6:12–20)

Questions in a letter from Corinth (7:1–11:1)

Various topics on marriage and Christian households (7:1–40)

Sexuality within marriage (7:1–7)

Apostolic celibacy (7:8–9)

Divorce and remarriage (7:12–16)

Maintaining pre-Christian relationships (7:17–24)

Additional advice to those not married (7:25–40)

Unmarried young women (7:25–28)

Celibacy to serve the gospel (7:29–35)

The betrothed (7:36–38)

The widowed (7:39–40)

On meat from pagan sacrifices (8:1–13)

Monotheism and the idols (8:1–6)

Impact of eating on faith (8:7–12)

Agapē as the principle of discernment (8:13)

Paul as example of Christian freedom (9:1–27)

Apostle's rights to material support (9:1–18)

The apostolic office (9:1–2)

Agricultural examples (9:3–12)

Priests and evangelists (9:13–15)

Renouncing the right to payment (9:16–18)

Apostle's strategy to win as many as possible for the gospel (9:19–23)

Comparison to runners in the stadium (9:24–27)

On participation in cult meals and banquets (10:1–11:1)

Cautionary *exemplum*: Israel in the desert (10:1–13)

Ruling against participation in temple banquets (10:14–22)

Concern for the faith of others at private dinners (10:23–31)

Imitating the apostle's example (10:32–11:1)

Problems in the community assembled for worship (11:2–14:40)

On the dress of women prophesying in the assembly (11:2–16)

Gender and the hierarchy of headship (11:2–5)

Rule: Veiled head of female prophets (11:6–15)

Social honor and shame (11:6)

Order of creation in Genesis (11:7–9)

On account of the angels (11:10)

Men and women in Christ (11:11–12)

Agreement on this rule (11:13)

Order of nature (11:14–15)

A universal custom in all the churches (11:16)

Against dishonoring the poor at the Lord's Supper (11:17–34)

Divisive behavior at the Lord's Supper (11:17–22)

Received tradition, the Lord's words (11:23–26)

Warnings against participating in the meal unworthily (11:27–34)

On spiritual gifts in the one community (12:1–31a)

The diversity of gifts from one Spirit (12:1–11)

Comparison of the community to a human body (12:12–31a)

Incorporation through baptism (12:12–14)

Fable of revolt by body parts (12:15–17)

Harmonious coordination of the body's parts (12:18–26)

Spiritual gifts in the body of Christ (12:27–31a)

On *agapē* as the greatest gift (12:31b–13:13)

Love's superiority to all other spiritual gifts (12:31b–13:3)

Encomium celebrating love (13:4–7)

Love's eternity (13:8–13)

On speech in the worshiping assembly (14:1–40)

Superiority of prophecy to tongues (14:1–5)

Principle of building up the community (14:6–12)

1 Corinthians 1:1–9

The Letter Opening

Introductory Matters

The length, style, and tone of Paul's longer letters distinguish them from most correspondence in antiquity. Private letters between family or friends often have a fuller opening and closing than letters involving business, administrative, or legal matters. The expanded greeting and thanksgiving in 1 Corinthians are closer to private correspondence than to official documents. Paul's letters adopt a tone of friendship, since they seek to sustain relationships in the new "household" of faith, the Christian communities (J. White 1986, 19).

While we read letters and email privately, Paul's correspondence was read aloud to the assembled church members. Consequently the letter could be considered a public performance. Assuming that Paul composed his letters with that public delivery in mind, scholars use categories from ancient rhetoric to illuminate the structure of 1 Corinthians (Mitchell 1993). Its opening expands both the greeting and the following thanksgiving or health wish typical of ancient letters. The thanksgiving sections often anticipate the content of a

> ### Cicero to His Brother Quintus
>
> A longer letter enables the recipient to experience the sender's presence:
>
> *"But when I read your letters I seem to hear you talk, and when I write to you it is as though I were talking to you. That is why the longer your letters the better I like them, and why I myself often write rather lengthily."* (Cicero, *Epistulae ad Quintum fratrem* 1.1.45; Klauck, 2006, 159)

Table 3
Thanksgiving Anticipates the Content of 1 Corinthians

Theme in thanksgiving	Later references
"enriched in speaking [*logos*]" (1:5)	"speaking [*logos*] of the cross" (1:18)
"enriched in knowledge [*gnōsis*]" (1:5)	"not all have knowledge [*gnōsis*] . . . knowledge causes vanity" (8:1, 7, 10); "speaking with knowledge through the Spirit" (12:8; 13:2, 8; 14:6)
"not lacking any spiritual gift [*charisma*]" (1:7)	"each has his own spiritual gift [*charisma*]" (7:7); "different spiritual gifts, the same Spirit" (12:4, 9, 28, 30, 31)

letter. Therefore one can compare the opening of a Pauline letter to the formal preamble to a speech (R. Collins 1999, 49).

Rhetorical theory taught students to use the introduction to establish the speaker's authority and create rapport with the audience. In the case of 1 Corinthians, Paul's objective is to incline his audience to accept the advice that follows. Many of the issues involved were quite contentious, as we shall see. The letter greeting emphasizes Paul's status as an apostle of Jesus Christ designated by God and reminds the Corinthians that they belong to a wider network of churches (1:1–3).

An ordinary thanksgiving section mentions the source of good news about the letter's recipients as the reason for giving thanks. Paul says nothing, however, about information received until he gets to the negative reports from Chloe's people (1:11). Instead he seeks to create goodwill by referring to characteristics prized among the Corinthians: spiritual gifts, knowledge, and "perfection" associated with their faith. The thanksgiving praises them for those characteristics (1:4–7). In the letter itself, Paul takes the Corinthians to task on each of these points. Consequently some scholars treat this thanksgiving as part of the body of the letter rather than its opening (Arzt-Grabner et al. 2006, 46).

Letters containing the friendly advice of a parent or teacher typically evoke words and actions that the recipients have witnessed, and friends might imagine themselves conversing with each other. Paul concludes the greeting by reminding the audience of the fellowship in Christ that they share (1:9). At key points during the long argument that follows, he calls on readers to imitate his example, as children copy parents (4:14–16; 10:31–11:1). However, letters are weak substitutes for personal presence. The rhetorical characteristics found in letters do not necessarily represent Paul's own style of preaching (Schrage 1991, 81–83). He acknowledges that some people experience a disconnect between his powerful letters and the unimpressive appearance that the apostle makes in person. Paul accepts the dichotomy but insists that his conduct when he is present is entirely consistent with what he writes in his letters (2 Cor. 10:10–11).

Tracing the Train of Thought

In the opening verses Paul highlights his own position: **Called to be an apostle of Christ Jesus through the will of God** (1:1). He uses even more words to describe the recipients of this letter. Comparing this greeting with the concise form in Philippians and even 2 Corinthians shows how overweighted the opening to 1 Corinthians is. The Corinthians had received at least one earlier letter from Paul (1 Cor. 5:9), so they may have caught the unusual notes in the opening verses.

> **1 Corinthians 1:1–9 in the Rhetorical Flow**
>
> ▶ The letter opening (1:1–9)
>
> Formal greeting and introduction (1:1–3)
>
> Thanksgiving for gifts received from God (1:4–9)

Paul does not remind the Philippians that he is an apostle as he does the Corinthians in both his letters to them. As we shall see, Paul's apostleship was being challenged in various ways throughout the Corinthian correspondence. Perhaps there were no other competitors for that designation in Philippi. The Corinthians have not, however, rejected Paul's authority entirely. He has received a letter from Corinth seeking advice on particular issues (1 Cor. 7:1).

Table 4
Greeting Formulas in 1–2 Corinthians and Philippians

	1 Cor. 1:1–3	2 Cor. 1:1–2	Phil. 1:1–2
Senders	Paul, *called to be* an apostle of Christ Jesus through the will of God	Paul, apostle of Christ Jesus through the will of God	Paul
	and Sosthenes the brother	and Timothy the brother	and Timothy, servants of Christ Jesus
Recipients	to the church of God that is in Corinth	to the church of God that is in Corinth	to all the holy ones in Christ Jesus who are in Philippi
	to those made holy in Christ Jesus	—	—
	to those *called to be* holy ones	—	—
	with all those who call on the name of our Lord Jesus Christ	with all the holy ones who are in all of Achaia	with overseers and deacons
	in every place, theirs and ours	—	—
Greeting formula	grace to you and peace from God our Father and the Lord Jesus Christ	grace to you and peace from God our Father and the Lord Jesus Christ	grace to you and peace from God our Father and the Lord Jesus Christ

Paul has the responsibility as the founder of this community to guide its development (4:14–15).

Paul identifies himself as **apostle of Christ Jesus** even though he was not one of the twelve apostles (Matt. 10:2–4; Luke 6:13–16; 17:5; 22:14) or among the larger circle of disciples taught by Jesus. In ordinary usage the Greek word *apostolos* designates the envoy or messenger sent by someone else (Luke 11:49; John 13:16). How can Paul claim to be dispatched by a person he has never met? His catalogue of witnesses to the resurrection of Jesus in 1 Cor. 15:5–11 provides a rationale. Paul's apostleship came later than theirs, and it came to one who actively persecuted the church (15:8–9). It came through a vision of the risen Jesus (9:1–2), which Paul insists is identical with the Easter experiences of Peter, the Twelve, James, and many others. Although he never describes his experience, Paul treats it as a commission to preach the gospel. Thanks to God's grace working in him, Paul has done so as effectively as the other apostles (1:10–11).

Because God's call established the Corinthians as a "fellowship" or "communion" (*koinōnia*) through Paul's preaching (15:11), he enjoys a special relationship with this church and others he founded, like that in Philippi. Sociological approaches to early Christianity focus on the apostle's authority to dictate the belief and conduct in the churches (Schütz 1975; Holmberg 1980; Clarke 1993). First Corinthians provides instances in which Paul defends his apostleship against misunderstanding or direct challenge. Studies of social conflict should not erase the theological basis for Paul's ministry (Fitzmyer 2008, 48–53). The gospel of Christ crucified shapes Paul's response to many of the practical problems addressed in the letter (Zeller 2010, 64–66). The apostle has shaped his life in response to the call received from God. His responsibility for the churches reflects that relationship with God.

The question of how Christians should understand their relationship to others recurs through the letter. Early Christians typically use familial language—brother, sister, or household—in speaking of fellow believers. The apostle is father to the children brought to faith through his ministry (Hvalvik 2005). Paul uses the term **brother** for his cosender, **Sosthenes**, as well as for the recipients of the letter (1:1, 10). **Brother** appears in the papyri both for coreligionists such as a fellow Jew and for persons who are friends, fellow citizens, members of the same guild, or persons of similar occupation (Arzt-Grabner et al. 2006, 38–40). Timothy was an important participant in Paul's missionary activities. He often acted as an emissary from the apostle to a church (1 Thess. 3:6), a role he is about to assume in Corinth (1 Cor. 16:10–11). In his case the designation **brother** could refer to his position in Paul's missionary entourage. The opening of Philippians includes Timothy as cosender, referring to both Paul and Timothy as "servants of Christ Jesus" (1:1). Sosthenes is a shadowy figure, not mentioned in other Pauline letters. An individual with that name appears in Acts 18:17, said to be a Jewish synagogue official roughed up before the Roman governor Gallio. Luke juxtaposes that episode with Paul's appearance before Gallio, but does not explicitly connect Sosthenes with the founding of the Corinthian church. Perhaps Paul's use of **brother** merely indicates that Sosthenes is a Christian from Corinth whose presence with Paul will strengthen the authority of the letter (Schrage 1991, 101).

The usual phrase in a greeting to a community, **church of God that is in Corinth**, has been supplemented with **those made holy** and **those called holy ones** (1:2). Paul employs both techniques of supplementing the community designation in 2 Corinthians and Philippians. He hints at an audience for the letter well beyond Corinth geographically. The phrase **all who call on the name of our Lord** and the locale **in every place, theirs and ours** suggest that this letter might be received by Christians anywhere. Yet, as the detailed outline shows, 1 Corinthians is not a global encyclical. Paul will be discussing a laundry list of issues peculiar to the local church. The theological insights that Paul brings to bear on these questions make the letter valuable for Christians in other times and places.

After the greeting, Paul expands the routine expression of gratitude, **I thank my God . . . for the grace of God given you** (1:4), so that it includes items that are causing divisions between Christians in Corinth: (rhetorical) **speech**, **knowledge**, and **spiritual gifts** (1:5, 7). This development allows Paul to meet the rhetorical requirement of an introduction. He can make the audience eager to hear what he has to say by affirming those attributes that the Corinthians most value. At the same time, Paul is beginning to correct a misunderstanding. He reminds his audience that any facility of speech or knowledge that someone possesses should not be credited to that person but to God. God has **enriched [them] in every respect** (1:5) so that they will be **blameless on the day of our Lord Jesus** (1:8). In what follows Paul will point out that the Corinthian misunderstanding of eloquence, knowledge, and spiritual gifts is actually destroying the community rather than strengthening it. The final verse picks up the divine call, **God is faithful through whom you were called** (1:9), introduced in the greeting (1:1–2).

Unfortunately, Paul was not able to resolve all the problems mentioned in 1 Corinthians. In addition to the letter and Timothy's visit, Paul himself paid a disastrous return visit to Corinth (2 Cor. 2:1–11). He faced even stronger resistance when other so-called apostles arrived in Corinth with letters of recommendation, stunning rhetorical prowess, spiritual endowments, and a lifestyle to match (2 Cor. 10–13). Despite all these hardships, Paul is determined to persevere in his vision of the apostle's life as an image of the cross. He remains opposed to those who adopt human strategies in preaching the gospel. Recognizing how committed Paul is to this vision of Christ should also temper our reading of the appeals to his role as the apostle-founder in this letter. The only real authority he possesses is the word. He has surrendered any means of acquiring social or economic control over others, something that elite patrons could have provided. Therefore even when Paul gives commands, he must engage in persuasion. Unless they accept the truth of what he is saying, nothing can compel the Corinthians to follow the apostle's recommendations.

Theological Issues

The creed says that we believe in "one, holy, catholic, and apostolic church." All of these marks of the true Christian church come into play in 1 Corinthians. "Holy," "catholic," and "apostolic" are mentioned in the opening section of the letter. The next verse introduces a major practical problem, the lack of unity among Christians in Corinth (1:10). With news media eager to report the religious scandal of the week, many Christians today hesitate to speak of the church as holy. Yet these verses emphasize the holiness of all who believe in Christ Jesus (1:2, 8). Holiness is a gift from God that could be lost, since salvation will not be complete until the second coming of Christ (1:8; 5:5; 2 Cor. 1:14; 1 Thess. 5:2; Phil. 1:10; Rom. 2:5). Consequently, the church must remain firm in its testimony to Christ and blameless on the final day (1 Cor. 1:6–7).

By speaking of the church as "called holy ones," Paul looks back to the picture of Israel in the Hebrew Bible. "Speak to all the congregation of the people of Israel and say to them: 'You shall be holy, for I the LORD your God am holy'" (Lev. 19:2 NRSV). Before they receive the law at Sinai, Moses must consecrate, that is, "make holy," the people (Exod. 19:14). Therefore one should not think of holiness as either ethical perfection or intense religious emotion. Holiness means being dedicated to God (Fitzmyer 2008, 122). In practical terms, holiness may feel like a high-wire act. On the one hand, Christian holiness remains the work of a God who is faithful (1 Cor. 1:9). On the other hand, believers often fall short of the obligation to express that holiness in their lives, so the apostle has a responsibility to encourage, instruct, and correct the churches. No one is more familiar with the tensions involved in leading a dedicated Christian life than Paul.

He will insist that his authority not be confused with the legal and social power exercised by the head of a household, the religious authorities in pagan temples, or the civic officials in Corinth. Apostleship does not lead to public honor or economic prosperity for those called by God. Instead the true apostle has turned his whole life over to the gospel paradox: the one most honored by God died on the cross (4:8–13; Horrell 1996, 200–204). Paul's practical expression for this theological conviction was a self-imposed social humiliation. Instead of accepting the support of patrons in the community, he engaged in manual labor like its lowliest members (9:1–14). He concedes that other apostles are supported by the churches, a right grounded in Scripture and in a saying of Jesus himself. Paul's conduct removed an obstacle to evangelizing the majority of the city's population but offended elite members of the church. They must have felt that Paul's apostolic hardships reflected poorly on them. After all, lowliness in its leader could be taken as evidence that the community itself lacked either resources or generosity (Horrell 1996, 207–16).

What does it mean to think of the church as apostolic? Because Paul associates his apostolic authority with founding churches, we often imagine the apostles as some sort of dynasty. That model does not, however, fit the Corinthian context. Since Paul had been called by the risen Jesus, the term "apostle" did not represent an office that could be filled by successors of the first generation. Later writers looked back on apostles as the foundation stones of our faith (Eph. 2:20; Rev. 21:14). Their preaching established the church. But the apostles did not create the Christian community in the sense that the "founding fathers" established the United States of America. God is the one who called the church into existence. Local communities sought God's guidance through the inspired words of Christian prophets (Acts 13:1–3), often mentioned along with apostles (Eph. 3:5; 4:11; 1 Cor. 12:28). Corinth had both men and women prophets (11:2–16). These individuals were unable, however, to resolve many of the questions facing the church. Consequently they dispatched a letter to the apostle for his guidance. Later generations will have to find other solutions to the problem of authority over church belief and practice. Though it might seem easiest to let each local church go its own way as the Corinthians are doing, Paul reminds them that the church God called into being is a holy people that exists in many places beyond Corinth (1:2). At the end of the letter, he asks the Corinthians to set aside contributions for the impoverished church in Jerusalem (16:1–4; also 2 Cor. 8–9). Because the apostle is not the bishop of a local church or region, he plays an important role in linking the small, scattered communities of faith to one another. Through the apostle, they learn what it means for the church to be universal, that is, "catholic."

1 Corinthians 1:10–2:16

Against Divisions: God's Wisdom

Introductory Matters

The opening ended on a harmonious note. Believers have been called into the *koinōnia* of God's Son, Jesus Christ (1:9). The Greek word can mean "fellowship," "communion," "participation in," or the attitudes of generosity, altruism, and friendly feeling appropriate to those who belong to such a group. In the commercial world, an association was a group of persons united for a common purpose. Paul refers to the church at Philippi as united with him in an "association for the gospel" (Phil. 1:5), that is, participating in his missionary efforts. The situation in Corinth is, however, far from such harmonious fellowship. As Paul turns from his introductory remarks to the business at hand, one learns that "divisions" (*schismata*; 1:10) and "conflicts" (*erides*; 1:11) have broken out in the community. These occupy this section (1:10–2:16) and the next (3:1–4:21) of the letter.

Divisiveness within the Community

The situation is serious enough that travelers from Corinth told Paul about it. Discussion of these divisions receives lengthy treatment. Paul concludes the first major section by referring to travel plans for two future visits: one by his associate Timothy (4:17) to remind them of what Paul teaches in all the churches, and a second visit by Paul himself to present the community with a choice. If the situation has been rectified, then that visit will be a joyful reunion. If not, the apostle will act like a school disciplinarian (4:21). Repetition of the opening appeal, "I exhort you [*parakalō*]" (1:10), marks 4:16–21 as the conclusion of this discussion. Because letters typically end with future travel plans, commentators suggest that this section was planned as a self-contained letter. Before Paul could find someone traveling from Ephesus to Corinth to deliver it, he received additional reports about questionable conduct at Corinth, and then representatives brought a letter from the church itself. Consequently the letter reads like a series of *responsa* on various topics in community life. In two sections, Paul identifies the source of his information: "people from Chloe's household" (1:11) and "concerning the things you wrote" (7:1). In the other sections, Paul chooses to remain vague ("people are saying"; 5:1) or give no indication at all. Perhaps the information about problems at the worship assemblies came from those who brought the Corinthians' letter to Paul at Ephesus (16:17).

What is behind the factions? This section of the letter provides two counterarguments. The introductory remarks (1:12–17) suggest partisan divisions or "fan loyalty" associated with different Christian leaders: Paul, Apollos, or Cephas (1:12; repeated in 3:4–5, 21–23; 4:6). Since Paul downplays the number of persons he baptized (1:17), these allegiances might have formed among those baptized by one or another apostle. The following section (3:1–4:13) will present Paul's arguments regarding the respective roles of Paul and Apollos in creating and building up the Corinthian church. Proper understanding of these apostles as humble servants of God should undermine the ego trip experienced by those who acclaim one as superior to the other. The Corinthians do not understand what it means to be apostles or "servants of Christ and stewards of the mysteries of God" (4:1).

The second line of argument suggests that there is more than ordinary social partisanship at stake in the false standards that the Corinthians use to evaluate apostles. Paul develops the antithesis between rhetorically sophisticated discourse ("wisdom of word"; 1:17) and preaching the gospel of Christ crucified ("word of the cross"; 1:18). God's wisdom revealed in the gospel cannot be evaluated or demonstrated by human wisdom. In 1:19 Paul threads a series of Scripture citations into this section as evidence for the superiority of God's wisdom to all forms of human reasoning or calculation (Isa. 29:14; 1:31; Jer 9:24; 2:9; Isa. 64:4; 52:15; Sir. 1:10; 2:16; Isa. 40:13). If fans are lining up behind one apostle or another based on the individual's verbal agility, then preaching the gospel is being placed in competition with the popular displays of public orators or sophists. Whoever can give the most subtle, moving, and persuasive speech advocating Christ as Lord will be deemed the wisest in the "mysteries of God." Because Paul was accused of weakness in such public speaking (2 Cor. 10:1–11), some interpreters suggest that he was at a disadvantage in comparison with Apollos. An education in Alexandria (Acts 18:24) could have provided Apollos with considerable skill in philosophical rhetoric and allegorical interpretation of the Jewish Scriptures that would appeal to the Corinthians (Welborn 1987, 102–3).

A Civic Duty to Exhort (*Parakalein*) Others

In a formal speech for honors bestowed by his city (Prusa), Dio Chrysostom (ca. AD 50–110) describes the philosopher-orator's obligation to urge others toward virtue:

"And I make this speech [logos] not simply on my own behalf but on that of others, those who attained great honor [doxa] by leaving home and gaining a great reputation as well as the free-born citizens who remain there and are in no way inferior to these [those who made their reputation abroad] in either words [logoi] or deeds. And I see that men become good and worthy of public notice [axiologos] in the city not only by means of speeches [logoi] but also by means of philosophy. So I, on their behalf, will not hesitate to exhort [parakalein] the young men both privately and publicly whenever the opportunity [kairos] arises." (Oration 44.10 AT)

Vocabulary and Themes

This section on God's wisdom and human standards (1:10–2:16) contains vocabulary and themes not found elsewhere in Paul's letters. Some of this terminology appears to be political. Both the partisan-sounding slogans—"I am of Paul, I of Apollos, I of Cephas" (1:12)—and the trumpeting of social status—"not many (are) powerful, not many of noble birth" (1:26)—sound like echoes of ordinary civic unrest between an urban elite and the populace. A second group of terms, those associated with wisdom and rhetorical skill, point toward the activities of human intelligence. They suggest the preoccupations of an educated elite seeking philosophical and religious transformation. Since this vocabulary differs from Paul's own theological language, the apostle appears to be adapting his arguments to categories in use among his audience.

The introductory formula opens with the Greek verb *parakalō*, often translated "request," "urge," "ask," or even "plead with." In other letters, Paul employs the verb to introduce practical advice about the conduct of Christian life (Rom. 12:1) or to make a specific request (1 Cor. 16:12, 15). Philippians 4:2 requests two women to "think the same thing in the Lord," that is, to restore a lost harmony in their efforts to spread the gospel. That situation comes closest to the opening in 1 Cor. 1:10. The difficulty in Corinth, however, goes well beyond a falling out between two individuals. The divisions and conflicts have infected the entire community.

A scholarly debate continues over the significance of the term *parakalō*. Does it designate a request that Paul's personal relationship to the recipients entitles him to make (Bjerkelund 1967)? Or is it a more formal term, the introduction to a topic about which the speaker asks the audience to deliberate (Mitchell 1993)? Documentary papyri provide examples of the verb *parakalō* introducing the subject of a petition and even a reference to the person from whom the request is made as "brother" (Arzt-Grabner et al. 2006, 58–59). Paul returns to the *parakalō* request in the concluding section of the larger unit (4:16), where he asks the audience to imitate him. Therefore, a request based on the personal relationship between the parties seems to be Paul's understanding of the term. He is not announcing the topic of a rhetorical deliberation in the assembly.

The language of political discord also creates difficulties for interpreters. Does Paul's use of the terms *schisma* and *eris* mean that Christians in Corinth are divided into identifiable factions opposed to one another like liberal and conservative or Democrat and Republican? The story about Paul's founding mission in Acts 18:1–18 describes discord between the Jesus believers and fellow Jews spilling over into a riot when a Jewish mob dragged the apostle before the Roman governor Gallio. Luke is well aware of the danger such civil disruptions caused for those involved. Acts 18:2 refers to the episode in which Claudius expelled Jews from Rome (Suetonius, *Claudius* 25.4). Other reports say that, fearing a riot, Claudius did not expel Jews from Rome but prohibited gatherings (Dio Cassius, *Historia romana* 60.6.6). Philo's claim that Augustus never took such measures against the Jewish community (*Legatio ad Gaium* 157) may be an indirect condemnation of actions taken by Claudius in both Rome and Alexandria (Pervo 2009, 446).

Given the danger that partisan discord within a minority community could lead to swift intervention by civic authorities (Hubbard 2005), one would expect Paul to address any issue of social conflict directly. He expects Christians to live peaceably under Roman rule (Rom. 13:1–7). Other religious associations made rules to prohibit factions among members. But Paul does not suggest that the conflicts in question might provoke a response from civil authorities. It is possible to understand Paul's language associated with political discord as a powerful rhetorical move rather than evidence of hard-core factions within the church (R. Collins 1999, 73). Paul is trying to get the audience to take the various points of discord and divided allegiance as seriously as they would any civic disturbance. As the letter progresses we see that Paul approaches a variety of issues as threats to the identity of the community itself.

Rhetorical skill, wisdom, and status within a civic community provide a connection between the threat of factions and the misunderstanding of wisdom. The peculiar phrases "word [*logos*] of wisdom" and "word of the cross" reflect the language of public oratory. Among the civic elite a reputation for powerful speech could reap

---

Rules against Schism in a Religious Association

A brotherhood of Zeus Hypsistos (69/68 BC) prohibited factions:

"And to no one of them is it permitted . . . to organize factions [schismata]." (Papyrus London 7.2193, in Arzt-Grabner et al. 2006, 66)

political influence and public honors. Most of the references to wisdom appear in the first three chapters of 1 Corinthians. Paul warns against the self-deception inherent in claiming to be "wise by the standards of this age" (3:18). That claim to be a wise person is associated with the boasting that Paul challenges at a number of key points in the letter (1:29, 31; 3:21; 4:6–7, 18–19; 5:2, 6; 8:1; Schrage 1991, 129). Since Paul has framed the debate in terms of rhetorical sophistication, it is unlikely that the Corinthians are pursuing the wisdom taught in philosophical schools or an allegorical interpretation of Scripture as a form of Christian wisdom. Enamored with the public performances of wisdom put on by orators or popular philosophers, the Corinthians are ready to apply the same standards to those who preach the gospel.

Text-Critical Problems in 1 Corinthians 2:1–5

Determining the earliest Greek text of 2:1 and 2:4 remains difficult. In each case plausible arguments can be advanced for alternative readings. In 2:1 the problem is the object of the participle "proclaiming" (*katangellōn*). Is it "mystery" (*mystērion*), as in our earliest papyrus ($\mathfrak{P}^{46}$ [ca. AD 200]), several major codices, and a number of Latin church fathers, or "testimony" (*martyrion*), as in other major codices, a number of Greek church fathers, and the medieval Byzantine text tradition? Either reading would fit the argument. The word "testimony" recalls a phrase from the thanksgiving section: "As the testimony of Christ has been strengthened among you" (1:6). The word "mystery" appears in the next section: "But we speak the wisdom of God hidden in a mystery" (2:7). On the one hand, anticipating "mystery" as the topic of the next section could lead scribes to substitute "mystery" for "testimony." On the other hand, since the "mystery" referred to in 2:7 is hidden and taught only to mature Christians, a scribe sensitive to the contradiction between restricted teaching and public proclamation could have changed the first *mystērion* to *martyrion* (R. Collins 1999, 118). Current editions of the Greek NT adopt "mystery" as the earlier reading.

First Corinthians 2:4 occurs in as many as eleven variations. Some represent scribes attempting to clarify what sort of wisdom Paul excludes from his teaching. They add an adjective "human" (*anthrōpinēs*) to modify the noun "wisdom." Other variations turn on the dative object of the preposition. Is it "persuasive words" (*peithois logois*)? That reading has Paul using an adjective related to the verb "persuade" (*peithein*), not otherwise attested for this period. The normal adjective would have been the Greek word *pithanos*. Or is the intended word the noun *peithō* ("persuasiveness, eloquence")? A scribe hurrying to copy the next word, "wisdom," which begins with the letter sigma in Greek, could have added a sigma to the dative of this noun (*peithoi*), converting it into an adjective modifying the noun "words" that comes after "wisdom" in the sentence. Early papyrus and other later manuscripts have the dative plural adjective *peithois* without the noun "words." Modern editions of the Greek text remain undecided. They marginally favor a text reading "in persuasive words of wisdom." But by bracketing the final sigma on *peithois*, thus converting it to the noun in the dative, and also bracketing "words," editors offer the option "in persuasion of wisdom" or, more colloquially, "by clever persuasiveness." A prepositional phrase beginning with Greek *en* followed by its dative object and qualified by another noun in the genitive matches the next phrase in the sentence, "in demonstration of Spirit and power." No such stripped-down reading appears, however, in the Greek manuscripts (R. Collins 1999, 119–20). Whatever the earliest reading of the text was, the point Paul makes is clear. He did not employ sophisticated rhetoric in proclaiming the gospel.

These textual problems suggest that even ancient scribes had difficulty following the tangled argument in this section of the letter. It is helpful to remember that Paul weaves together three distinct threads: (1) factions within the church (1:10–17; 3:4–5, 21–23; 4:6); (2) fascination with a mode of preaching the gospel that meets cultural standards for human wisdom (1:8–2:16; 3:18–20; 4:10); and (3) misunderstanding of the ministry given to the apostle and others (1:17; 2:1–5; 3:1–4:13). On the last point, Paul is forced to respond to criticism addressed to him personally (Fitzmyer 2008, 127). Paul unfolds the theological issues at stake as he progresses through each section of the argument.

If, as I suggest, the various divisions are not hardened ideologies, the opening section (1:10–17) may have sounded relatively benign, something like a coach trying to get a divided team back on the same page. Its final verse (1:17b) introduces new terms that shape what comes next: "to preach the gospel," "not in verbal wisdom," and "the cross." The next section (1:18–25) opens with a phrase that Paul creates as the antithesis to the verbal or rhetorical wisdom, "word of the cross." Paul draws on an antithesis between wisdom and folly in Scripture to establish the opposition between human wisdom and God's wisdom. Having generated that antithesis, Paul turns to his audience. God calls persons who are weak by human standards. They should be paying attention to what comes from God (1:26–31).

Then Paul moves to his own case. He did not preach the gospel with the kind of rhetorical sophistication that some Corinthians are advocating. He could not do so, since the cross is the core of the gospel (Marcus 2006). Therefore, faith is based on God's power, not human wisdom (2:1–5). One might expect the chain of argument to end at that point. His audience's ears must have pricked up with the opening words of the next section: "Wisdom we speak" (2:6–16). To match the gospel proclaimed, this wisdom is not a variant of the human wisdom that Paul rejects (2:13). Paul introduces an anthropological distinction between those open to God's wisdom, "spirit-endowed" (*pneumatikos*; 2:12, 13, 15), and the ordinary, "natural," or biological human being (*psychikos*; 2:14). The section concludes with a robust affirmation of Paul's authority as an apostolic teacher: "We have the mind of Christ" (2:16).

Tracing the Train of Thought

Against Valuing One Apostle over Another (1:10–17)

1:10–17. Paul opens with phrases familiar to his audience: **all say the same thing**, and **restore the same mind and the same opinion**. Such phrases were employed to calm social tensions or encourage devotion to communal goals. Paul indicates that his information came from **associates of Chloe**. Whether these individuals were slaves, business associates, or household members of the aforementioned woman, it is impossible to tell. Since the audience apparently knew who Chloe was, either she or Paul's informants belonged to the Corinthian church unless these unnamed associates were from Ephesus and had stayed with Christians while in Corinth on business for their mistress.

Paul's opening may reflect uncertainty about conditions in Corinth. He attaches partisan slogans to three well-known missionaries—**I belong to Paul . . . Apollos . . . Cephas**—and adds a fourth: **Christ** (1:12). The addition of Christ enables him to introduce a logical absurdity in speaking of such divisions: **Is Christ split up? Was Paul crucified for you?** (1:13). Paul clearly presumes an audience familiar with the standard baptismal catechesis and his own teaching that Christians are baptized into Christ and that baptism means participation in the death and resurrection of Christ (Rom. 6:1–4; Col. 3:1–4). All baptized Christians receive a share in God's Spirit (1 Cor. 12:13). Given this theology of baptism, it sounds odd to hear Paul sidestepping his role in baptizing members of the church: **I thank God that I did not baptize any of you except Crispus [Acts 18:8] and Gaius [19:29; Rom. 16:23]** (1 Cor. 1:14). That rhetorical tactic unravels before the facts as Paul immediately issues a disclaimer to add the important **household of Stephanas** (cf. 16:15) and anyone else he may have forgotten (1:15–17a).

Did the Corinthians form factions around individual apostles on the basis of who had baptized them? Nothing in the standard baptismal catechesis points to a special relationship between a baptizer and the baptized. Some scholars propose analogies with mystery cults. In that model the apostle conveyed special wisdom to those being initiated. Nothing in Paul's discussion of baptism fits that model. In addition the slogan form creates difficulties for the proposal. All believers are baptized into Christ, so **I am Christ's** (1:12) could not separate one group from another. That objection is not fatal to the

---

1 Corinthians 1:10–2:16 in the Rhetorical Flow

The letter opening (1:1–9)

▶ Against divisions: God's wisdom (1:10–2:16)

   Against valuing one apostle over another (1:10–17)

   Preaching Christ crucified against human wisdom (1:18–25)

   The weakness of believers (1:26–31)

   Preaching the gospel against rhetoric (2:1–5)

   The wisdom of mature believers (2:6–16)

theory, since Paul may have added that phrase as a parody of Corinthian behavior. Though Peter (Cephas) was apparently well known in Corinth, there is no clear indication that he had visited Corinth (9:5). Paul uses himself and Apollos as examples in the discussion of apostolic ministry in the next part of this division (3:1–4:13). So if advocacy was correlated with baptism, any actual fans would have to be on the side of Paul or Apollos. Paul does not, however, make Apollos responsible

> **Fan Favorites**
>
> Graffiti from Pompeii show fans declaring their favorite members of a visiting troupe of actors: "Actius, star of the stage"; "Here's to Actius, come back to your people soon." (Beard 2008, 258)

for divisions in question. At the end of this section Paul shifts from baptism to his main concern, that **rhetorical skill not void the cross of Christ** (1:17b).

Preaching Christ Crucified against Human Wisdom (1:18–25)

1:18–25. The opposition between rhetorical skill and the cross of Christ introduced in 1:17b requires explanation. Why isn't it valuable to present the gospel in a mode that everyone in the city values? First Paul shifts to how people react upon hearing the **preaching [*logos*] about the cross. Those destined to perish** treat it as **foolishness.** But we **who are saved** consider it **the power of God** (1:18). This distinction takes readers back to that fundamental fact of their identity as a people "called by God . . . into fellowship with his Son" (1:9). Citing Isa. 29:14 LXX, Paul establishes the antithesis between divine and human wisdom. He has modified the quotation to fit his argument by replacing "I will hide" in the second strophe with **I will set aside** (1 Cor. 1:19). A rhetorical series of five contrasts between "the wise" in human terms and believers culminates in a theological statement: **God's folly is wiser than human beings** (1:25).

Even though the relationship between the divisions in Corinth and the Corinthians' fascination with rhetorical wisdom remains unclear, Paul's response is clear. Human intelligence and the wisdom of God's plan for salvation do not belong to the same order of reality. Paul's own experience as a devout, zealous Jew had taught him firsthand that the cross contradicted even the best Jewish learning (Gal. 1:13–14; Phil. 3:3–11). Paul extends that experience to embrace all human wisdom. He invokes the authority of Scripture to make the point (1 Cor. 1:19, 31; 2:9, 16). A series of five antitheses hammers home the question about the limits of human intelligence. The objections of Jews who refuse to believe in the gospel place them on the negative side of the ledger (1:21–23). As Paul sees it, Jews and non-Jews have different reasons for rejecting the message of salvation in the cross: **Jews demand signs and Greeks seek wisdom** (1:22). Though signs can mean miracles, it would be wrong to press Paul's elegant rhetorical phrases into the service of a cultural divide between Jewish religion and Greek philosophy. Jews who had grown up in cities like Tarsus, Corinth, Rome, and Alexandria had assimilated much of the surrounding Greco-Roman culture (Niehoff 2001), so they might not have drawn the antithesis as sharply as Paul does here. Of course, the gospel that Paul is preaching among the gentiles negates the distinction (Fitzmyer 2008, 152). God has called believers from both Jews and Greeks. They acknowledge **Christ the power of God and wisdom of God** (1:24). The final verse (1:25) in this section employs neatly constructed parallel phrases that both sum up the argument so far and link it to the next section:

A **the foolishness of God**
  B **is wiser than human beings**
A′ **the weakness of God**
  B′ **[is] stronger than human beings**

The Weakness of Believers (1:26–31)

1:26–31. Paul quickly turns this depiction of God's wisdom into a warning for his audience. **Consider your calling**, he reminds them (1:26). Not many fit the categories of the city's elite: **wise, powerful, of noble birth**. A series of rhetorical antitheses in 1:27–28 demonstrates the rationale for calling such persons:

Table 5
The Objects and Purposes of God's Call

God called "the lowly"	Purpose of God's call
"things considered foolish by the world"	"to shame the wise"
"things considered weak by the world"	"to shame what is strong"
"things considered inferior by the world"	—
"things that are despised"	—
"things with no existence"	"to abolish things that are"

Paul makes a subtle shift from speaking about persons of exalted or lowly and despised social status to speaking of **things**. Members of the elite might use accusations of lowly birth, despicable behavior, association with persons of the lower classes, or lack of noble physical bearing or characteristics to bring down an opponent (Clarke 1993). Paul initially presents God as though he were standing against all such persons. They are shamed or humiliated by God's chosen people.

Why move from speaking of persons (1:26) to things? The final antithesis in the list provides a clue. When Paul thinks of God's saving plan, he incorporates a cosmic dimension that Christians today (and likely the Corinthians; 15:20–28) forget. God's triumphant reign in Christ will bring the universe as we know it to an end. God will **abolish the things that exist** (1:28). Paul also has another reason for making this shift. It is too easy for some in Corinth to consider this divine boost to the status of marginalized individuals **in human terms** (*kata sarka*, "according to [the] flesh"; 1:26). Individuals treated with contempt by the larger community might use their personal resources or even their spiritual gifts to claim status and power over their brothers and sisters in the new Christian community. Many of the practical issues addressed in the letter that follows play out as conflicts over social status (Theissen 1982). Paul does not, however, focus on the socioeconomic structures in play. He is anxious for his audience to grasp the theological principles that should inform their life together.

By shifting focus from contention between humans to God's power over all of creation, Paul states a general principle. God has undermined these status categories so that **no living being** [*sarx*, "flesh"] **can boast before God** (1:29). Paul then concludes this section of the argument by substituting the proper way of considering what God has done for believers (1:30). Christ is the source of those attributes that enable God's people to put to shame the intellectual and civic elites who dominate life in Roman Corinth: **wisdom, righteousness,** and **holiness,** and **being set free.** Then Paul concludes this section as he did the previous one, with a Scripture quotation (Jer. 9:23 LXX). Of course, for the Christian reader the phrase **let him boast in the Lord** can have a double meaning, since **the Lord** can refer both to the God who creates all things and to the Christ through whom all are redeemed. As the next step in the argument turns toward the antithesis between the apostle and the gospel of salvation through the cross, the emphasis in this verse is on Christ as Lord.

Preaching the Gospel against Rhetoric (2:1–5)

2:1–5. Paul draws his audience, **brothers** (2:1; cf. 1:26), back to their first encounter with the gospel. He did not present himself as a Sophist with rhetoric or wisdom to be exchanged for money or civic renown (Winter 2002, 143–59; Krentz 2003). Nor did Paul engage in the self-promotion typical of orators who traveled from one city to the next: **I came not claiming superiority in speech or wisdom** (2:1b).

The section consists of two sentences composed of parallel phrases. Each one opens with **and I** (*kagō*) and then gives a description of Paul's arrival among the Corinthians consisting of the negative and positive characteristics of his speech. The concluding phrase (2:5) explains the purpose behind such preaching. It grounded the **conviction** or **faith** of the Corinthians **not in human wisdom but in [the] power of God.**

If the Corinthians prefer apostles who present the gospel employing the verbal cleverness and the physical mannerisms of trained orators or the trappings of philosophical wisdom, believers are risking the divine foundations of their faith. Of course, those entranced by rhetorical sophistication probably recognized that orators often claimed to be repudiating rhetorical deceit. Even

Table 6
Paul's Style of Preaching in Corinth

	1 Cor. 2:1–2	1 Cor. 2:3–4
Paul's presentation	"when I came to you"	"was with you in weakness, fear, and trembling"
His speech (negative)	"not with superior speech or wisdom"	"my speech and my preaching did not employ persuasive [words of] wisdom"
His message concerned	"the mystery of God"	—
His speech (negative)	"not to know anything among you"	—
His message concerned	"Jesus Christ and that one crucified"	"with demonstration of spirit and power"

though Paul could not win a head-to-head contest with such famous orators as Dio Chrysostom (Anderson 1998), he crafts his words with some skill (Winter 2002, 155–59). So the audience may not have taken these disclaimers at face value. He makes fun of the air of mastery and self-control expected of an elite orator (Gleason 1995) by describing his presence as **in weakness and in fear and in trembling** (2:3). Paul is setting the audience up for an even more stunning contrast between boastful Corinthians and humiliated apostles in 4:6–13. But in the same sentence that Paul denies employing rhetoric, **persuasive [words of] wisdom** (2:4a), he employs another standard rhetorical term *apodeixis*, **proof** or **demonstration**, accomplished through the spirit and power of God. An audience might be forgiven if it concluded that the apostle is engaged in rhetoric with a Christian overlay.

Those listening to 1 Corinthians being read to the church have an advantage later readers lack. They can remember what those first days were like. They know whether Paul appeared to be weak and fearful. In the rough and tumble of rhetorical competition, people sought to detect such flaws in an opponent. The traveling missionaries who sought to discredit Paul in Corinth somewhat later made invidious comparisons between his letters and his personal presence (2 Cor. 10:9–11). Such accusations do not necessarily correspond to the actual situation.

The Wisdom of Mature Believers (2:6–16)

Having just denied that he employs the sort of verbal sophistication (*sophia*, "wisdom") expected of a public orator or teacher, Paul states that he teaches **among the mature [*teleioi*] a wisdom that is not of this age.** He shifts from the first-person singular of the previous section to the first-person plural **we**. The argument divides into two sections, each concluding with a quotation from Scripture (2:6–9, 10–16a). The final sentence, **and we have**

the mind of Christ (2:16b), leaves no doubt about Paul's authority to teach such wisdom.

2:6–9. The first section picks up the antithesis, introduced in 1:18–25, between God's wisdom, manifest on the cross, and human wisdom. Having discussed conflict between the sorts of proof that learned humans demand and the cross, Paul now broadens the scope of his argument to an apocalyptic perspective. It is **the rulers of this age that are being abolished** (2:6), whose ignorance of God's plan of salvation led them to **crucify the Lord of Glory** (2:8).

Jewish apocalyptic texts use "mystery" (Aramaic *rāz*; Greek *mystērion*) for God's preordained plan of salvation revealed to the elect in the last days.

Table 7
Mystery as God's Plan of Salvation

Dan. 2:28 LXX	"There is a God in heaven revealing mysteries, who has shown King Nebuchadnezzar what must come to pass in the last days." (AT)
1QpHab 7.4–6 (on Hab. 2:2)	"Its interpretation concerns the Teacher of Righteous, to whom God has made known all the mysteries of the words of his servants, the prophets." (García Martínez and Tigchelaar 1997, 17)
1QpHab 7.7–8 (on Hab. 2:3)	"Its interpretation: the final age will be extended and go beyond all that the prophets say, because the mysteries of God are wonderful." (García Martínez and Tigchelaar 1997, 17)
1QpHab 7.10–14 (on Hab. 2:3b)	"Its interpretation concerns the men of truth . . . [who] will not desert the service of truth when the final age is extended beyond them, because all the ages of God will come at the right time, as he established for them in the mysteries of his prudence." (García Martínez and Tigchelaar 1997, 17)
1QM 3.9	[To be written on one of the banners:] "God's mysteries to destroy wickedness" (García Martínez and Tigchelaar 1997, 117)
2 Esd. [4 Ezra] 14:5	[Included in God's revelation to Moses on Sinai:] "I told him many wondrous things, and showed him the secrets of the times and declared to him the end of the times." (NRSV)
2 Baruch 81.4	[Visions that God gave the seer mourning the evils that have befallen Israel:] "The Most High . . . made known to me the mysteries of the times, and showed me the coming of the periods." (trans. A. F. J. Klijn in *OTP* 1:649)

In an apocalyptic framework, only the elect to whom God has revealed the plan by which the ages or periods of history will reach their conclusion know the meaning of events they experience and what is to come. The expression **rulers of this age** (2:6) has a double meaning. It can refer to actual human rulers, in this case those responsible for the death of Jesus (Fitzmyer 2008, 175). It can also refer to evil powers behind their actions, which God permits to remain active in the last days (1 Cor. 15:24; Zeller 2010, 124).

By inviting his audience to see both visions—the political rulers faced with the degraded criminal and the cosmic powers confronted with an angelic manifestation of God's rule—Paul is laying out the mystery of salvation. The

---

The "Lord of Glory" in *1 Enoch*

"In those days, the governors and kings who possess the land shall plead that he may give them a little breathing spell from the angels of his punishment . . . that they shall fall and worship before the Lord of the Spirits, and confess their sins before him. They shall bless and glorify the Lord of the Spirits and say, 'Blessed is the Lord of the Spirits— the Lord of kings, the Lord of rulers . . .—the Lord of glory and the Lord of wisdom.'" (*1 Enoch* 63.1–2, trans. E. Isaac in *OTP* 1:44)

---

cross marks the beginning of the end for the powers that dominate the world. Had they known God's plan, the rulers would never have acted as they did.

For God's elect who have patiently endured the evils of a world coming to an end, this event is good news; salvation is under way. Paul introduces that perspective as a preordained plan **for our glory** (2:7) and **what God has prepared for those who love him** (2:9c). That phrase is the third in a three-part citation introduced as Scripture, though it cannot be identified with any known passage.

Table 8
Scripture Citations Related to 1 Corinthians 2:9

Isa. 52:15 LXX	"Thus many nations will be amazed at him, and kings will constrain their mouth; that those to whom tidings about him have not come will see, and those who have not heard, will perceive." (AT)
Isa. 64:3 LXX	"From ages past we have not heard nor have our eyes seen a god except you and your works, which you will do for those awaiting mercy." (AT)
Ps. 31:19 LXX	"How great is the multitude of your goodness, Lord, which you have hidden for those who fear you." (AT)

Since antiquity exegetes have suggested that Paul was quoting from an apocryphal work (*Apocalypse of Elijah*; Origen, *Commentarium in evangelium Matthaei* 27.9), though no such citation is known. The first two phrases are organized around a series of bodily references: **what *eye* has not seen and *ears* have not heard and has not entered the human *heart***. Paul may have formulated the citation as a pastiche of remembered phrases, a technique found in apocalyptic texts (R. Collins 1999, 131–32).

Rhetorically this section invites the audience to consider themselves among the elect who know the mystery of God's plan. Paul may have adopted from the Corinthians themselves the terminology of *teleioi* ("perfect" or **mature** persons) initiated into a wisdom unknown to most humans (Pearson 1973). Second-century Valentinian authors exhibit a similar interest in discovering a knowledge of higher truth behind the Gospels that transforms individuals into immortal, spiritual persons, and they found 1 Corinthians a congenial text (Klutz 2003, 208–15; see *Gospel of Philip* 77.15–30). The next stage in Paul's argument, however, introduces anthropological distinctions that will challenge those who consider themselves a spiritual elite.

2:10–13. The next section opens with a statement of principle: **God has revealed to us through his Spirit** (2:10a). Knowledge of the mystery of salvation cannot be attained without that gift. Paul appears to taunt the Corinthian fascination with knowledge or wisdom in the next series of statements (2:10b–11) based on the premise that **no one knows divine things except the Spirit of God** (2:11b). The logical sequence is unclear. First Corinthians 2:10a fails to specify the object of divine revelation. Instead the possibility of revelation through the Spirit is justified through the omnipresence of the Spirit, who **searches all things, even the depths of God** (2:10b). The phrase articulates a common view of *pneuma* (**spirit**) in ancient Stoic cosmology. *Pneuma* is both the underlying material substance from which all things come into existence and the principle of rationality that grounds the cognitive abilities of the mind (Engberg-Pedersen 2009; 2010, 62–65). The two parallel expressions in 2:11 link the anthropological function of the *pneuma* within a human and the possibility of knowing **the things of God**. Listeners familiar with Stoic philosophy might conclude that Paul's disclaimers were only rhetorical. He is using human wisdom to explain the gospel. The missing subject of revelation in 2:10a must be **the depths of God**. Therefore the divine Spirit that Christians possess enables believers to know everything that exists.

Clearly this Stoic interpretation does not distinguish the divine spirit from the wisdom of human intelligence. To avoid that conclusion, Paul reiterates the distinction. First Corinthians 2:10 opened with *hēmin de* (**now to us**); 2:12 begins with the same phrase, *hēmeis de* (**now we**), and repeats the antithesis between human and divine wisdom: **We have not received the world's spirit but the Spirit that is from God.** By denying that the Spirit that Christians have received is **the spirit of the cosmos**, Paul disables any Stoic interpretation of

---

Stoic Cosmology

"The Stoics declared that god is an intelligent substance—an artistic fire that pursues a path to the genesis of the cosmos, embracing all the seminal principles [logoi] according to which all things come to be according to fate—and, on the one hand, a spirit [pneuma] pervading the whole cosmos and, on the other hand, taking on names according to the alterations of the matter [hylē] through which it passes." (Aetius 1.7.33, in *Stoicorum veterum fragmenta* 2.310 AT)

the relationship between God, Spirit, and cosmos. That correction also forces a reconsideration of 2:10. Paul does not mean to suggest that God's Spirit revealed the hidden nature of God, **the depths of God** (2:10), to believers. Instead Paul explains that the gift of the Spirit enables believers to **know the gracious things done for us by God** (2:12b).

Every time the audience might anticipate some form of higher teaching or evidence that the apostle is skilled in human wisdom, Paul comes back to the gospel. Paul's disclaimer, **we speak not in words taught by human wisdom but in those taught by the Spirit** (2:13a), presents his audience with a new challenge. Though the apostle engages in **explaining spiritual matters to those who are spiritual** (2:13b), they may not all qualify as **spiritual people**. This phrase substitutes the word *pneumatikoi* (**spiritual people**) for the *teleioi* ("mature people") of 2:6. The **spiritual matters** are identical with the **wisdom** and **mystery** about which Paul has been speaking.

2:14–16. Paul closes this argument with a new variation of the antithesis between those who accept God's wisdom and those who judge according to human standards: **The ordinary person [*psychikos anthrōpos*] does not accept what comes from the Spirit of God** (2:14a). Paul employs adjectives from the Greek words for "spirit" (*pneuma*) and "soul" (*psychē*) to differentiate the two groups. In ancient philosophy, the intellectual or reasoning faculty of humans was "mind" (*nous*). "Soul" referred to the functions of living beings common to humans and animals, such as the ability to direct one's movements according to desires. "Body" (*sōma*) referred to the physical entity in and through which these processes occur (C. Gill 2006). A philosopher would consider *pneuma* the organizing power that unifies the various functions and faculties. It is not limited to the rational intelligence employed by the wise person. Paul's **spiritual person [who] evaluates all things but himself is not evaluated by anyone** (2:15) is neither the Stoic philosopher nor an individual with a highly developed intellectual capacity.

For Paul a **spiritual person** judges matters in accord with God's Spirit. Hence anyone who cannot grasp God's wisdom belongs to the category *psychikos*. Translators have struggled to find appropriate terms for the ways in which Paul employs that designation. The NRSV settled on "unspiritual" to represent the contrast. In contemporary English usage, however, the term "unspiritual" carries negative overtones that a first-century audience would not associate with the word *psychikos*. Paul's argument at this point appears to be straightforward: confronted with the gospel, human reasoning will judge it to be **foolishness, because it is evaluated spiritually** (2:14b). Therefore *psychikos* designates ordinary or natural human capacities.

Paul concludes with another citation of Scripture (Isa. 40:13 LXX): **Who has known the mind of the Lord, who will instruct him?** (1 Cor. 2:16). Like the quotation that ended the previous section, the reply to this one is unambiguous. No human knows God's mind or can serve as God's teacher. Ambiguity in the Christian use of **Lord** to refer both to the God of Israel and to Jesus Christ exalted at God's right hand with dominion over all the powers in the universe (Phil. 2:9–11), however, enables Paul to attach a surprising addendum: **But we have the mind of Christ** (1 Cor. 2:16c). Although the question posed in Isaiah expects the answer, "No human being has the mind of God," Paul's affirmation comes as a surprise. Initially, that expression appears to be a direct claim to authority to teach in the name of Christ. But for Paul, **the mind of Christ** refers to the self-emptying that the Son of God accepted on the cross (Phil. 2:5–8). Thus Paul has not let his audience off the hook. God's wisdom has been revealed on the cross. The second half of Paul's treatment of divisions will apply that perspective to understanding the ministry of the apostles.

Theological Issues

How far does the antithesis that pits God's wisdom against human intelligence extend? Treating the opposition as a lofty rhetorical counter to a specific Corinthian problem or to inflated interest in oratory or popular philosophy limits its scope. One might find a contemporary analogy to that situation in media studies, public relations, or marketing. By opposing rhetoric, Paul implies that Christians should be wary of using the marketing tools of any age to sell the gospel. On that analogy, it is easy to see why a faith grounded in something equivalent to consumer choice cannot be secure. There is always another brand with its own marketing team seeking attention. Even old, familiar items that we grew up with feel compelled to update their image or add varieties, providing the health or environmental buzzword of the moment. Religions, churches, spiritual paths, and self-improvement gurus are also part of the marketplace. Though the Corinthians may have favored one apostle over another, there is no evidence of defection from the faith they have embraced. Paul insists that the gospel message itself challenges the human judgments employed by marketing campaigns.

But the challenge to human wisdom does not stop with the abuses of persuasion. Human intelligence runs two risks: claiming to know or control what it does not and endowing those who have knowledge with inflated self-importance. Paul employs an apocalyptic theology to lay out that discontinuity between human and divine wisdom (Zeller 2010, 149–50). The parameters of this theology are explicitly laid out in his letter to the Romans (Rom. 1:18–8:38; Dunn 1998, 79–181). All of humanity has fallen away from God: non-Jews from the God visible in the created order, Jews from the gift of an enlightened knowledge of God in Torah and covenant. But human sin did not derail God's saving purpose, which is being accomplished in Christ. The hidden plan of salvation is not something that philosophical speculation or even Torah interpretation could arrive at without revelation. As Paul puts it, the mysteries of God must be made known to God's elect through God's Spirit. Because the message of salvation through Christ crucified requires a gift of the Spirit to be recognized as wisdom rather than absurdity, its truth cannot be demonstrated by any system of human reasoning: learned exegesis of Jewish Scriptures, elegant rhetorical sophistication, or the wisdom of one of the popular philosophical schools.

The sharp antithesis between God's revealed truth and human wisdom poses a challenge for Christians today. If God's saving truth can be known only by those whom God calls to a relationship with God-self, then believers have little to say to contemporary intellectuals who reject faith as irreconcilable with scientific knowledge. In this modern Stoicism, the human spirit achieved all the attributes we celebrate on its own. Physician Sherwin Nuland said in an interview:

> That quality, which I call spirit, has permeated our civilization and created the moral and esthetic nutriment by which we are sustained . . . largely of our own making . . . the human spirit is a quality that *Homo Sapiens* by trial and error gradually found within itself over the course of millennia. . . . It lives while we live; it dies while we die. It is neither soul nor shade—it is the essence of human life. (Tippett 2010, 49–50)

That representation of wisdom about the cosmos has no place for the God who breaks into human history and calls people into a relationship with God-self. Rather than attempt to reformulate Christian teaching in categories taken from the biological or human sciences, Paul insists that God's wisdom belongs to a different order of knowing.

Each of these modes of thought has its criteria for evaluating individuals who claim to possess that form of intelligence. Paul has argued that God does not require persons with the talents prized among the socioeconomic or educated elite. Most of those God has called hardly meet the criteria for inclusion among such an elite (1 Cor. 1:26–31). Furthermore, Paul never presented himself in a manner that could lead people to infer that he claimed to be one of the wise (2:1–5). Therefore anyone who tries to evaluate the apostle or the gospel he preached by these standards is acting like an ordinary (*psychikos*) person (2:14). Paul's attack on human wisdom does not mean that Christians should have nothing to do with all that human intelligence can discover about the universe. Paul may not have been much interested in such learning, as he thought that the world as we know it was closing in on its end (7:29–35). Nor is he claiming that God has revealed scientific information in the Scriptures. Paul is contesting the use of such wisdom to evaluate the message of salvation.

1 Corinthians 3:1–4:21

Against Divisions: Paul and Apollos as Exempla

Introductory Matters

Paul returns to the practical problem of dissension with which the letter opened (3:3–4; cf. 1:10–12). He now focuses on himself and Apollos. The earlier references to baptism, to an "of Christ group," have vanished, and the "Cephas" possibility appears only in a list (3:22). This shift leaves three parties under discussion: the Corinthians as a group and the two apostles. At the conclusion of the argument, Paul introduces a fourth individual, his associate Timothy (4:17). The latter, however, is clearly subordinate to Paul as "my beloved child." Apollos is not under Paul's authority. He has a ministry that is comparable to that of the apostle: "We are servants and stewards" (4:1).

   Some scholars think that Apollos had introduced the Corinthians to the concept of Christianity as a higher form of wisdom that made its initiates "the wise" or "the spiritual ones" or "the perfect" (Horsley 1979). Paul takes great pains to undercut any such self-aggrandizing views in this section of the letter. The Corinthians are still on baby food when it comes to Christian truth, he alleges (3:2). But Paul never accuses Apollos of contributing to the distorted view of wisdom prevalent in Corinth. Had Apollos been responsible for false teaching, Paul's description of the relationship between his ministry and that of Apollos would not be credible. Paul laid down the foundation on which Apollos later built (3:4–4:13). Rather than suggest a single ideology behind the problems in Corinth, a wisdom spirituality being taught by Apollos, for example, we will take Paul at his word. He and Apollos continue to labor at the same task. In other words, they possess the "same understanding and same opinion" (1:10) that Paul hopes the Corinthians will adopt. We do not know how detailed Paul's information was. He may have received more than one report about the situation (Arzt-Grabner et al. 2006, 63). Perhaps several factors lay behind the divisiveness in question.

Will the letter alone restore the unity appropriate to "fellowship in Christ"? Paul may hope so, but he hardly leaves the matter to chance. Personal interventions are called for. Paul's associate Timothy will arrive soon. He can remind the community of Paul's teaching and conduct in all the churches (4:17). Within a few months (16:5–8) that visit will be followed by one from the apostle himself. If the situation has not been resolved, Paul will be forced to act like a schoolmaster rather than a loving father (4:13–14, 21).

Assessing the role assigned to Apollos presents several problems, since the extended comparisons that Paul makes in this section appear intended to downgrade a potential competitor. Taking 16:12 at face value, one might conclude that Apollos is present in Ephesus at the time Paul writes 1 Corinthians. Paul wants the Corinthians to conclude that it is Apollos himself and not Paul who has decided not to revisit Corinth in the near future (Murphy-O'Connor 1996, 274–76). Therefore the audience is to infer that Apollos concurs with the depiction of his apostolic ministry being presented by Paul. It is the Corinthians as a group or some unidentified leaders within the local church who got it wrong. But other interpreters see the rhetorical agenda of this section differently. If Apollos built on the results of Paul's founding mission, he did so as a higher-level teacher corrects and enriches what students learned in preliminary studies (Horsley 1979). Since not all church members had the opportunity (or ability?) to receive such instruction, Apollos was responsible for at least one division within the church, the separation between Christians who have received instruction in the higher mysteries of the faith and a majority of ordinary believers.

This tension illuminates the sharp tone that Paul adopts in the transitional passage (3:1–4; Zeller 2010, 150). Some commentators treat these verses as part of the previous section (Fitzmyer 2008, 170). Paul punctuates the new beginning by opening with a sharp "but I" (*kagō*; also 2:1). The previous section extended the possibility that Paul might be about to share his knowledge with the audience. They certainly would have put themselves in the category of "Spirit-endowed people." Suddenly Paul pulls the rug out from under them. The divisions between the "of Apollos" and "of Paul" camps prove that the audience is not capable of receiving grown-up instruction.

We do not know how much time has elapsed since either man had visited Corinth, possibly several years. Since sailing on the Corinth-Ephesus route ended in early fall and 1 Corinthians is being written just as sea travel resumes in early spring, Apollos has been in Ephesus for almost a year (Murphy-O'Connor 1996, 275). The Corinthians have received at least one letter from Paul since he left the city (5:9). Perhaps neither the version of events that the Corinthians remember nor that which Paul has asked them to remember (2:1–5) is accurate. Clearly Paul is pulling out all the stops to reconstruct how the Corinthians remember the role of both apostles in their founding. He does so in anticipation of his own return to Corinth at some future time (4:21). That visit turned out to be a disaster that further soured Paul's relationships with this church (2 Cor. 1:12–2:11).

The first half of Paul's revisionist argument asks readers to "remember" Apollos as one who cultivates what Paul has planted or who builds according to Paul's architectural plan

Baker Photo Archive

Figure 10. Theater Ruins.

(1 Cor. 3:6–17). The second half employs a rhetorical technique of comparison (*synkrisis*) to set the "wealthy, privileged, ruling" Corinthians over against the poor, humiliated apostles (4:6–13). No one can miss the heavy tone of sarcasm in these verses. The question remains: how close are they to describing actual persons or events? Since the degrading associations attached to manual labor (4:12a; see "Christianity in an Urban Setting" in the introduction) were attached to Paul's working at his trade in Corinth (9:12b–18), many readers assume that everything in this depiction of the apostles reflects Paul's personal biography. But if that were true, could the same be said of Apollos? Not necessarily.

An alternative interpretation of Paul's rhetorical agenda suggests a scenario comparable to that of campaign videos posted on the internet. Just as today's candidates look for a striking image that will generate buzz, like politician Sarah Palin's "mama grizzlies," Paul invokes familiar tropes. The terminology of "becoming a fool" (3:18), "being put on display [*theatron*] before the entire world" (4:9), and "fools, weak, dishonored on account of Christ" (4:10) proves that the entire scenario is imagined in terms of popular entertainment. The Corinthians with their alleged wisdom are compared to the social elite who have special seating, privileges, even their own entrances to theaters and amphitheaters. They are far removed from the populace, not to mention performers or victims whose suffering provides entertainment (Toner 2009, 93–122). Yet Paul is treading on treacherous ground rhetorically. One of the pleasures that the populace took in athletic contests, theatrical shows, and spectacles in the arena was just what Paul is condemning: conflicts between factions. While the Roman elite saw the behavior of such "soccer hooligans" as evidence of social decline, the crowds relished it (Toner 2009, 115–16).

What sort of display or spectacle does Paul have in mind? The remarks about the apostles being displayed "last" as "condemned men" (4:9), combined with the earlier emphasis on the cross (1:18, 23; 2:8), lead most readers to imagine the display of condemned captives in a Roman triumph (Schrage 1991, 342; Fee 1987, 174) or gladiator show (Thiselton 2000; Dunkle 2008, 172–73). Painted scenes depict the victor's conquest, captured booty, enslaved captives, and defeated nobility—some headed for immediate execution—being led through the streets (Tyldesley 2008). And, more important for those who would never witness a triumph, many more people were familiar with its representations in literature and art (Beard 2007). Perhaps the descendants of Julius Caesar's veterans who had settled at Corinth had heard of his triumph in Rome from their fathers or grandfathers. Even if they had never seen a Roman triumph firsthand, Paul's audience knew the difference between turning out to witness the humiliation and execution of the once-proud scion of a noble house and the execution of ordinary criminal types during a regional gladiator show. So, if God intends to put condemned apostles on display, they have to have exactly the characteristics of noble bearing that Paul says that he did not have (2:1–5).

Recognizing the difficulties in the Roman-triumph interpretation of Paul's imagery, scholars propose alternatives. By taking the word *theatron* as a reference to theatrical performances, one can rescript this entire section as an allusion to Roman *mime* or lowbrow comedy, which has something of a slapstick character. Slaves and other seedy types are depicted in such farces. Crucifixion serves as an occasion to mock the victim. Sometimes the fool manages to outwit or deceive the elite master (Welborn 2005, 2–3). The assorted hardships catalogued in this section reflect what happens to characters in this sort of comedy. Thus the participle *diōkomenoi* (4:12) should not be translated "persecuted," as though for confessing Christ, but "harassed" like the poor victim in a mime (Welborn 2005, 79). This proposal also presents historical difficulties. It presumes a level of engagement with Roman cultural expression that one would not expect of Paul, since Jews did not perform this type of mime (Goodman 2007, 298).

After surveying the evidence and difficulties with both the spectacle interpretation—whether the spectacle in mind is a triumph or a gladiator show—and the mime interpretation, Nguyen concludes that the only option left is the display of prisoners to be executed in the arena (2007; 2008). This hypothesis still presumes close cultural ties between characteristically Roman behavior in making a spectacle of executions (Kyle 1998) and what was the case in first-century Corinth (Nguyen 2008, 37). Roman historians seeking to demonstrate the brutality of emperors they despised, like Caligula and Nero, employ this image. They accuse these emperors of forcing citizens and even members of the elite to perform (and die) in degrading exhibitions (Suetonius, *Caligula* 27.3–4; Dio Cassius, *Historia romana* 61.17.3). Read as though God were the "producer" of the spectacle in which God's apostles die in the arena, Paul's argument becomes truly shocking (Nguyen 2008, 47). Of course, later Christians know many stories of heroic martyrs subjected to gruesome public execution, but the Corinthians did not. We lack chronological evidence for the spread of spectacle executions of "despised persons" to the Roman east by the mid-first century AD. Therefore, we are uncertain to what extent theories advanced by Roman historians concerning the negotiations of status between the populace, the local elite, and their rulers in the arena represent the social code at play in first-century Corinth.

Nguyen's proposal has the advantage of disentangling Paul's images from later martyrdom tales of heroic death. In doing so, it illuminates the shock to the cultural sensibilities of a first-century audience represented by Paul's words. But Paul's rhetorical ploy carries its own risks. Rather than question their cultural assumptions, the Corinthians might find this picture revolting. If Apollos had provided a different model of the mature Christian as wise or spiritual, Paul's description might persuade the undecided to jump to the Apollos group. The Roman-triumph or spectacle metaphor is less likely to alienate hearers. It only asks the audience to forget what Paul had said about his "fear and trembling" earlier. It indulges the Corinthians' natural inclinations to view the apostles as elite persons. The heroic death of someone who was once a proud king deprives the victor of the honor he seeks by humiliating the enemies of Rome. Paul saves that image for the sarcastic conclusion to this rhetorical comparison (4:6–13): "You are rich, without us you have become kings—would that you were kings so that we might rule along with you" (4:8).

Finally the comparison of Paul's images with low comedy takes a completely different view of the emotional trade-offs being negotiated in this section. Paul is out to shake up the boasting and self-importance of some in Corinth by adopting the role of the abused fool and casting his audience as self-important braggarts. Turning the world upside down and mocking those who ruled their lives was a central feature of popular entertainment. In Rome itself social hierarchy was tossed to the winds during the Saturnalia festival, closer to public celebrations we know as carnival. In that setting slaves might act like freedmen and the despised strut about like kings (Toner 2009, 92–95). Since neither the role of braggart pretending to be king ascribed to his audience nor the role of a beaten and abused fool ascribed to Paul (and Apollos) has any resemblance to their actual social situation, both sides can laugh at the caricature and return to the business at hand.

What begins as a simple legal metaphor—only the master can evaluate the work of his managers (4:1–2)—concludes on an eschatological note, the divine judgment of all humanity (4:5). The intervening verses introduce the possibility that the Corinthians ("you") or some other human entity might pass judgment on Paul (4:3). He insists that there are no possible grounds for a guilty verdict by any human judge; only the Lord can render the final judgment in his case (4:4). What sort of judgment is being envisaged? The verb *anakrinein* can refer to an inquiry or examination of a question, an inquiry aimed at discovering facts in a legal setting, or a judicial case (BDAG 66). Therefore Paul does not envisage the sort of judgment awarded to or withheld from skilled orators or those who perform in the arena in which the stakes are a victor's crown. He must have a legal proceeding in view. The peculiar expression "by a human day" must refer to any human court in contrast to God's "day" of judgment (3:13).

Paul's several imprisonments would be reason enough for concern over condemnation by civil authorities (e.g., Phil. 1:12–14; 2 Cor. 11:23–25; 2 Tim. 4:16–18). Other interpreters detect an allusion to Job 27:6 LXX in the reference to Paul's own clear conscience (R. Collins 1999, 173): "And attending to righteousness [*dikaiosynē*], I will not let go; for I am not conscious of [*synoida emautō*] disgraceful actions." In other words, the defendant swears an oath affirming his innocence of any charges, though unlike Job's oath, Paul's extends only as far as any human court. He is willing to permit God to have the final word in the matter.

The images that Paul employs in this section of the letter are critical to its emotional impact on the audience. Paul is not playing it safe. He risks giving offense at several points. The opening transition (1 Cor. 3:1–4) shatters the audience goodwill that Paul might have achieved in the prior section by hinting that he conveys the Spirit-endowed wisdom he possesses (2:6–16). "You are not old enough," he tells them and returns instead to the previous discussion of factions. The first major section (3:5–23) picks up the slogan list of 1:12. The comparisons establish the proper hierarchical order: Paul sets out the plan, Apollos helps execute it (3:5–17), but both are subject to the Lord (3:5, 9). Paul reminds the audience that God reverses the standards of wisdom and folly prevalent in the world. Therefore boasting in human status should be rejected (3:18–21; 1:18–25). The section concludes with a return to the opening list of three human figures—Paul, Apollos, and Peter—and "Christ, the messiah of God," to whom all believers belong (3:22–23).

The ordering implicit in this section appears to solve the problem of factions. For all its turmoil the Saturnalia reaffirms the sociopolitical hierarchy that is mocked. Paul's images provide suitable roles for himself and Apollos while insisting on God as the source of any success. He also invites the community to see itself as the temple of God's Spirit (3:16–17), an image to which he will return (6:19). Rhetorically one might consider the issue of factions resolved by this return to order. Yet Paul will not let it go. The opening section focused on Paul and Apollos in relation to each other. He now turns to a comparison between the pair—Paul and Apollos—and the Corinthians: "I have used these things as a pattern for myself and Apollos because of you" (4:6).

As this discussion of the images shows, its emotional register is complex. It opens with the legal metaphor supporting the master's right to judge his household servants (4:1–5). That comparison is intended to ward off criticism of Paul's conduct (4:4). Then Paul draws the complicated comparison in which he and Apollos are possibly captured enemies on display in a Roman triumph, criminals slated for execution in an arena, or actors on the comic stage (4:6–13). The audience may be alternatively inspired by noble bearing, in awe of Roman power, disgusted by routine criminals, or amused by comic reversal. The success of Paul's argument depends on the audience's emotional response. Paul acknowledges the fragile situation (4:14–15). They could be offended. He hopes that they will recognize him as a loving father in Christ and will, like beloved children, copy his example (4:16). Since the travel plans that conclude this section (4:17–21) present a desired—"in love and a spirit of gentleness"—and less desired—"with a rod"—tone to Paul's visit, the apostle is uncertain about the impact of his words.

Tracing the Train of Thought

Factions as Signs of Immaturity (3:1–4)

3:1–4. Paul's **but as for me, brothers, I cannot address you as enlightened/spiritual persons** (3:1) comes as a shock to an audience that considers itself enlightened or spiritual persons who "evaluate all things" (2:15). Paul sharpens the contrast between a mature Christian faith and the attitudes of Christians in Corinth with two antitheses: **spiritual** (*pneumatikos*) or **enlightened** over against **desiring** (*sarkinos*), and adult Christian over against a **baby** (*nēpios*). Whereas Paul previously contrasted the insight proper to a mature Christian as *pneumatikos* over against ordinary human understanding, *psychikos* (2:14–15), Paul demotes his audience even further by using adjectives based on the Greek word for "flesh" (*sarx*) in this section. Since the parallel phrase refers to the audience as **babies**, his point appears to be that such persons are acting out of the basic desires that govern an infant's behavior. This is certainly an insult to any adult. The antithetical pair *spirit-flesh* is characteristic of Paul's own theological vocabulary (5:5; 2 Cor. 7:1; Rom. 8:4–6, 9, 13; Gal. 3:3;

> **1 Corinthians 3:1–4:21 in the Rhetorical Flow**
>
> **The letter opening (1:1–9)**
>
> **Against divisions: God's wisdom (1:10–2:16)**
>
> ▶ **Against divisions: Paul and Apollos as *exempla* (3:1–4:21)**
>
>   Factions as signs of immaturity (3:1–4)
>
>   The role of apostles, planting and building (3:5–23)
>
>   Responsibility of apostle servants to the Lord (4:1–5)
>
>   Apostles as "fools for Christ" (4:6–13)
>
>   Paul's concern for the community and travel plans (4:14–21)

Ancient Authors on Infant Behavior

Bodily Desires Expressed

"For my desires were internal; adults were external to me and had no means of entering my soul. So I threw my limbs about and uttered sounds and signs resembling my wishes.... When I did not get my way, ... I used to be indignant with my elders for their disobedience, and with free people who were not slaves to my interests; and I would revenge myself upon them by weeping. That this is the way of infants I have learned from those I have been able to watch." (Augustine, *Confessionum* 1.6, trans. Chadwick 1998 [modified])

Milk as Child's Food

"Who could the adult [anthrōpos] in each of us be but the mind [nous] whose job is to reap benefits from all that is planted. But as milk is nourishment for babies [nēpios], while for adults [teleios] there is wheat bread, there must be a form of milklike food for the soul, that is elementary schooling, while for adult men instructions leading to wisdom [phronēsis], self-control [sōphrosynē], and all virtue." (Philo, *De agricultura* 9 AT)

Emotional Outbursts

"Will you sit and cry like little children [paidion]? What did you do at school?... Why did you record yourself as a philosopher when you might have put down the real state of affairs as: 'I studied a few introductions ... but I did not get in the door of a philosopher.' ... Are you not willing, finally, like little children to be weaned and eat more solid food and stop crying for your mammas and nurses?" (Epictetus, *Diatribai* 2.16, 34, 39 AT)

4:29; 5:17; Fitzmyer 2008, 186). Ordinarily he uses the noun and adjective "flesh" for the domination of sin in human life (e.g., Rom. 7:13–25; Dunn 1998, 62–70). Those overtones are only moderately present in this passage, as Paul connects the designation *sarkinoi* with the **jealousy and strife** in the church (1 Cor. 3:3a).

Paul turns to a commonplace of moral exhortation. One must give up childish ways to achieve the virtues of rational self-control in philosophic teaching or to express genuine devotion to God in Jewish or Christian teaching. Paul's statement that **jealousy and conflict** prove that the Corinthians **are still not capable** of digesting **solid food** belongs to this familiar paradigm.

Although Philo compares the preliminary studies one must master before the "higher learning" of philosophical pedagogy to an infant's **milk**, Paul does not propose a "higher level" of Christian instruction with this comparison. He is chiding the Corinthians for failure to engage the moral conversion expected of Christians. Instead they continue **to act like ordinary human beings** (3:3).

The Role of Apostles, Planting and Building (3:5–23)

3:5. Since the divisions in question center on Paul and Apollos, Paul redefines their role as **servants** [*diakonoi*] **through whom you came to believe.** Just as the letter opening reminded readers that they were called by God (1:2, 9), so those who preach the gospel take no credit for the faith of those who hear the preaching. Both Paul and Apollos simply carry out their assigned tasks, **to each one as the Lord has allotted** [it]. As Paul develops the metaphor in what follows, he and Apollos are not engaged in the same operation. God has entrusted Paul with the establishment of what is to be grown or built. Apollos is the servant who must take care of what has been established.

3:6–9. The relationships among the three parties are reinforced by a series of elegantly crafted parallel phrases. The first two (3:6–7) sets highlight God's role in the process:

A **I planted, Apollos watered**
  B **but God caused the growth**
A′ **so that the one who plants is not important, nor the one who waters**
  B′ **but God who causes the growth**

Then the relationship between the apostles is depicted as that of hired agricultural workers (3:8–9a):

A″ **the one who plants and the one who waters are equivalent** ["one"]
  C **each will receive his wage appropriate to his labor**
  B″ **for we are coworkers with God**

The conclusion (3:9b–c) wraps up this comparison by referring to the community as **God's cultivated field** and then shifts to a new metaphor, **God's building.**

3:10–11. Though the metaphor of agricultural workers does not distinguish one from another in terms of knowledge or skill, simply the labor involved, the building image does. Paul is superior to Apollos: **as the skilled** [*sophos*] **architect to lay the foundation, while someone else builds.** Suddenly Paul is willing to claim that contested term *sophos* ("wise"), which in this instance refers to the skill required for the architect of a building project. Of course, as Paul goes on to insist, **no one can put down any other foundation beside that which has been laid, namely Jesus Christ** (3:11). Once again he brings the audience back to the gospel that he had preached in Corinth, Christ crucified (1:17; 2:2).

Community as God's Planting and Building

The *Community Rule* found at Qumran depicts the community of God's holy people as an eternal planting and building. Paul may have a similar picture in mind in juxtaposing the two metaphors (R. Collins 1999, 147):

"To be an everlasting plantation, a holy house for Israel" (1QS 8.5, trans. García Martínez and Tigchelaar 1997, 89)

"And he has given them an inheritance in the lot of the holy ones. He unites their assembly to the sons of the heavens in order (to form) the council of the Community and a foundation of the building of holiness to be an everlasting plantation." (1QS 11.7–8, trans. García Martínez and Tigchelaar 1997, 97)

3:12–15. Since Paul has laid the true foundation, any flaws in the building must be laid at the feet of those responsible for building the superstructure. The list of building materials, **gold, silver, precious stones, wood, straw, reeds** (3:12b), initially seems to be ordered by value. The first three were used only on public buildings, temples (1 Chron. 29:2), or palaces; the second group were used in ordinary homes or dwellings cobbled together by the poor. The list ignores the rough-hewn stone and mud brick required for walls. Paul's focus is not, however, on actual buildings but the fate of each group of materials in a fire. A series of short phrases rubs in the warning (3:13):

A the work of each one will become clear
  B for the day will show that it is revealed by fire
A′ the work of each of what sort it is
  B′ the fire will test it

Paul's audience may respond to this image on two levels. The fire might be the devastating outburst in the poorly built urban tenement or the deliberate destruction of a wealthy person's house or a temple in a riot. For those familiar with biblical images, it might be the end-time fire of God's judgment (Mal. 3:2; Dan. 7:9; 2 Esd. [4 Ezra] 13:10; 1QS 4.13; 1QpHab 10.13; Matt. 3:10–12). The awkward description of builders receiving their wages in the next sentence works only if the metaphor refers to divine judgment. A builder whose construction survives **will receive wages; if a person's work is burned up, it is lost, but the individual will be saved** (3:14b–15b). A builder might forfeit some penalty if the work was not up to code (Thiselton 2000, 308), but testing by fire before paying the workmen hardly makes sense. If the builders in question are missionaries like Apollos, who built on Paul's foundation, then the awkward distinction between the lost work and a "saved" builder is clear. God may not reject the individuals in question. But for those whose faith is constructed out of the shoddy materials, their teaching provides a risk of being lost in the judgment. Paul expresses a comparable anxiety about his own efforts when he refers to the danger of "having labored in vain" (1 Thess. 3:5; Phil. 2:16).

3:16–17. The valuable materials of the building metaphor could evoke images of a temple. Paul shifts to the second-person plural, addressing the audience directly: **Do you not know that you are God's sanctuary, and the Spirit of God dwells in you?** (3:16). This image of the community as the Spirit-filled sanctuary returns frequently in the letter. Moral laxity corrupts the holiness of a sacred space (e.g., 6:19–20). An axiom that destroying a temple might evoke divine wrath highlights the necessity of holiness within the community: **If someone ruins the sanctuary of God, God will ruin that person** (3:17a).

3:18–23. Paul returns to the situation in Corinth, partisanship for one or another apostle rooted in esteem for those cultural achievements that mark

---

Urban Fire Damage in Ancient Rome

Cicero's house was torched when he was sent into exile (58 BC): "Unless you somehow imagined when you were tearing down walls and tossing your criminal torches on roofs that some part of my (real) property was being ruined or going up in flames . . ." (*Paradoxa Stoicorum* 3.28 AT).

The following famous temples were damaged or destroyed by fire:

Temple of the Nymphs (Cicero, *Paradoxa Stoicorum* 3.31)
Temple of Castor (Cicero, *In Verrem* 2.1.129–54)
Temple of Jupiter Optimus Maximus (Suetonius, *Julius Caesar* 15)
Temple of Magna Mater (Ovid, *Fasti* 4.251–72)
Temple of Apollo (Suetonius, *Augustus* 29; Pliny, *Naturalis historia* 36.24–32)
Temple of Mars Ultor ("the Avenger") (Suetonius, *Augustus* 29; Ovid, *Fasti* 5.545–98; Pliny *Naturalis historia* 36.102)
Temple of Vesta (Dio Cassius, *Historia romana* 54.24)

The great fire of 19 July AD 64, which raged for nine days, damaged or destroyed a number of important shrines, including those of Vesta, Apollo on the Palatine, and Juno Moneta (Tacitus, *Annales* 15.36–41; Suetonius, *Nero* 38; Dio Cassius, *Historia romana* 62.18). For a historical evaluation of these events, see Champlin 2003, 171–200.

Augustus claimed to have repaired eighty-two temples in 28 BC alone and built or restored fourteen others during his reign (*Res gestae divi Augusti* 19–21; Beard, North, and Price 1998, 1:196–201). These achievements in caring for sacred places that lay in ruins show that "it was not enough to place humankind in his debt; he obligated even the gods" (Ovid, *Fasti* 2.57–70 AT).

Jupiter Complains about Augustus's New Temple

Augustus built a new temple to Jupiter Tonans near that of Jupiter Optimus Maximus, one of those he restored after fire damage (Beard, North, and Price 1998, 1:201). The lavish gifts made to restoring the Temple of Jupiter Optimus Maximus included 16,000 pounds of gold, along with pearls and precious stones valued at 500,000 gold pieces (Suetonius, *Augustus* 30). According to Suetonius, the older Jupiter objected to a decline in traffic:

"One day after he [Augustus] had been frequenting the Temple of Jupiter Tonans [the Thunderer] that he himself had established on the Capitoline Hill, Capitoline Jupiter appeared to him in a dream complaining that the newcomer was stealing worshipers. He replied, 'I put the Thunderer close to your temple because I had decided you should have a janitor.' When Augustus woke up, he hung bells from the front of the new building to make it look like an entry door." (*Augustus* 91 AT)

---

an individual as wise (*sophos*). Having argued that the wisdom of this age is contrary to God's wisdom displayed on the cross (1:18–20; 2:8–9), Paul suggests, **"If someone among you appears wise according to the standards of the present age, let him become a fool in order to actually be wise"** (3:18). His own ministry was just such an act of deliberate status reduction. Even in the metaphors of temple building, Paul does not insert himself or Apollos as the wealthy patron who seeks architectural immortality. Though the skilled architect ranked above the actual builders, both belonged to the class of paid laborers (Horrell 1996, 202).

Citations of Job 5:12–13 and Ps. 94:11 in 1 Cor. 3:19–20 support the premise that **this world's wisdom is folly with God**. At this point the listener anticipates **so that no one can boast in human beings** (3:21a) and the list of names **Paul, Apollos, Cephas** (3:22a) that sparked the whole discussion (1:12). But Paul adds what appears to be a concession to those who adopt the policy **all things are yours** (3:21b) in addition to the named apostles: **the universe, life, death, present, future, all things are yours; you are Christ's and Christ is God's** (3:22b–23). The expression **all things are yours** echoes a slogan familiar to Stoic moralists. Cicero chides those who burned down his house when he was condemned to exile with falsely thinking they had attacked what was his. The possessions of a wise person are not external but are reason and tranquility of spirit (*Paradoxa Stoicorum* 28–31).

Paul is not recommending such Stoic detachment. Using paradox to dislodge the audience's views is comparable to Stoic tactics of moral improvement. But Paul's rationale for rejecting the ordinary, worldly standards of honor differs from the logical arguments advanced by philosophical pedagogues. The audience possesses **all things** because they belong to Christ.

Responsibility of Apostle Servants to the Lord (4:1–5)

4:1–5. Though the Corinthians claim a special relationship to the apostles in Christ, Paul denies that any human is competent to evaluate whether his ministry is faithful to the God who called him. The apostles are **house slaves** or **estate managers** entrusted with **the mysteries of God**, that is, with preaching the gospel of the crucified (2:6–9). Everyone knows the basic job requirement for estate managers—**that a person be found trustworthy [*pistos*]** (4:2). The *oikonomos* (**estate manager**) possessed the authority to manage an owner's agricultural estate or workshop in the master's absence. In the urban context an *oikonomos* might be a business agent, city treasurer, or the treasurer of a private association (Fitzmyer 2008, 212). Thus managers possessed authority over other slaves attached to the household (Columella, *De re rustica* 1.8.3; Harrill 1995, 103–10). Columella encourages owners to visit their farms periodically to check on conditions and moderate any abuses by the slave who serves as estate manager (*De re rustica* 1.8.17–18).

Paul jumps from the commonplace that slaves are judged and punished by their owners to divine judgment: **For I am not aware of any failing on my part, but I am not justified on that account, for it is the Lord who evaluates me** (4:4). This judgment is more searching than that of any human master, since it is **the Lord who brings what is hidden in darkness to light and reveals the plans of the heart** (4:5a–b). Moralists encouraged human masters to treat slaves justly and moderate the harsh punishments that slaves often suffered (Philo, *De decalogo* 167; *De specialibus legibus* 2.90–92). No one has to fear such arbitrary treatment when the Lord is judge. Since Paul concludes that **the praise will be accorded each one from God** (4:5c), he clearly refers to God's eschatological judgment. The image is not simply a surprise inspection by the owner.

Apostles as "Fools for Christ" (4:6–13)

4:6–7. The point Paul hopes to make is clear enough, **that one of you not arrogantly set one person above another** (4:6c) or treat as one's own achievement what is God's gift, **and if you received, why boast as though you did not receive [it as a gift]?** (4:7b). The introduction that leads to this conclusion bristles with difficulties. **These things I have spoken figuratively about myself and Apollos for your sake** leaves the referent of **these things** ambiguous. Paul could be alluding to everything he has written up to this point or to the discussion of their respective roles that began at 3:5. In that case, **these things** designates the collection of images and analogies presented up to this point: planting, building construction, temple destruction, and slaves entrusted with responsibilities for the owner's property. The verb *meteschēmatisa* (**I have spoken figuratively**) is also problematic. It ordinarily means to change shape or to disguise oneself, pretending to be something else. Whose shape is being changed? By the end of the section, it appears to be the Corinthians who must reshape themselves to fit the model of the apostle: "become my imitators" (4:16; Fitzmyer 2008, 214). At this point Paul could be using such overtones to suggest that these analogies are providing a different form or shape to the apostles in order to correct the way in which the Corinthians understand what it means to be an apostle of Christ.

That solution still leaves the opaque phrase that Paul uses to indicate the purpose of his speech: **So that you may learn with our help "not beyond what has been written"** (4:6b). Ordinarily phrases of the sort "it is/was/has been written" in one of Paul's letters refer to passages from Scripture. The reader would expect a citation or paraphrase of one to follow, as is the case with the two citations in 3:19–20: "For it has been written." Therefore the simplest solution to this enigmatic phrase is to consider it a verbal shorthand directing the audience back to those verses, or perhaps to the whole series of citations about God's wisdom contradicting human wisdom that began at 1:19 and includes 1:29, 31 (Fee 1987, 167–68). That solution could accommodate the possibility that Paul also intends to focus on the whole argument being presented. If the expression **not beyond what has been written** was a familiar shorthand, we have no other examples to determine its meaning (Schrage 1991, 336).

However the elliptical phrase works, the following clause indicates the purpose of this exhortation: **that you not be puffed up each one over another** (4:6b). Paul follows it with a series of ironical questions to suggest that no one in the audience has any grounds for superiority over others (1:26–31). **Who sets you apart?** (4:7) he asks. The reference to an inflated sense of self might be keyed to the previous comments about managers and their owners as well as the comic depictions of slaves. Slave managers for wealthy owners often copied their masters in lording it over those under them. Agricultural handbooks are as concerned with the behavior of slave managers as with that of owners. The manager could put those under him in prison. Harsh and abusive practices create risks of rebellion that could destroy the whole enterprise (Harrill 2006, 105–12).

The accusation of boasting over what is not one's own achievement but something received (4:7) refers to their faith. The letter's thanksgiving opens with "I give thanks to my God always on your behalf for the gracious gift of God given you in Christ Jesus, that you have been enriched in every way in him" (1:4–5a). The arrogance that Paul has in view does not come from the social or economic status of the audience. It is a consequence of their Christian calling. The letter is not clear about how that faith and the partisanship for one or another apostle are connected.

4:8–13. Paul is not finished with his attack on the inflated self-importance of some in Corinth. Just as his earlier images separated apostles from the elite by comparing them to laborers and slaves, he now contrasts the lowly, even despised, condition of the apostles with the exalted claims of his audience.

Table 9
The Corinthians and the Apostles Compared

Boastful Corinthians	Lowly apostles
full, wealthy (4:8a)	hungry, thirsty, and clothed in rags (4:11a)
(alleged) kings (4:8b)	condemned men (4:9)
intelligent (*phronimos*) in Christ	fools for Christ (4:10)
strong	weak (4:10)
honored	dishonored (4:10)
—	harassed, homeless, cursed, persecuted, slandered (4:11b–13a)
—	like garbage, scum (4:13b)

Few of the Corinthians were from the elite, learned, or wealthy classes (1:26–31). Most, like Paul himself, would have **worked with their hands** (4:12a). Have the Corinthians really found such status enhancement in joining the new movement? Perhaps not to the extreme that Paul's rhetoric suggests. The standard comic trope of a braggart incorporates the element of self-deception.

The situation is less stereotyped in the case of the apostles. At least some of the hardships mentioned were the consequences of traveling from city to city preaching the gospel (2 Cor. 11:16–33). Whether overland on foot or in steerage on ship, travel was difficult and dangerous. Suspicions about the new movement meant arrest and exile from a city, not the honors paid to leading citizens or skilled orators, whose public performances made them wealthy. The catalogue of hardships on Paul's side of the ledger shifts from reality to imagination only at the extremes when he mentions being put on display as **last of all** and despised as the world's **refuse** (1 Cor. 4:9, 13). But how does Paul's audience come to be so thoroughly identified with the wealthy and powerful elite?

Some scholars suggest that a misrepresentation of the gospel that presented Christianity as a form of human wisdom fostered that attitude. Philosophical traditions ascribed true kingship to the wise, whose souls have been drawn away from sense perception and pleasure to the divine. Adapting that view to a Jewish religious context, Philo allegorizes the story of Abraham as an example of the soul's transformation: "It will not remain in Haran, the senses, but withdraws into itself. . . . Amid such vessels of the soul as the body and senses it was not able to hear the principles and rules of kingship, for we say the wisdom is kingship and the wise man, a king" (*De migratione Abrahami* 195–97 AT).

Welborn (2005, 121–39, 232–42) takes a theatrical approach to this section. Not only are the apostles the slavish, degraded figures of Roman mime, but the self-absorbed audience also comes in for a drubbing. By adopting the perspective of the masses, comedy also portrays the abusiveness of the wealthy and powerful. This perspective allows an indirect criticism of Paul's audience. If they consider themselves "rich, wise, kings," they might be cast as the domineering kings who drag the poor, oppressed slaves along only to make an exhibition of their suffering (Welborn 2005, 232). Paul does not, however, adopt the pose of a degraded character in Roman comedy. When the apostle faces hostility, he responds as Christians were exhorted: **When cursed, we bless; when persecuted, we endure it; when slandered, we comfort** (4:12b–13a; cf. Rom. 12:14–18). Perhaps Paul intends this reminder of Christian teaching about how one responds to hostility as a conciliatory gesture toward his audience. If any of them have cursed or slandered him, he will respond with patience and kindness (Fee 1987, 179). A neatly turned chiasmus in 4:13b brings this segment to a close with verbal insult (Fitzmyer 2008, 220):

A we have become
  B as refuse
  B′ of the world
A′ scum up to the present time

Paul's Concern for the Community and Travel Plans (4:14–21)

4:14–15. Since the previous verse ended with an example of taunting or hate speech that was or could be directed at the degraded apostle, an audience might anticipate a response. Instead he steps back, giving the audience a glimpse of the writer puzzling over the words to put on the page: **I am not writing these things as a way of shaming you** (4:14a). The parental image that introduced this section of the letter (3:1–2) returns. The imagined audience is no longer nursing infants but school-age children supervised by slave pedagogues, **instructing you as my dear children, for you have millions of pedagogues in Christ but not many fathers** (4:14b–15a). This distinction establishes the special authority that Paul as the founding apostle enjoys in relationship to the Corinthian church.

4:16–17. As their father, Paul expects compliance with his directives: **become my imitators** (4:16). The injunction to imitate a parent or a revered teacher was commonplace in ancient moralists. It was assumed that the philosopher provided his students with the living example of his teaching. But the effectiveness of imitation depends on living in the presence of the exemplary teacher, not reading the occasional letter. To fill the gap left by his long absence from Corinth, Paul must call on a substitute, one of his closest associates: **I sent you Timothy, my beloved child who is trustworthy in the Lord, who will remind you** (4:17).

The chronology of this visit relative to the composition of 1 Corinthians is unclear. Had Timothy already departed for Corinth prior to the reports Paul has received? Did he leave after those reports but prior to the letter from Corinth that Paul will begin answering in 1 Cor. 7? Has he been there and returned,

---

On Imitating a Father's Virtues

Emperor Marcus Aurelius (died 180) reflects on the example of his adopted father, Antoninus Pius (died 161), as the ideal Stoic ruler:

"Be careful not to be turned into a 'Caesar,' not dyed with the imperial purple. . . . Remain . . . the friend of justice, pious, kind, with strength for your own work. Wrestle to continue as the person philosophy wished you to become. . . . In all things like a pupil imitate Antoninus; his consistent way of acting in accord with reason . . . his gentleness, his disregard for glory. . . . How he let nothing go without first investigating and understanding it . . . would suffer those who blamed him unjustly . . . refused to entertain slander . . . not putting on a show of being a wise man; how he was content with little, in lodging, . . . dress, food . . . loved work and was long-suffering." (Meditations 6.30 AT)

---

providing Paul with additional information about the situation? Or does the past tense imply that Timothy will be sent along with the letter? That seems improbable, as Timothy is not included in the letter greeting (1:1), and 16:10 suggests that Timothy may not reach Corinth before the letter does. Therefore it would appear that Paul had already instructed Timothy to leave for Corinth, a visit that will occur in close proximity to their receipt of this letter.

Timothy's presence will provide the Corinthians with an example of Christian virtues: **my way of living in Christ** (4:17b). Since the Corinthians have been contrasting Paul with Apollos, Paul emphasizes the universality of his teaching: **as I teach everywhere in every church** (4:17c). By the time 1 Corinthians is completed, a number of important figures in the Corinthian church have visited Paul in Ephesus (16:17). Upon returning to Corinth, Gaius, Fortunatus, and Achaicus will be able to testify that the content of 1 Corinthians corresponds to Paul's teaching and practice in all the churches (also 11:16; 14:33b). This claim to universality is not simply a way to enhance the apostle's authority. A first-century audience would recognize the implicit refutation of rhetorical skill as desirable in an apostle. Rhetoricians adapt their words and conduct to each audience. Paul does nothing of the sort. He remains the same in every community.

4:18–21. Paul concludes with another familiar image of parental authority, a father disciplining his son: **Shall I come to you with a rod or with love and gentleness?** (4:21).

He hopes to visit Corinth soon and find out for himself about the situation, as **some [are] puffed up with self-importance** (4:18). The contrast between the **speech of self-important people** and **power** (4:19b) allows Paul to formulate a maxim: **The kingdom of God is not in speech but in power** (4:20). This maxim recalls the contrast that he has been making throughout between

On Disciplining Schoolboys

Augustine describes his experiences as a schoolboy. His father added to the teacher's punishment. Even God will not spare him the rod:

"I was next sent to school.... If ever I was lazy at learning, I was beaten. This method was approved by adults.... As a boy, I began to pray to you, 'my help and my refuge' (Ps. 93:22).... Though I was only a small child, I begged you passionately that I not be beaten at school. When you did not listen so as 'not to give me to foolishness' (Ps. 21:3), adults, even my own parents, used to laugh at my bruises, which at the time were torture to me." (Confessionum 1.14 AT)

Childhood itself is a punishment worse than death for an adult:

"Boys are compelled, under pain of severe punishment, to learn trades or letters. Yet the learning to which they are driven ... is itself such a punishment, that they often prefer the pain that forces them to learn over the learning itself. If anyone were offered the choice between death and becoming a child again, who would not shrink from the second and choose to die?" (De civitate Dei 21.14 AT)

conventional human wisdom or clever speech and God's wisdom or power. Of course, however difficult it was for Paul to make a commanding public appearance, his letters employ familiar rhetorical devices (2 Cor. 10:10–11). Using or formulating proverbial sayings makes one's speech memorable (Aristotle, *Rhetorica* 3.10–11). Of course, the "power" in Paul's kingdom saying is God's power, not that of some human authority.

If the Corinthians continue to behave like errant schoolboys, they have chosen the rod. Before Paul arrives in person, however, his letter and Timothy's visit will provide the opportunity to rectify the problems in the community. Paul hopes for that outcome.

Theological Issues

For contemporary readers this section raises questions about Paul's authority that would not have occurred to a first-century audience. The apostle has manipulated the metaphors used to describe himself, Apollos, and Timothy to consolidate his own position as the absent father in a patriarchal family (Wanamaker 2007). The opening disclaimers that Paul did not employ rhetorical sophistication in preaching link his ministry as founder with God's own power, awakening faith in the hearts of his audience. Consequently one should infer that opposing Paul would be equivalent to rejecting God's word (Castelli 1991). Yet Paul's vigorous defense of his unique relationship to the church in

Corinth indicates that his position had been challenged. Obviously those who informed him about the problems in the church as well as the letters received from Corinth (5:9; 7:1) expect a response that carries weight with the church. His advice is not being sought or offered as simply one option to be weighed against others in an open debate among church members.

To what extent might the church dissent? Some scholars treat 1 Corinthians as an example of deliberative rhetoric. The speaker seeks to persuade an audience to adopt his or her point of view or recommended course of action but either lacks or will not exercise authority to compel a desired outcome (Mitchell 1993). Paul cannot exercise direct authority in Corinth for two reasons. First, he has been absent for some time, and even the timing of a future visit remains uncertain. Second, he has no permanent representative in Corinth to whom his authority is delegated. The closest he comes to establishing some form of local leadership is the recommendation that the community defer to persons associated with the household of Stephanas (16:15–18). The rationale Paul provides for such deference echoes two motifs in this section of the letter: they were among the earliest converts ("firstfruits of Achaia") and have served others ("charged themselves with service to the saints"; 16:15). Though Paul himself baptized members of this household (1:16), such personal ties to individual apostles created discord in Corinth (1:10–17). His recommendation that members of this household have authority within the church is not based on their personal ties to Paul. The criteria—being among the first believers and devoted service to others—mirror what Paul says of himself. His preaching laid the foundations of faith in Corinth. The humiliation and hardships he endures as an apostle of Christ mirror the gospel message itself, Christ crucified.

Paul reminds his audience that neither he as the architect nor Apollos and others as builders are like the wealthy patrons who put their names on temples, amphitheaters, markets, and other public structures. Civic preferment and honor will not be theirs. Like estate managers and construction workers, the apostles must face the judgment of a master, the Lord (4:1–5; Thiselton 2000, 373). Although Paul clearly expects the audience to acknowledge his authority in the concrete cases that follow, he must persuade them to accept his recommendations. The imagery of a father's relationship to offspring at varied stages of development from infancy through childhood to the adult son, Timothy, who reminds others of his father, supports Paul's basic plea: learn by imitation. Imitating the apostle provides the pattern for imitating the Lord.

Interpreters committed to a hermeneutic that is suspicious of all claims to authority over others protest that posing as the model for imitation reinforces the power of the individual in question (Castelli 1991, 103). The apparently underage Corinthian children are, however, as much beloved as the adult Timothy (4:16–17; Aasgaard 2007, 146–49). Paul's use of the pervasive social fact of paternal authority is neither abusive nor an effort to stunt the spiritual and moral development of his audience. He acknowledges that perhaps his own absence contributed to the situation in Corinth. He has not been present to serve as a living model. Timothy's arrival could refresh memories clouded by absence and conflicting claims of those who are puffed up (4:17–19).

1 Corinthians 5:1–6:20

Reports about Unholy Conduct among Believers

Introductory Matters

Rather than dispatch a shorter letter in response to what he had learned from "Chloe's people" (1:11) about strife and factionalism in the church (1 Cor. 1–4), Paul decided to compose a much longer letter that would address a number of additional problems. He fails to indicate the source of his information in this section. Paul has heard about specific instances of conduct that undermine the moral integrity of the community: a prominent member of the church marrying his stepmother (5:1–5), Christians taking one another to court (6:1–8), and sex with prostitutes (6:12–20). He alleges that the first case is both shocking and commonly known (5:1; Hartog 2006). At the same time, Paul also knows that his advice in a previous letter to Corinth is being misinterpreted (5:9). If that conclusion was based on the letter to which he begins responding at 7:1, then the unnamed source of this information may have been those who brought that letter from Corinth to Ephesus.

The specific moral lapses treated in this section involved complex social and economic relationships that make Paul's solutions problematic for at least some in his audience. Social class played a large role in determining whether a relationship was legally recognized as marriage. Technically Roman soldiers on active duty were not permitted to marry. Nor were slaves. But evidence for long-term marriage and family bonds exists in both cases. Marriage between members of the elite and lower classes, especially freed persons, was actively discouraged (Crook 1967). Yet marriage to her owner is the most common reason for the manumission of a female slave. Therefore social historians conclude that marriage in Roman law does not fully represent the range of relationships that ordinary people would have considered marriage (Osiek and MacDonald 2006).

The outrage that Paul expresses over "someone [who] has his father's wife" was evidently not felt by all members of the Corinthian church (5:2). For Paul the matter may be settled by Lev. 18:6–18, which prohibits sexual relationships with a wide range of female kin. But what if the woman in question was a sort of wife, a concubine? Cleopatra's ties with Julius Caesar and Mark Antony provided a celebrity case, even in the face of a legal wife in Rome (Kleiner 2005). Most exegetes presume that the father in question is deceased. It is possible, however, that the woman in question is divorced from the father who is still living (Fitzmyer 2008, 233–34). Paul does not provide enough information to pin down the social or legal context more precisely.

Since the illicit marriage is something of a cause célèbre and its resolution is not to send the woman packing, it is likely that one or both parties are high-status individuals. One must factor in the possibility that status asymmetry favors the wife in this case. She could be part of the city's wealthy elite who defied convention by first taking one of her freedmen as a husband and subsequently his son. The second case, recourse to lawsuits, also presumes parties with some wealth and social status. But the final example, frequenting prostitutes, involves the ordinary male populace. The well-bred elite would avoid association with the bestial sounds emanating from brothels (Toner 2009, 139). Wealthier persons had slaves as readily available sexual outlets. Most would have seen no moral issue at all in sexual relations with their own property. Since the majority of Paul's audience was not from the elite class (1:26–31), they may have relaxed as Paul took on moral failings characteristic of the wealthy. But when he shifts to the brothels, *porneia* is no longer high-profile incest but the hoglike snorting and grunting coming from rooms around the local baths. And what of the Christian slaves forced to work there or to be subject to the sexual demands of their owners? Paul ignores their plight (Glancy 2002; M. MacDonald 2007).

Patronage in Ancient Associations

Christian communities were private associations whose activities depended on the contributions of members. No inscriptions list the names of their members, officers, rules about meetings or burials, assessments, or fines such as one finds for other groups. Their gatherings must have occurred in homes or other spaces not devoted solely to the social and religious activities of the group (L. White 1990). Consequently there would have been no occasion to produce such an artifact.

In addition to spaces in which to assemble, the churches had other material needs: contributions for the poor and assistance to Paul and other traveling missionaries (16:1–4, 17–18); food for the Lord's Supper (11:17–34); and perhaps even resources for the burial of members (15:1–19), a provision that was common in other associations (Walbank 2005). The pride that Paul alleges the community takes in the individual who has married his father's wife (5:2) suggests that he (or the woman in question) is one of the elite. That status is the reason for apparent indifference to the individual's situation, not some pride in members whose lifestyle flies in the face of moral conventions (Clarke 1993, 77). If the wife was a member of the elite married to the offspring of one of her ex-slaves, then having him in the church provided access to a wealthy household. If Chloe was not a believer, then the social hierarchy would be similar. Members of her household belonged to the church and provided valuable communication links between churches as they went about her business.

The dynamics of patron-client relationships is the elephant in the room. Much as he hopes they can find a better solution, Paul does not issue a blanket prohibition of Christians taking each other to court. Could expelling the man married to his father's wife have social or economic consequences for the Christian community? Paul does not say. Perhaps tiptoeing around the sources of his information was Paul's attempt to avoid alienating some important members of the church.

Sexual Immorality through Jewish Eyes

Although the sexual impropriety of a man marrying his stepmother is said to be offensive even to gentiles (5:1), the subsequent case of males engaging in sexual relations with prostitutes, slaves, or other unmarried women was morally indifferent to most inhabitants of a city like Corinth. Paul's rhetorical "even gentiles" alludes to a common Jewish view that idolatry breeds sexual immorality (Rom. 1:18–32). Idolatry enables other vices such as violence, bloodshed, and deceit. Jewish apologists treat the sexual restraint of pious Jews as one example of the moral integrity bestowed by the Torah (2:17–22).

Paul's statement "not even gentiles" has the rhetorical force of shaming his audience. His source for the moral judgment on incest is Scripture. The Levitical prohibitions against incest include stepmother as a blood relative (Lev. 18:8; 20:11). The catalogue of forbidden sexual relationships in 20:9–21 opens with the prohibition against dishonoring parents. Leviticus includes marriage with a stepmother among those offenses that call for the death of both parties, not merely their expulsion from the community as in other cases.

Pursuing Greed in the Courts

What sort of lawsuit might be involved (1 Cor. 6:1–8)? The primary vices referred to in this section of the letter are sexual immorality, greed, and idolatry (Horrell 1996, 79). Paul invokes idolatry by distinguishing Christian believers, "the holy ones," from judges in the city courts, described as "unjust persons." Of course the courts were notorious for injustice, as the wealthier parties

Sexual Immorality Associated with Idolatry

"Then it was not enough for them to err about the knowledge of God. . . .
For whether they kill children in their initiations, or celebrate secret mysteries, . . .
they no longer keep either their lives or their marriages pure,
but they either treacherously kill one another, or grieve one another by adultery,
and all is a raging riot of blood and murder, theft and deceit, . . .
confusion over what is good, . . .
defiling of souls, sexual perversion,
disorder in marriages, adultery, and debauchery.
For the worship of idols not to be named
is the beginning and cause and end of every evil."

(Wis. 14:22–27 NRSV)

"You do not fear the existing God who guards all things. . . .
Alas for a race which rejoices in blood, a crafty and evil race
of impious and false double-tongued men and immoral
adulterous idol worshipers who plot deceit. . . .
They will have no fidelity at all. Many widowed women
will love other men secretly for gain;
and those who have husbands will not keep hold of the rope of life."

(*Sibylline Oracles* 3.33–45, trans. J. J. Collins in *OTP* 1:362–63)

"And she [Potiphar's wife] kept saying to me, 'If you want me to abandon the idols, have intercourse with me. . . .' But I kept telling her that the Lord did not want worshipers who come by means of uncleanness, nor would he be pleased with adulterers, but with those who were pure in heart and undefiled in speech." (*Testament of Joseph* 4.5–6, trans. H. C. Kee in *OTP* 1:820)

"The cloven hoof . . . is a sign of setting apart each of our actions for good. . . . The symbolism conveyed by these things compels us to make a distinction in the performance of all our acts, with righteousness as our aim. This moreover explains why we are distinct from all other men. The majority of other men defile themselves in their relationships . . . and . . . take pride in it: they not only procure the males, they also defile mothers and daughters." (*Letter of Aristeas* 150–52, trans. R. J. H. Shutt in *OTP* 2:22–23)

could employ bribes to secure a favorable verdict (Winter 1991). A poor person or one without social standing had little hope of prevailing. Therefore anyone who initiated the proceedings must have been one of the wealthier persons in the Corinthian community.

Attempts to link the lawsuit in question with the case of sexual immorality are not convincing. They presume that charges have been brought against the man. The situation would be considered adultery if the son married a divorced stepmother while his father was still living. Other potential charges are misappropriation of a woman's dowry, a dispute over inheritance, or even prostitution by the stepmother (Deming 1996). The sexual charges seem implausible, as the man's father would have to be involved. Property disputes after the father's death involving either a dowry (pressed by her relatives) or inheritance (by other children) could be involved (Aasgaard 2007, 138). The marriage of a woman and her stepson, however noxious to moral conventions, might have been orchestrated to preserve property within the family (Clarke 1993).

Though a failed lawsuit in civil courts that brought such sordid details to light might explain the outrage Paul exhibits (Deming 1996, 296–98), one would expect that topic to be treated before demanding

> **A Legal Dispute Settled by Mediators**
>
> "I, ... Nikantinoos, ... made a settlement with you, ... Phoibammon and Anastasia, his wife, through you, ... Apollos, chief citizen in the civil courthouse of the area concerning the debt, now paid by me, on behalf of the redemption of a deed of security ...before a court case and before preliminary hearings, in the end good friends having become mediators for us, and having taken up the matter." (*Papyrus Vatican Aphrodite* 10, trans. Rowlandson 1998, 153)

expulsion of the offender (5:4–5). Therefore it seems more likely that Paul is referring to some other case. The dispute probably involved property. Whether it pitted a creditor against a debtor or two individuals contesting business dealings or inheritance, Paul does not say. Although Paul's antithesis of "holy" versus "unjust" makes the proposal of communal mediation (6:5) appear unusual, mediation by a friend of both parties could terminate a legal process. Other cases of mediation show that the process was employed to preserve relationships between those involved and head off any further hostilities.

Preserving the Holiness of the Church

A desire to preserve the holiness of the church links all three episodes in these chapters. The requirement of a moral and ritual integrity to ensure the holiness of God's people appears in the Torah (Lev. 19:2–4; 20:25–26; Deut. 14:2). Paul expects his gentile churches to follow such moral prescriptions of the law as the Ten Commandments (Rom. 13:8–10), even though they are not obligated to observe Jewish ritual laws (Gal. 2:11–21). A metaphorical transposition of the community into the "body of Christ" or "temple of the Holy Spirit" elicits the same concern for holiness that the ancients attached to sacred places, persons, and objects generally.

Jews who lived far from their sacred site, the Jerusalem temple, typically linked the idolatry of their non-Jewish neighbors with sexual immorality.

Worshipers of the One God

"Happy those human beings who love the great god, . . . trusting in piety. They will reject all temples when they see them, altars too, . . . dumb stones defiled with the blood of animals. . . . They will look to the great glory of the one God and commit no wicked murder, nor deal in dishonest gain. . . . Nor do they have disgraceful desires for another's spouse or for hateful and repulsive abuse of a male." (Sibylline Oracles 4.24–34, trans. J. J. Collins in OTP 1:384)

Jewish worship of a God not represented in lifeless statues correlated with lives of moral holiness (Sanders 1997). Paul seeks to create similar convictions in the minds of his gentile converts. They must exhibit the same concern for the internal holiness of the church that devotees show toward sacred precincts. This boundary between those who belong to the body of Christ and those who do not requires a different approach to fellow believers than to nonbelievers. Believers contaminate the church's holiness when their actions mirror those of idolaters. Nonbelievers do not impinge on the holiness of the church (5:6–13). Therefore Christians do not have to avoid contact with outsiders.

This emphasis on holiness and protecting the boundaries of the community is most pronounced in the first case. Paul demands a formal procedure by which the individual is separated from the community (5:1–5). He anticipates protest from those who take pride in the patronage link this member provides. To justify his measures, Paul makes a metaphorical connection between excluding the man and the Jewish custom of clearing all yeast products out of the house in preparation for Passover (5:6–8).

Before going on to the next specific case, Paul takes the opportunity to clear up the confusion about his earlier advice (5:9–13). He did not advise breaking off relationships with nonbelievers. That would make life impossible. The point is to avoid association with immoral believers. The section is divided by two references to Paul writing—"I wrote to you in the letter" (5:9–10) and "now I've written to you" (5:11)—and concludes with a reaffirmation of Paul's authority to render judgment against the believer who is flagrantly immoral. Exclusion is confirmed by the authority of Scripture (5:12–13; Deut. 17:7).

Paul returns to specific cases as abruptly as he began this section: "Does someone of you with a [legal] matter against another dare . . ." (1 Cor. 6:1). In this case, Paul does not impose a solution. He indicates the preferred resolution, mediation by fellow believers (6:1–6). Then he elaborates, hoping to show that such behavior is a moral "setback for you." In recommending the alternative, a preference for suffering evil rather than doing it, Paul may be making an indirect allusion to sayings of Jesus (see "Theological Themes in 1 Corinthians: Jesus Tradition in Paul" in the introduction). As in the previous section (5:11), Paul picks up a vice catalogue to reinforce the negative evaluation attached to the behavior he is correcting (6:9–10; Oropeza 1998). Instead of concluding with a Scripture quotation, this section ends with an appeal to become holy and righteous "in the name of the Lord Jesus Christ and in the Spirit of our God" (6:11).

While the first two cases dealt with a limited number of persons, the final case could involve most members. Paul opens with a slogan that may have been widely bandied about, "all things are permitted me" (6:12a), which he corrects. What one does with the body is not indifferent because it has a special relationship to the Lord. Paul first defines that relationship in terms of its eventual destiny, resurrection (6:13–14). He then shifts to the church as "body of Christ." A rhetorical question puts the absurdity of uniting a bodily member that belongs to Christ with a prostitute (6:15–17). Scripture confirms the unique relationship between sexual partners (Gen. 2:24). Then the concluding verses open with "flee sexual immorality" as contaminating the body that is the temple of God's Spirit. The overlapping boundaries of self, body, community, and temple come together in support of the final exhortation: "Glorify God in your body" (1 Cor. 6:18–20).

Tracing the Train of Thought

An Incestuous Marriage (5:1–8)

5:1–2. Paul abruptly shifts to a shocking topic: **sexual immorality of the sort not even found among the gentiles.** Even worse, this situation is not hidden. People know about it. Paul suggests that the community takes some pride in the situation: **You have become arrogant rather than mourning.** Marriage to a stepmother was generally considered incestuous even if the father had died, which is the situation most commentators assume to be the case (R. Collins 1999). The complexities of marriage in the first century provide, however, a number of other possibilities. Boasting is a consequence of status claims. There is no reason to presume that the Corinthians are boasting about a spiritual freedom to set aside social mores and ethical propriety. Rather the individuals involved

> **1 Corinthians 5:1–6:20 in the Rhetorical Flow**
>
> The letter opening (1:1–9)
>
> Against divisions: God's wisdom (1:10–2:16)
>
> Against divisions: Paul and Apollos as *exempla* (3:1–4:21)
>
> ▶ Reports about unholy conduct among believers (5:1–6:20)
>
> An incestuous marriage (5:1–8)
>
> Misunderstanding of a previous letter (5:9–13)
>
> Lawsuits between believers (6:1–11)
>
> Sexual relations with prostitutes (6:12–20)

probably belonged to the city's elite. However distasteful to ordinary believers, their wealth and influence put such persons beyond the law.

5:3–5. Paul avoids naming the individual involved but demands a harsh penalty: **that the man who has done this deed be removed from your midst** (5:2). He then invokes a quasi-judicial proceeding in which the gathered community effectively ratifies his decision rendered in absentia (5:3–4): **As though I were present, I have condemned the one who has done this.** Though Paul invokes not only his own spiritual presence along with **the name of our Lord Jesus [and] the power of our Lord Jesus** (5:4), something is clearly amiss. In contrast to the formal procedure described in Matt. 18:15–18, the offender is nowhere present. Nor are there witnesses to any efforts to correct the situation privately.

One cannot rule out the possibility that there had been attempts by some members of the church to rectify the situation. But factors of social and economic asymmetry possibly made it evident to all concerned that the individual in question would not or could not divorce his wife. Paul's characterization of the consequences of this communal action bristles with problems. To be outside the community places one under **Satan for the destruction of the flesh** (5:5a). Perhaps the expression is no more than a dramatic metaphor for the

---

Discipline and Expulsion from the Community

"With justice you shall judge your neighbor.... You shall not hate in your heart anyone of your kin; you shall reprove your neighbor, or you will incur guilt yourself." (Lev. 19:15, 17 NRSV)

"One should reproach one another in truth, in meekness and in compassionate love for one's fellow-man.... No-one should raise a matter against his fellow in front of the Many unless it is with reproof in the presence of witnesses." (1QS 5.24–25; 6.1, trans. García Martínez and Tigchelaar 1997, 83)

"Whoever goes round defaming the Many shall be expelled from their midst and will never return. And whoever complains against the foundation of the Community shall be expelled and will not return.... The person whose spirit turns aside from the foundation of the Community to betray the truth and walk in the stubbornness of his heart, if he comes back, shall be punished for two years; during the first year he shall not approach the pure food of the Many." (1QS 7.16–19, trans. García Martínez and Tigchelaar 1997, 87)

"Take one or two others along with you, so that every word may be confirmed by the evidence of two or three witnesses. If the member refuses to listen to them, tell it to the church; and if the offender refuses to listen even to the church, let such a one be to you as a Gentile and a tax collector." (Matt. 18:16–17 NRSV)

world outside the holiness of God's people. But **destruction of the flesh** remains a troubling phrase. Does Paul imagine the consequences to be actual illness or death? Some scholars even entertain the possibility that some zealous believer might invoke Deut. 17:2–7 and kill him (Gaca 2003, 140).

Destruction of the flesh correlates with a positive outcome, preservation of the spirit, **that the spirit be saved on the day of the Lord** (5:5b). Whose spirit is preserved? That of the individual? Or God's Spirit that dwells in the community? Since Paul used the body/spirit division to describe his own absence and presence, **the spirit** could refer to the man being disciplined. Paul's overall concern with preserving the holiness of the Christian body as the dwelling place of God's Spirit makes, however, the latter interpretation more likely. Or Paul might be overlapping both realities, the flesh/spirit of the offender and the body/Spirit of the church (D. Martin 1995, 170–74).

5:6–8. Paul anticipates resistance to this instruction. **Your boast is not [in something] admirable** (5:6a). The adjective *kalos* has a wide range of meanings, from physical beauty to the nobility of an aristocrat to moral excellence. Paul employs an analogy between excluding the wayward member and cleansing one's house of **leaven** in preparation for Passover (5:7; Exod. 12:15; Mishnah, tractate *Pesaḥim* 1.1). A **tiny amount of leaven leavens the whole lump [of dough]** (1 Cor. 5:6b). How much emotional resonance this image had for Paul's gentile audience is unclear. Paul acknowledges that their link to Passover is the death of Christ: **Our Passover has been sacrificed, Christ** (5:7b). That comment does not necessarily equate the Christian meal with a Jewish Passover sacrifice. The eucharistic formula recited speaks of "the new covenant in my blood" (11:25).

The metaphor shifts from support for expulsion from the community to ethical reform: **not with leaven of evil and wickedness but with unleavened [words] of sincerity and truth** (5:8). This shift anticipates the broader question of how to preserve the holiness of the believing community (1:2; 5:9; 6:19). Though expelling the incestuous individual is necessary to that task, the Corinthians have other sources of contamination to address.

Misunderstanding of a Previous Letter (5:9–13)

5:9–10. Since conversion involved rejecting one's past life of sin and idolatry, the conclusion that one should break with former associates is hardly surprising. Yet Paul insists that this view was not his intent: **not at all the wicked of this world or the covetous and greedy or idolaters or you would certainly have to leave the world** (5:10).

5:11. Instead Paul expands the typical vice list to require that Christians exclude immoral believers from table fellowship—the **wicked, covetous, idolater, slanderer, drunkard, greedy**. The Essenes excluded members of their fellowship from the communal meal for infractions of their rules. This catalogue could hardly serve as a set of rules determining participation in communal activities.

Some items will be treated in what follows: covetousness in pursuing lawsuits (6:1–11), idolatry in questions of meat from sacrifices (8:1–13; 10:1–22), and the drunkenness of wealthier members at the Lord's Supper (11:17–22). Although Paul concludes this list with **do not eat with such a person** (5:11b), he does not propose withdrawing table fellowship in the specific cases that follow.

5:12–13. Paul concludes by distinguishing between judging the conduct of believers and judging that of outsiders: **God judges those outside** (5:13a). Christians must, however, preserve the holiness of God's people. Therefore the judgment against the incestuous man stands. Although Paul does not use a citation formula such as "as it is written" to introduce the citation of Deut. 17:7, **drive the wicked one out from among you**, he must presume that his readers recognize it as Scripture.

Lawsuits between Believers (6:1–11)

6:1–3. The verb "to judge" carries Paul from the general statement that concluded the previous section (5:12–13) into this new case: **Is there someone among you who dares to have his case against another judged before the unjust and not the saints?** (6:1). What sort of lawsuit remains obscure. Although Jews employed elders in the community to settle their disputes, the non-Jewish converts in Corinth did not have such a custom. If those involved belonged to an elite accustomed to pursuing their own interests in the courts, Paul's qualms may have come as a surprise.

Paul opens these verses with a series of compressed arguments in the form of questions intended to press the absurdity of the situation. The horizon is expanded from a contest between two individuals who happen to be **brothers** because they are part of the Christian fellowship to a contrast between **the unjust** and **the saints**. The rhetorical **do you not know?** (6:2, 3) makes it appear that those engaged in lawsuits have somehow forgotten prior teaching, but this form of punctuation may represent Paul's own way of adding developments to that teaching or drawing a conclusion by analogy (3:16; 5:6; 6:2, 3, 9, 15, 16, 19; 9:13, 24; 12:2). Paul subtly downgrades the significance of the cases in question from the generic *pragma* (**matter, affair, subject of a lawsuit**; 6:1) to *elachista* (**trivial things**; 6:2) and *biōtika* (**the stuff of daily life**; 6:3). If the matters being litigated are trivial, then preferring mediation by fellow believers is not overly problematic. If the cases involve socioeconomic asymmetry, an elite individual against one

> **Jews Settle Their Own Disputes**
>
> "In any place where you find Gentile law courts, even though their law is the same as the Israelite law, you must not resort to them since it says, 'These are the judgments you shall bring before them' (Exod 21:1), that is to say 'before them' and not before the Gentiles." (Babylonian Talmud, tractate Giṭṭin 88b, trans. in Fee 1987, 231)

of the poorer community members, then the weaker party would have a better chance with fellow Christians. But if both parties are among the elite, they may prefer a system they can control.

Paul introduces an eschatological note to justify this new idea: **the saints will judge the world** (6:2a). With the logic of an argument from the more important to a lesser case, it follows that **if the world is to be judged by you, how much more . . . lesser things.**

> ### Judgment by the Saints of God
>
> *"Judgment was given to the saints of the Most High."* (Dan. 7:22 LXX AT)
>
> *"They shall judge nations and rule over peoples."* (Wis. 3:8 AT)
>
> *"God will judge all the nations by his elect."* (1QpHab 5.4 AT)

First Corinthians 6:3 repeats similar logic using the pair **angels** and **everyday matters**. Presumably the angels to be judged are fallen angels (2 Pet. 2:4). The phrase **everyday matters** suggests that, whatever its particulars, the plaintiff's lawsuit does not require the expertise of a civil court (Fee 1987, 234). That conclusion rests, however, on Paul's rhetorical craft. He provides no evidence about the matters at hand.

6:4–6. Having established the principle that believers should be competent judges, Paul shifts his tone. He hopes to **shame** (6:5) the Corinthians for not asking fellow believers to mediate in these cases. The somewhat contorted rhetorical question in 6:4 is a present general condition. Its meaning turns on the identification of *tous exouthenēmenous* (**persons viewed with contempt**). The word is used to speak of the lowliness of the majority of church members in 1:28. God has chosen what the world holds in contempt. If the term refers to church members, then the question would be an ironical counter to Paul's view. The expression, however, makes more sense as a degrading remark about civil judges (Fitzmyer 2008, 252–53), possibly even the Roman proconsul Gallio (see "Gallio as Proconsul" in the introduction). Despite the esteem in which outsiders hold these persons, Christians consider the civil elite as no better than the poorest urban trash. **Brother sues brother and that before unbelievers** (6:6). Paul may even be needling them. For all their alleged wisdom, the Corinthians suddenly have **no one wise enough to render a judgment** (6:5b).

6:7–11. Paul raises the stakes. **Lawsuits [*krimata*] with each other [are] a complete defeat** (6:7). The Corinthians risk joining the ranks of the **unjust [who] will not inherit the kingdom** (6:9a) because these legal proceedings involve **injustice** and **fraud** (6:8). It is difficult to tell whether that assumption is based on details about the cases in question or is a generic assumption about the legal system. Such judgments reflect the ordinary experience of poorer persons hauled into court by the wealthy. Better to steer clear of the courts as Jesus advises in Matt. 5:25–26. Or Paul may have in mind the stipulations about just treatment of the neighbor from Lev. 19:11–18 in formulating this remark (Zeller 2010, 215–16). Paul's suggestion that it would be preferable to **suffer injustice** and **be defrauded** is comparable to the more striking saying of Jesus: "If anyone would sue you and take your tunic, give him your cloak as well" (Matt. 5:40). Paul does not, however, enlist the authority of a word of the Lord to halt legal wrangling between believers. Instead, Paul rehearses for the third time a list of vices that characterize **the wicked** (*ponēros*).

Table 10
Vice Lists in 1 Corinthians 5–6

5:10	5:11	6:9b–10
wicked	wicked	wicked
covetous	covetous	covetous
greedy	greedy	greedy
idolater	idolater	idolater
—	slanderer	slanderer
—	drunkard	drunkard
—	—	adulterer
—	—	catamite
—	—	pederast
—	—	thief

Note: The sequence of terms has been altered to highlight similarities.

Each repetition adds terms to the list. In addition to theft, the final iteration inserts a grouping associated with sex: **adulterer**, *malakos* (the passive, "female" partner in a homosexual act), and *arsenokoitēs* (the pederast or active partner; Fitzmyer 2008, 255–58). At this point, Paul represents the ordinary views of Jewish moralists. Scripture (Gen. 1:26–27; 2:18–25) defines the purpose of human sexuality. The worst of the batch is to play the role of a female and be penetrated by another male (D. Martin 1995, 33). Attempts to restrict the meaning of Paul's terms to homosexual prostitution or homosexual abuse of young children cannot be defended linguistically. Paul never discusses concrete cases of homosexuality among believers; the examples in 1 Corinthians all involve heterosexual relationships. In addition, the vice list genre is not engaged in defining its individual elements. The rhetorical point is to incorporate items that the audience will spontaneously reject.

Paul returns to address his audience with the familiar "once/now" schema that describes their conversion (Zeller 2010, 218): **And some of you were such people** (6:11a). As "saints," God's holy people, **justified by the name of the Lord Jesus and the Spirit of our God** (6:11c), believers have cast off the vices of their past life. Indirectly Paul suggests that they do the same with lawsuits. Legitimate grievances can be settled through mediation by members of the community. It is important, however, to recognize the importance of the passive voice in the drumbeat sequence of three verbs, each introduced by the particle *alla*: **but you cleansed yourselves [in baptism], but you have been made holy, but you have been made righteous** (6:11b). The transformation from a past marked by sin to holiness cannot be claimed as one's own achievement. It reflects the power of God's Spirit (Zeller 2010, 219).

Sexual Relations with Prostitutes (6:12–20)

6:12–13. Paul jolts the audience to attention with a sudden shift into the first-person repeated twice: **Everything is possible for me but . . .** (6:12). Most scholars think that the phrase is a slogan being employed by Corinthians. Paul employed several such rhetorical shifts to the first-person, however, without citing slogans (e.g., 4:6, 16–17; 10:28–11:1). Therefore he could have composed the opening phrase to back up the initial point that **not everything is to our advantage; I am not enslaved by anything** (Dodd 1995, 46–54). As a general statement, these phrases remind Paul's audience that Christian freedom is not a license for self-indulgence (Gal. 5:13). The phrase **everything is possible** could refer to the specifics of the previous cases of incest and lawsuits (Deming 1996, 302–3). Whether **everything** refers back to the previous cases or anticipates the prostitute question that is to come does not make much difference. In either case, Paul expects the community of believers to take actions not demanded by the laws of the city or the ethical mores of the larger society.

The expulsion of the man married to his stepmother is a unique situation, and if the lawsuits involve church members from the social elite going at one another, those cases may not have concerned many in the church. The socioeconomic context for urban prostitution makes this final case quite different. It potentially involves most of the adult males in the audience—and, though Paul does not acknowledge them—female slaves as well. Paul creates an elaborate pair of chiasms in 1 Cor. 6:13:

A food is for
   B   the stomach and
   B′   the stomach is for
A′ food, but God will destroy
   B″   it and
A″ these things [food]
   B‴   the body is
       C   not for sexual immorality
          D   but for the Lord
          D′   and the Lord
   B⁗   for the body

Stomach, food, and sexual immorality all belong to the perishable realm. No ancient moralist would find surprising the caution not to let the passions for food and sex generated by the physical body enslave an individual. Perhaps the Corinthians concluded that because the physical drives for food and sex do not endure, they have no relevance for one's life as a Christian (D. Martin 1995, 126).

6:14–15. Paul's argument takes a surprising turn. While food, sex, and stomach do perish, the body does not. It has an enduring relationship with the Lord because **God raised the Lord and will raise us** (6:14). Since Paul must confirm resurrection as the core of Christian faith in 1 Cor. 15, the recipients may not be in a position to pick up his logic at this point.

Paul employs a drumbeat of **do you not know** (*ouk oidate*) phrases to punctuate the argument (6:15, 16, 19). The first establishes an image that will be picked up again later in the letter, the community as body of Christ (10:16–17; 11:27, 29; 12:12–27): **your bodies are members of Christ.** By transferring the significance of one's body to Christ's, Paul makes the offensiveness of sex with a prostitute clear. Behavior that is culturally accepted and not covered in the vice lists contaminates Christ's body.

6:16–18. The second step introduced by **do you not know** challenges a widely held view that sex with a prostitute is insignificant to one's identity. Paul quotes Gen. 2:24, **the two will be one flesh,** as evidence that **the man who unites with a prostitute becomes one body** (1 Cor. 6:16). Employing a passage from Genesis about marriage to describe sex with a prostitute probably sounded odd to the audience (D. Martin 1995, 177). Paul expands the metaphor with a parallel phrase about union with the Lord (6:16–17):

   A **the man joined to the prostitute**
     B **is one body** [with her]
   A′ **the man joined to the Lord**
     B′ **is one spirit** [with him]

(In this instance I depart from the gender-neutral rendering of the masculine participle as "the person" or "one" to make it clear that Paul is discussing the sexual behavior of male members of the community. When he turns to questions about marriage and celibacy raised by the Corinthians in the next chapter, Paul explicitly includes women in the discussion.)

The conclusion to this step of the argument proves somewhat puzzling. It opens with an imperative that covers both the unique case of immorality (*porneia*) in 5:1–5 and this more general situation of sex with a prostitute (*pornē*): **Flee *porneia*!** (6:18a). Paul distinguishes sexual immorality from all other sins. Other sins are **outside the body, but the man who engages in sexual immorality [*porneuōn*] sins against his own body** (6:18). The vice lists include as sexual immorality the legal crime of adultery and the offense against proper male behavior in homosexuality. But they are silent about sex with prostitutes at a banquet, local bar, or bathhouse as well as sexual relations with one's slaves. In the lists the sexual offenses mentioned are of the same order as other offenses such as idolatry and greed. What leads Paul to this unusual conclusion? Some scholars conclude that Paul must be correcting a slogan being tossed around at Corinth (Fitzmyer 2008, 269). The citation of Gen. 2:24 in 1 Cor. 6:16 provides a clue. Paul's thinking on gender and sexuality is governed by his reading of the creation story. The sexual union of man and woman reflects Eve's originating from Adam's body. Paul returns to Genesis as evidence for the hierarchy of male over female in 1 Cor. 11:2–16. Here Gen. 2 leads Paul to suggest that the communication involved in sexual immorality attaches to the core of the individual (Byrne 1983, 612–13).

The parallel phrases in 1 Cor. 6:16–17 expose an ambiguity in the argument. It would make the morality of sex with prostitutes applicable only to Christians who are joined to Christ in **one spirit**. That assumption also figures in the final iteration of the argument in 6:19–20. Yet 6:18 presents *porneia* as a vice that belongs on the generic lists, indeed as a vice that should come with a special warning label. With the exception of idolatry (see "Theological Themes in 1 Corinthians: Turning Away from Idols to the True God" in the introduction), anyone in Corinth would agree that the contents of the vice lists represent immoral behavior. But Paul's gentile converts must have been puzzled by restrictions on sexual behavior by males—barring adultery or incest, of course (Sanders 1997, 70–73). The argument that Paul presents is not based on a biological account or a philosophical analysis. It applies the Christian experience of salvation to the issue. As a consequence of the gifts of holiness and righteousness that God bestowed on them, Christian men should acknowledge the impropriety of sex with prostitutes.

6:19–20. The final **do you not know** sentence reinforces the restrictions on sexual activity with two additional analogies concerning the body of a Christian. It is **a temple of the Holy Spirit** and the property of another (6:19). The idea that sexual activity might pollute religious rituals was common enough in antiquity. Initiates into mystery cults or priests engaged in temple rituals could be required to abstain from sexual activity for a specified time prior to engaging in specific rites. Paul employs that cultural conviction to support his condemnation of sex with prostitutes. Since the believer's body/temple has the **Holy Spirit that you received from God**, the holiness temporarily required by ritual must become permanent.

Paul's second analogy, in 6:20a, draws on the metaphor of salvation as paying the price for a slave (Fitzmyer 2008, 270): **You have been purchased for a price**. Therefore, contrary to the opening slogan (6:12a), believers are not free to do as they like. Their bodies belong to God, just as the slave's body belongs to her or his owner. Unlike human masters who procured and abused slaves for sexual purposes (Harrill 1995, 129–33), God asks believers to refrain from sex with prostitutes. Although Paul does not condemn the sexual slave trade explicitly, if his ethical view spread beyond the tiny Christian minority, it would undercut such exploitation of humans. The inclusion of "effeminate" and "penetrating" homosexual activity in the vice list (6:9b–10) suggests that Paul would have objected to other facets of the sex trade, such as the physical alterations and abuse of young boys. Such cases do not come into the discussion because they were not of immediate concern for his audience. Paul brings this section of the letter to a close by stating a general principle: **Glorify God in your body** (6:20b).

Theological Issues

To what extent does the church challenge the accepted cultural and social mores of its day? Paul's distinction between letting God judge nonbelievers and calling Christians to account for failing to live as God's holy people would have been familiar to Diaspora Jews. They followed the holiness code prescribed in Torah. God would deal with their idol-worshiping and sexually immoral neighbors in God's own time. Transferring the moral conviction that Jews attach to such religious symbols—"holy ones," "temple of God's Spirit," God as redeemer, or even the new symbol, "body of Christ"—to gentile converts proved difficult. They evidently did not see such religious symbols as guideposts for conduct in such basic areas as sexuality, lawsuits, or conflict resolution. Instead they took their bearings from philosophical slogans or popular culture.

Today Christians struggle with modern variants of the same issues. "I can do whatever" and "It's *my* body" are common slogans in the hookup dating culture of both teens and adults. Undesired pregnancy is the only negative, and abortions are considerably safer than they were in first-century Roman Corinth! Paul does not try to formulate a philosophical argument to address the sexual perversions of his day, though philosophers did so. The culture is what it is. But he does insist that the believer's calling to be part of God's sanctified people, members of the body of Christ, changes the game. They know from Scripture that the sexual relationship between a man and a woman is not the casual encounter of two bodies. It involves the person as an embodied being in his or her relationships with others and with God. Paul does not reduce his moral injunction to "flee *porneia*" to another slogan: "Just say no." He tries to give his audience a vision of what is really at stake. If they interiorize that vision, then sexual immorality will feel as absurd as eating the family pet for dinner.

Those who interpreted Paul's previous letter urging a life of holiness (5:9–10) reacted by opting for the other extreme: protect the moral integrity of Christians by isolation from nonbelievers. Christians would marry only fellow believers. The man married to his stepmother could not have been received in the first place. Certainly lawsuits in civil courts and use of the city's prostitutes would be unacceptable. Therefore Paul's injunction to "not even eat with such a person" (5:11b) would become a general community rule. No table fellowship with outsiders. Penalties might be put in place to exclude from the common table those who conducted themselves like outsiders. Paul refuses to adopt that solution to protecting the holiness of God's people. "For you would have to go out of the world" (5:10), he protests.

One could see Paul's rejection of the "holiness by isolation" policy as a practical matter. The tiny Christian house-churches would never have survived, let alone attracted new members, if they had barriers to contact with outsiders. As we turn to questions that the Corinthians raised in their letter to Paul (7:1–11:1), this issue of boundaries recurs in such key areas as attending pagan religious celebrations and marriage. As a holy people (6:11), the Corinthians are no longer "gentiles" (12:2) or alienated from God. They are obliged to "keep the commandments of God" (7:19). The task Paul faces in 1 Corinthians may seem Herculean. He must persuade the congregation to draw the correct ethical and practical conclusions from Christianity's core symbols and beliefs. In some cases, the links between theological symbol and ethical conduct may not have been obvious or persuasive (Barclay 1995, 153). Paul does not institute a stripped-down version of the Torah to govern Christian life or a group of authorized interpreters, Christian Pharisees, to control behavior. This freedom from rules does not leave much of life outside Christ where one may do as one pleases, "everything possible." Instead, by drawing the physical body of believers into Christ as the temple of the Spirit, Paul effectively argues that everything the Christian does is marked by holiness (Barclay 1995, 157).

This open-ended strategy allows the churches—and the apostle himself (9:20–21)—maximum adaptability across cultural boundaries. At the same time, it will demand constant conversation and negotiation over the relationship between "in Christ" and "the world." Although 1 Corinthians sometimes reads as a long series of theological and moral put-downs, it could be treated as an invitation to a different kind of Christian maturity. The apostle is inviting his audience to engage in a process of ethical discernment. Guided by the Spirit, they will learn to assist one another in becoming the body of Christ.

1 Corinthians 7:1–11:1

Questions in a Letter from Corinth

Introductory Matters

Paul now turns to issues posed in a letter that he has received from Corinth (7:1). He does not indicate whether the whole community is behind the questions raised or whether a group within the church has dispatched a letter to elicit Paul's assistance on one side or other of some conflict. The introductory formula "now concerning the . . ." (*peri de*), which recurs in this section (7:1, 25; 8:1, 4), highlights particular topics: whether to marry (7:1–40) and whether to participate in sacrificial banquets (8:1–13). The topic of sacrificial meat and cult banquets continues in 10:1–11:1. An excursus in defense of Paul's apostolic freedom (9:1–27) provides content (9:19–23) for the concluding appeal to imitate Paul as he imitates Christ (11:1). A similar exhortation to imitate the apostle brought the first section of 1 Corinthians to a close (4:16).

What Questions Did the Corinthians Pose?

Paul does not explicitly identify the issues or arguments in the letter he received from Corinth. The subsequent *peri de* phrases follow sections in which Paul has introduced his own opinions with "I say" (*legō de*; 7:8, 12) or "I am saying this" (*touto de phēmi*; 7:29). That break in the chain might indicate that Paul has added these topics on the basis of other information he has received (Fitzmyer 2008, 330). Consequently scholars often select phrases that appear to be either quotations or paraphrases of what the Corinthians had said. These expressions take the form of brief assertions to which corrections have been added, as in the case of 6:12. But they do not come explicitly marked as

Corinthian opinions. By contrast, Paul attributed the partisan slogans to his audience in 1:12 and 3:4. Similarly the phrase in the opening of this section, "it is good for a man not to touch a woman" (7:1b), provides the content for the opening clause: "Concerning the things you wrote about" (7:1a). In the other cases, identification of a particular phrase as a Corinthian slogan often depends on how a given interpreter carries out two tasks: (a) determining what is actually being debated, and (b) identifying religious or philosophical assumptions at play in the discussion.

Since the Corinthians themselves appear to have held diverse opinions on most of these issues, the view encoded by a particular phrase was probably only one of several familiar to Paul's audience. Rhetoricians were taught to employ or even invent maxims to make a point. Paul could be responsible for generating the sloganlike phrases with their attached corrections. He may even anticipate the repetition of his versions by members of the audience. A neatly crafted slogan pair began the earlier discussion of sex with prostitutes (6:12):

> All things are permitted me,
> but not all things are advantageous.
> All things are permitted me,
> But I will not be controlled by anything.

It will be repeated with a slight variation in the final unit of this section (10:23):

> All things are permitted,
> but not all things are advantageous.
> All things are permitted,
> but not all things build up.

Presumably the Corinthians charged with either boasting about or engaging in sexual immorality in the previous section of the letter (5:2; 6:13) do not hold the opinion with which this section opens: "It is good for a man not to touch a woman" (7:1).

Further evidence that the so-called slogans represent only one of several positions in play comes from the next major topic in this section: participation in banquets that followed sacrifices to the gods and consumption of sacrificial meat sold in the market. Earlier Paul indicated that the Corinthians had misunderstood his previous instructions, treating the exhortation not to associate with "sexually immoral persons" as though it meant avoidance of nonbelievers (5:9). But anyone who pursued that policy would not have the concerns mentioned in this later section. A strict barrier against association with nonbelievers would exclude the possibility of participating in banquets linked to sacrificial offerings or concern with "idol food" (8:1, 10).

The idol-food issues become more complex when one notes the contexts for consuming sacrificial meat: somewhere in the precincts of a temple (8:10),

---

Stages in a Public Sacrifice

a. Parade of sacrificial victims to the altar
b. Officiant prays, libation of wine, incense
c. Officiant pours wine-and-grain mix over animal's head
d. Slaves slaughter the animal
e. Entrails examined for omens
f. Parts of the animal burnt on the altar
g. Participants banquet on the remaining meat

(Beard, North, and Price 1998, 2:148)

---

meat purchased in the market (10:25), at a banquet to which one has been invited (10:27–28). Were the meals in question really honoring a deity or placating the demons of the lower regions—say at the temple of Demeter and Kore—or were they social occasions that maintained an individual's relationships with family and the larger community (Newton 1998)?

Does Paul's Jewish background insulate him from the concerns of his gentile audience? He reaches back to the story of Israel's idolatry in the wilderness to warn against participation in feasting associated with pagan deities (10:7; Exod. 32:6). Similarly Paul's convoluted remarks about the holiness of children in a marriage that involves a Christian and a non-Christian (1 Cor. 7:12–16) depend on fairly arcane distinctions of Jewish law concerning licit marriage (Gillihan 2002). Within a Jewish context illicit marriage or marriage to a non-Jew puts the holiness of God's people at risk (Loader 2007, 93–101). Paul's earlier argument—that sexual relations with a prostitute defile the body that belongs to Christ or temple of the Spirit (6:15–19)—would suggest that believers should divorce unbelieving spouses. When it comes to the remarriage of a Christian widow, Paul will advocate marriage within the group (7:39). Therefore in several of the particular questions being discussed, Paul adopts images and premises familiar to a Jewish audience, but not necessarily transparent to non-Jews. Jews routinely lump idolatry and various forms of sexual immorality together when speaking of non-Jews, just as Paul does in Rom. 1:18–32. So "flee *porneia*" in 1 Cor. 6:18 will be matched with "flee from idolatry" in 10:14. Yet Paul introduces a new tone at this point in the letter. He no longer chides the audience for claiming a wisdom they do not have, as he did in the first part. Instead he addresses them as individuals who possess practical wisdom (*phronimoi*), quite capable of judging (the truth of) what he is saying (10:15).

Cult Meals and Fellowship

Paul draws the line against participation in meals connected with sacrifices to the gods on the grounds that doing so implies a fellowship with demons (10:19–22). The Christian rite of blessed wine and bread creates a fellowship in the body and blood of Christ (10:16). Just as sexual relations with a prostitute defile the members of Christ's body, so drinking a cup associated with demons undermines the holiness of the Christian table fellowship. Based on Paul's analogy, scholars once assumed that the gods associated with the cult meals were thought to be participants in the banquet. This conclusion was supported by artistic representations of a funeral meal in which a deity appears to be reclining on one of the couches.

More recent scholarship questions that interpretation of the evidence. Fellowship with the deity or human hero or emperor does not follow from making a sacrifice. Only a small group of individuals witnessed the animal's death. The feasting that follows at public festivals such as the Isthmian Games involves both persons and food distinct from the events at the altar. Furthermore, studies of Roman triumphs challenge the impression gained from literary sources that the populace at large participated in the banqueting. It would appear that only the elite were invited. The masses may have received portions of food to take away or an equivalent in cash (Beard 2007, 260–62). Comments in ancient moralists also suggest that private banquets among the elite be limited to a few guests so that the company would remain unified (Smith 2002, 24–25).

These studies demonstrate that for the masses any food or money distributed at festivals had little connection with the deities being honored. On the one hand, whether such grants occurred often enough to be of economic or nutritional significance cannot be ascertained. For the elite, on the other hand, invitations to recline at a banquet might be declined at the risk of severing family or social ties (P. D. Gooch 1993, 38–45). Class distinctions probably do not correlate with religious scruples about eating idol meat, with the elite claiming it to be an indifferent matter and the poor masses being superstitious (contra Theissen 1982), since food distributed to the masses did not come directly from the altar. But social differences could have contributed to the confusion at Corinth, since the elite are more likely to have been invited both to the sacrificial banquets mentioned in 10:14–22 and to the private dinners in 10:23–11:1. It is not even possible to determine whether the meat served at a banquet in the dining facility linked to a larger religious complex such as the Asclepeion at Corinth came from sacrificial animals (P. D. Gooch 1993, 24–26). Therefore the questions to which Paul responds do not appear to represent a head-to-head clash of ideological positions. Rather, they stem from the confusions of familial, social, and religious obligations faced by non-Jewish believers. Since Paul has rejected the option of sectarian isolation, Christians must continue to wrestle with the problem of figuring out how much they can conform to the culture around them.

The apostle has taken up two examples of sexual immorality in the previous section (5:6–7; 6:12–20). The first involved an illicit marriage. The second concluded with a ringing summons to "flee *porneia*" (6:18). Picking up questions about marriage and celibacy posed by the Corinthians forms a natural line of continuity in the letter. If Paul had not indicated the shift to matters about which they had written to him, the initial slogan, "it is good for a man not to touch a woman," might read as a diatribe-like objection to the image of the body as the temple of God's Spirit with which the previous section ended (6:19). On the one hand, Paul commends marriage as a divinely sanctioned institution within which the sexual desires of both women and men have a legitimate place (7:1–5). Marriage is supported by the Lord's saying that prohibits divorce (7:10–11). On the other hand, Paul himself has opted for celibacy as a preferable mode of life in which to serve the Lord. And he clearly encourages others, both (widowed) women and men, to do the same if they are able.

Much of the chapter on marriage and celibacy has this character of choosing between options, either of which is acceptable. Although Christians should not divorce each other, the situation of a Christian with a nonbelieving spouse is different (7:12–16). Although remaining unmarried to serve the Lord is preferable, widows may remarry after the death of their husbands (7:39–40). In the middle of this back-and-forth discussion, Paul appeals for social harmony. His suggestion that Christian slaves not agitate for their freedom has drawn considerable controversy (7:17–24).

The deliberative tone carries over into the treatment of idols, idol meat, and social relationships in 1 Cor. 8 and 10. Paul sets out some straightforward principles. On the one hand, one cannot participate directly in banquets perceived to honor a god or goddess. That is equivalent to the idolatry depicted in the Scriptures (10:1–22). On the other hand, there are situations in which Christians need not have any concerns: buying what is sold in the market or eating dinner at a private home (10:23–11:1). Just to make the situation more complex, Paul finds some contexts in which these indifferent matters become problems. He can imagine—or perhaps has been told of—cases in which individuals who witnessed or followed the lead of those who ate idol meat lost their faith. Since it does not matter whether one does or does not eat, Paul counsels restraint. Better to give up the freedom to participate than to have another lose his or her faith (8:7–13; 10:23–30).

Paul interrupts his discussion of the complex problems created by the religious environment (see "Religious Activities in the City" in the introduction) with a defense of his own freedom as an apostle (9:1–2). Rhetorically, 1 Cor. 9 constitutes a digression or excursus. The transition is quite abrupt in this instance. Paul asserts that he is presenting a defense (*apologia*)

---

1 Corinthians 7:1–11:1 in the Rhetorical Flow

The letter opening (1:1–9)

Against divisions: God's wisdom (1:10–2:16)

Against divisions: Paul and Apollos as *exempla* (3:1–4:21)

Reports about unholy conduct among believers (5:1–6:20)

▶**Questions in a letter from Corinth (7:1–11:1)**

Various topics on marriage and Christian households (7:1–40)

On meat from pagan sacrifices (8:1–13)

Paul as example of Christian freedom (9:1–27)

On participation in cult meals and banquets (10:1–11:1)

to those who might criticize him (9:3). His argument is composed as a barrage of nineteen rhetorical questions (Fitzmyer 2008, 354–55). After explaining how he conducts himself as an apostle (9:1–18), Paul presents his freedom to adapt to the cultural situation of his audience as desirable in winning others to Christ (9:19–23). Finally, the digression concludes with images of boxing and track from the games. The apostle's freedom is highly disciplined, not just knocking about (9:24–27).

Tracing the Train of Thought

The questions posed in the letter Paul had received from Corinth suggest some radical positions. Perhaps Christians should renounce sexuality even within marriage (7:1–7). Since the gods and goddesses worshiped in the city have no reality, why shouldn't believers join everyone else in festivities connected with the various temples (8:1–13; 10:23–11:1)? How many of the topics discussed under the two main heads of marriage and idol meat came from the Corinthians' letter is unclear. Paul may even have generated some of the possibilities himself. Even the excursus defending the conduct of his ministry could be understood as a return to the comparisons between Paul and Apollos in the first section of the letter (3:4–4:13). That excursus need not indicate that Paul feels pressure from Corinth to defend himself, since his apostolic freedom serves as an example for the audience as they negotiate the choices they must make (9:1–27). The tone of principles and exceptions or of a choice between options that emerges in the opening section on marriage is distinct from that in the previous two sections of the letter.

> ### An Outline
> ### of 1 Corinthians 7:1–40
>
> **Various topics on marriage and Christian households (7:1–40)**
>
> **Sexuality within marriage (7:1–7)**
>
> **Apostolic celibacy (7:8–9)**
>
> **Divorce and remarriage (7:12–16)**
>
> **Maintaining pre-Christian relationships (7:17–24)**
>
> **Additional advice to those not married (7:25–40)**
>
> Unmarried young women (7:25–28)
>
> Celibacy to serve the gospel (7:29–35)
>
> The betrothed (7:36–38)
>
> The widowed (7:39–40)

Various Topics on Marriage and Christian Households (7:1–40)

7:1–2. The expression **it is good** designates a morally preferable option. Since Paul had just taken the Corinthians to task for sexual immorality (6:12–20), the proposal **not to touch a woman** appears to be an alternate position to those who thought that it did not matter what one did with the body. Paul opens with the principle that marriage exists **on account of sexual passion [*porneia*]**

107

(7:2). Because the phrase "flee *porneia*" (6:18) appears as the catchword slogan in prohibiting sex with prostitutes, *porneia* as the reason for recommending marriage is problematic. Readers often conclude that Paul considers marriage little more than legalized *porneia*. All of the apostle's views on gender and sexuality are, however, derived from Genesis. Therefore the negatives in this section—*porneia* (7:2), opportunity for Satan (7:5), and the famous phrase **better to marry than to burn** (7:9)—do not tell the whole story. They are part of a response to the initial claim that the morally preferable option is for males never to have sexual relations. Paul is not attacking the scriptural claim that marriage is a good (Fitzmyer 2008, 275). In 7:2 Paul uses the plural form of the noun *porneia* to indicate that he has situations of sexual immorality in mind. The catchphrase in 6:18 used the singular to indicate the condition in general.

7:3–5. Some philosophers distrusted the passions associated with sexuality but argued that a man had the duty to society to establish a family. Though he mentions children in the context of believers married to nonbelievers (7:14), Paul does not discuss the social obligations of marriage beyond the general advice not to change the status in which one was called (7:17–24; Mitchell 1993, 121).

Advice on marriage was addressed to men as heads of household, as is Paul's general rule in 1 Thess. 4:4 (Yarbrough 1985, 7). The Corinthians' question also concerned the sexual behavior of men. But in replying Paul formulates his advice on sexual relations within marriage to address women as well as men. Adopting another philosophical topic, marriage as a partnership (R. Collins 1999, 255), he uses a series of parallel statements to underline the mutual obligations of husband and wife: **The wife does not have authority**

Observations on Marriage and Sexuality

*"There is a time for having intercourse with one's wife,
and a time to abstain for the purpose of prayer."*
(*Testament of Naphtali* 8.8,
trans. H. C. Kee in *OTP* 1:814)

"The law [of Moses] recognizes no sexual relations except the natural one of husband and wife, and that for the purpose of producing children." (Josephus, *Contra Apionem* 2.199 AT)

"'Look at me,' he [the Cynic philosopher] says, 'I am without a home, without a city, without property, . . . I have neither wife nor children, . . . but only earth and sky and one rough cloak. Yet what do I lack? Am I not free from pain and fear? Am I not free?'" (Epictetus, *Diatribai* 3.47–48 AT)

over her own body, but her husband, and likewise the husband (7:2–4). Suspension of sexual relations for religious reasons (7:5a–b) occurs in both Jewish and non-Jewish contexts. Paul insists on limiting that practice **lest Satan test you through your lack of self-control** (7:5c).

7:6–7. Paul's own preference for unmarried celibacy (7:7) could have led some Corinthians to refrain from sexual relations even within marriage. Paul clearly rejects that position. He even treats the **for the purposes of prayer** suspension as an option that is not absolutely necessary: **I say this as a concession, not a command** (7:6; Yarbrough 1985, 98–100).

7:8–9. Paul expands his initial response with a series of alternate cases. This section of the letter resembles a minitreatise on marriage. Where a philosopher might have appealed to Roman law and rational argument, Paul employs the teaching of Jesus (7:10), Jewish rules on legitimacy (7:12–14), and his own evaluation of various cases (7:25–40).

Paul admits that his own example favors renouncing all sexual activity. Though the phrase **it is better to marry than be aflame [with sexual passion]** (7:9) seems a negative judgment on marriage, Paul is recommending marriage. He does not propose that a rational disciple extinguish passion as some philosophers did. Nor does he imagine an ascetic regime of isolation, prayer, and fasting as in monastic traditions. Therefore those to whom God has not given this gift of self-control should marry (Deming 2004, 124–29).

7:10–11. Paul opens the discussion of divorce with Jesus's teaching **that a woman not be separated from her husband** (Loader 2005, 88–92, 165–66). In the first century AD divorce did not require legal or religious intervention. The responsible party could simply announce that he or she was abandoning the marriage (Jackson 2005, 343–47). Paul's **not be separated** reflects the Jewish law that limited divorce to husbands (Deut. 24:1), though first-century Jewish women seem to have enjoyed the same freedom to divorce as their gentile counterparts (Satlow 2001; against this interpretation, see Fitzmyer 2008, 289). Jesus tradition challenged the ordinary reason for divorce in antiquity—the desire to marry another (e.g., Matt. 5:32). Paul clearly agrees in principle that the divorced woman should either remain unmarried or be reconciled with her husband.

7:12–16. The complex situation of marriages in Roman Corinth leads Paul to consider cases not covered by Jesus's teaching. Paul distinguishes couples who are both believers from those in which only one party is a Christian. He employs his own insight to come up with a solution for cases of what we often refer to as mixed marriages: **if a believer has a wife who is not a believer** (7:12). The Christian has no reason to dissolve an existing marriage to the nonbeliever on religious grounds. Some may have thought that marriage to a nonbeliever, someone who worshiped idols, contaminated a Christian's holiness in a way comparable to what Paul said about sex with prostitutes (6:18–20). Or they may have worried that their offspring would be illegitimate, that is, unable to participate in the worshiping community. Paul employs terms from Jewish law concerning illegitimate marriages and their offspring (Gillihan 2002). "Holiness" in regard to the nonbelieving spouse and children is not the same as "believing." So at the end of the day, Paul is able to conclude that both the nonbelieving spouse and the children are acceptable.

Paul acknowledges, however, that divorce may be initiated by a nonbeliever unwilling to live harmoniously with a Christian spouse. Requiring the Christian in such a situation to **remain unmarried or be reconciled** (7:11), as in the previous case, would make celibacy a law rather than a gift. In that instance, **do not let the brother or sister be enslaved to such persons** (7:15). Paul does not explicitly state that the Christian who has been divorced by an unbelieving spouse should or will remarry (Deming 2004, 145). Presumably they will be guided by his earlier advice (7:7). Paul's conclusion returns to the advice to believers not to divorce an unbelieving spouse. As long as the marriage continues, the nonbeliever may convert, **be saved** (7:16; R. Collins 1999, 272). In the course of this discussion, Paul refers to the social goal of harmony within the household as the divine intent for all marriages: **God has called you to peace** (7:15; Fitzmyer 2008, 303).

7:17–20. Both Paul's earlier advice not to isolate oneself from nonbelievers (5:9–10) and the injunction not to divorce them (7:12) point toward the general principle: **Let each continue to live in the situation in which God called** (7:17, 20, 24). First Thessalonians demonstrates that Paul teaches this principle in all his churches (4:11–12; 5:12–15). The moral renewal brought about by baptism and the Holy Spirit does not mean that Christians should disrupt prior social relationships. Given the divisiveness evident at Corinth (1 Cor. 1:11),

---

Do Not Be Concerned about External Circumstances

Indifference to one's circumstances exemplified superiority to most of humanity in Cynic and Stoic moralists.

"Therefore one should not try to change circumstances, but rather prepare oneself for them as they are, just as sailors do. . . . And as for you <regard> your present situation, use [it]. You have grown old?—do not seek the things of a young man." (Teles, "On Self-Sufficiency," frag. 2.10.65–80, in Deming 2004, 157)

"Exercise yourself in that which is in your power. Each person's master is the one who has authority over what the person wishes or does not wish, so as to provide it or take it away. Therefore whoever wants to be free should neither wish for nor flee any of the things that are controlled by others; otherwise he is necessarily enslaved." (Epictetus, *Enchiridion* 14 AT)

this rule is crucial to both communal and political harmony (Mitchell 1993, 123).

The first example involves the distinction between Jew and non-Jew symbolized by circumcision: **Circumcision is nothing and lack of circumcision is nothing but keeping the commandments of God** (7:19). There is no indication that conflict over the extent to which non-Jewish believers should adopt a Jewish way of life was being debated at Corinth (Fee 1987, 312–13). Paul rejected an opposition that demanded circumcision of non-Jewish believers in Galatia (Gal. 2:1–9; 5:2–6). On the other side of the equation, some Jews sought to remove the evidence of being circumcised (1 Macc. 1:14–15; *Assumption of Moses* 8.3; Martial, *Epigrams* 7.82).

7:21–24. The second example has elicited considerable debate. Distinctions between **slaves, freed persons [former slaves]**, and **free persons** (7:22) had important social and legal consequences. Paul cites a liturgical formula—"whoever has been baptized into Christ, has put on Christ. In Christ there is no Jew or Greek, slave or free person, no male and female"—to support his argument against Judaizing in Gal. 3:27–28 (also 1 Cor. 12:13). The irrelevance of such distinctions within the Christian fellowship was undoubtedly familiar to his audience. Reading through the questions posed to the Egyptian oracle at Astrampsychus in the second century AD shows that the two questions repeatedly posed by slaves were: "Will I be sold?" and "Will I be freed?" The oracle frequently responds "yes" to the first question but pushes off the timing of the second with such replies as "not yet," "after some time," or "once you've paid" (Toner 2009, 46–49).

The problem in this text appears in the second part of Paul's advice to slaves (7:21b): **but if it is possible to become a free person, rather make use [of it].** His response is worthy of an ancient oracle and may represent a comparable take on the social realities involved. Presumably Paul's elliptical expression encourages slaves to seize an opportunity to gain their freedom (Fitzmyer 2008, 309). If the decision to manumit a slave was initiated by the owner, however, slaves had no choice in the matter (R. Collins 1999, 282). So what sort of use does Paul expect slaves to make of their new situation? His general principle, **each in the situation [calling] in which he was called, let him remain in it** (7:20), excludes taking measures to secure manumission. Perhaps Paul has a different situation in mind, one in which being freed entails some hardship or loss for the individual involved (Bradley 1994, 154–56). Ancient comedy inculcated an image of the slavish character as wicked, lazy, conniving, deceiving the master, expected to obey automatically, subjected to capricious violence. In some tales, the good slave emerges as a contrast to the ordinary types. The good slave internalizes the master so that he can anticipate what his owner desires (Harrill 1995, 20–28, 66–83).

Freed persons had obligations to former owners. Paul deftly crafts the slave-and-master dynamic to bind all believers to Christ: **A slave who has** been called is a freed person of the Lord, similarly a free person who has been called is a slave of Christ (7:22). Regardless of a person's social status, he or she is the good slave to Christ. When Paul says **each in [the situation] in which he was called, let him remain in this** (7:24), the final phrase **before God** indicates that **remain** does not mean acting as most people do. To do so constitutes becoming **slaves of humans** (7:23b).

7:25–28. Paul returns to advice on marriage, addressing *hai parthenoi*, young women not yet married. (On occasion the term *parthenos* might be used for a young man.) He qualifies what follows as **opinion**, not a **command of the Lord** (7:25). Paul's opinions on these topics are not, however, casual. He presumes that they carry his authority as "father"—that is, apostle and founder—of the church (Fitzmyer 2008, 315). Paul addresses young men and concludes that the same applies to young women: **If the young woman marries, she does not sin** (7:28b). Those already engaged should not break it off (7:27a; Loader 2005, 175). Paul, however, still advocates remaining unmarried (7:26b). His reasons are puzzling: **because of the present necessity** (7:26) and **these [persons who marry] will have affliction in the flesh, and I would spare you [that]** (7:28b). Since the word *anankē* (**necessity**) can be used of suffering or bodily affliction, the two phrases are synonymous. What bodily affliction is associated with marriage? The only candidate applicable to both men and women is sexual passion itself. If marriage is the prescription for those afflicted by such passion (7:9; D. Martin 2007, 678–79), then Paul appears to edge back from his earlier remarks. In stating that the unmarried would do better to choose celibacy, he is close to the slogan he rejected (7:1).

7:29–35. Paul introduces another consideration: the eschatological situation. Believers are living in the final days before the end time: **the time has grown short** (7:29a); **the outer form of the world is passing away** (7:31b). These references frame a list of parallel phrases that indicate that ordinary behaviors should be reversed (7:29b–31a):

> those who have wives as though they did not have
> those who weep as not weeping
> those who rejoice as not rejoicing
> those who buy as not possessing
> those who use the world as not making use

Paul's eschatological timetable distinguishes his call to detachment from the ordinary relationships and concerns of life from comparable statements in Cynic or Stoic moralists (R. Collins 1999, 291).

Paul returns to the question of whether the person who has a choice should marry. He presents celibacy as preferable because it frees individuals from **concern over worldly things, how to please** a husband or wife (7:33b–34). The unmarried man, woman, or young woman **is concerned about things of the**

Cynic Detachment

"Diocles reports how Diogenes persuaded Crates to give up his fields to sheep pasture, and throw into the sea any money he had. . . . He [Crates] entrusted a banker with a sum of money on the condition that, if his sons proved ordinary men he was to pay it to them, but if they became philosophers, then to distribute it among the people: for his sons would need nothing. . . . He used to say that one should study philosophy to the point of seeing in generals nothing but donkey-drivers. . . . When Alexander inquired whether he would like his native city rebuilt, his answer was, 'Why should it be?'" (Diogenes Laertius, *Lives* 6.88–93, trans. LCL)

Lord, how to please the Lord (7:32b, 34b). With this orientation toward Christ, Paul's emphasis on avoiding the concerns that most people face might be taken for the routine harangue of a Cynic philosopher. Paul's remark that the unmarried woman's concern is **being holy in body and spirit** (7:34c) appears to contradict his earlier statements about marriage (7:1–5). It suggests that even within marriage sexuality detracts from holiness (D. Martin 1995, 209–10). Paul hesitates long enough to claim that his advice is **for your benefit; I am not laying a burden on you** (7:35).

7:36–40. Paul is not, however, done with possible cases. He continues to present celibacy as preferable to marriage (D. Martin 1995, 211). At the same time, Paul reminds readers that these cases are **in my opinion and I think I have the spirit of God** (7:40). The second of the two cases, a woman who finds herself widowed, is clear (7:39–40a). But the first, **if someone thinks he is disgracing his young woman [*parthenos*]** (7:36a), remains a puzzle. Is Paul referring to a father or other male relative who might feel responsible for arranging a marriage for a daughter or niece? Or is he speaking of a man who has contracted an engagement with a young woman? In any case, the girl in question has no role in determining the outcome. Whether she marries or remains as she is will be decided by the man in question. A girl of marriageable age (about fourteen to sixteen years old in that culture) does not have the same choice as the widow. Unless they were pawns in the political or economic interests of wealthy families, widows often had a say in whether they remarried. Paul advises them to choose a Christian spouse if they wish to remarry (7:39).

An Outline of 1 Corinthians 8:1–13

On meat from pagan sacrifices (8:1–13)

> **Monotheism and the idols (8:1–6)**
>
> **Impact of eating on faith (8:7–12)**
>
> ***Agapē* as the principle of discernment (8:13)**

On Meat from Pagan Sacrifices (8:1–13)

Paul introduces another question raised by the Corinthians. Can a believer eat meat from an animal that has been sacrificed to one of the city's many gods and goddesses? The first case refers to eating at a banquet within temple precincts (8:10). Our best evidence for the setting of such an activity suggests that only wealthier Christians would have been invited (see "Religious Activities in the City" in the introduction). Since few Christians belonged to that demographic, Paul may not have addressed this particular question before. In 1 Cor. 10 Paul adds two additional situations: meat sold in the market and meat served in a private home (10:23–27). As in the section on marriage, Paul will begin with the opinion held by some people, which he corrects. It remains difficult to determine how much of what follows represents questions from the church in Corinth and how much is Paul's own reflection on the issue (P. D. Gooch 1993, 82–84).

8:1–3. The slogan-plus-correction pattern suggests that the phrase **all have knowledge** (8:1a) summarizes an argument from the Corinthian letter. Paul's **knowledge inflates** recalls the earlier argument against the community's fascination with wisdom and rhetorical sophistication (4:6–19; 5:1). The correction **but love builds up** anticipates the advice he will offer on using spiritual gifts to build up the community in the next section of the letter (13:4; 14:4, 17). Paul then develops the knowledge and love contrast with two parallel phrases that remind readers to consider how God views them:

Individual's attitude	God's perspective
thinks he knows something	knows as one should know
loves God	is known by him [God]

8:4–6. A second introduction to the topic leads to a more theological explanation. The **knowledge** in question was based on the monotheistic belief that **no one is God except one** (8:4), which the Corinthians had embraced upon their conversion (cf. 1 Thess. 1:9–10). That conviction is shared by everyone in the church. So is the initial conclusion that follows from it: **An idol has no reality in the world** (cf. Isa. 44:9–20).

Paul expands this monotheistic slogan in two stages. He acknowledges that believers live in a city full of entities that everyone else worships, those **called gods in heaven and on earth** (1 Cor. 8:5). Then he contrasts these false gods with the true God, who created all things, **one God, the Father, from whom all things [come into being]** (8:6a). To this point Paul follows the depiction of idols and their worshipers familiar to first-century Jews. The concluding phrase, however, incorporates Christ as Lord into the creative process: **one Lord Jesus Christ through whom all things** (8:6b). Each phrase concludes by incorporating the believers to the Father (**us into him**) and to the Lord (**us through him**).

What is the basis for incorporating the Lord Jesus into the creative activity of the one God? One possibility is an early identification of the exalted Christ with God's preexistent Wisdom (Dunn 1996, 165). Another possibility treats the incorporation of the Lord Jesus into the formula as a reflection on the role Christ plays in salvation (Murphy-O'Connor 2009, 59–75). In either case, Paul uses the revised formula as the foundation for the solutions he will offer. Even though the gods and goddesses have no reality, participation in activities designed to honor them is not indifferent. Believers have obligations to the Lord Jesus, into whom they were baptized.

8:7–9. Though all Christians make the same dual confession of God as one creator Father and of Jesus as Lord, they differ over eating meat from sacrificial offerings. Paul wishes to correct the position being advanced by those who concluded that Christians could participate in banquets that followed a cult sacrifice. Even though access was somewhat restricted, Paul presumes that their presence was open to observation by nonparticipants: **If someone sees you, a person with knowledge, reclining in a temple precinct** (8:10). Those who saw no problem with accepting an invitation to dine in a temple area asserted that food had nothing to do with one's relationship to God: **Food will not establish us with God** (8:8a; Murphy-O'Connor 2009, 76–86). The rest of the sentence is ambiguous: **neither in want if we do not eat nor have a surplus if we do** (8:8b–c).

The Absurdity of Idol Worship

"With their hopes set on dead things, are those
who give the name 'gods' to the works of human hands,
gold and silver fashioned with skill,
and likenesses of animals,
or a useless stone, the work of an ancient hand. . . .
One preparing to sail and about to voyage over raging waves
calls upon a piece of wood more fragile than the ship that carries him."
(Wis. 13:10; 14:1 NRSV)

God's Creative Wisdom

"For she is an initiate in the knowledge of God,
and an associate in his works.
If riches are a desirable possession in life,
what is richer than wisdom, the active cause of all things?
And if understanding is effective,
who more than she is fashioner of what exists?"
(Wis. 8:4–6 NRSV)

"Wisdom, by whose agency the universe ["the All"] was brought to completion." (Philo, *Quod deterius potiori insidari soleat* 54, trans. LCL)

115

If the phrase is paraphrasing a Corinthian argument, then the point may have been that eating or refraining from such food makes no difference to one's spiritual gifts.

Paul's approach to the question introduces a different consideration—the impact of one's choice on fellow believers. He acknowledges that a lifetime of participation in sacrificial meals as an act of worship leaves its mark on the conscience (8:7). He describes that situation as a weakness: **and their conscience being weak is defiled** (8:7c). Unlike those who experience no change in their relationship with God, these individuals find themselves condemned as idol worshipers. Paul warns those who insist on a right to eat at a sacrificial meal that their example could endanger the faith of others: **Watch out lest that authority of yours cause those who are weak to stumble** (8:9). With only cryptic information about the situation in Corinth, exegetes often treat this situation as another dispute between two factions: those who eat sacrificial offerings without any qualms (**the strong**) and those who are criticizing such behavior (**the weak**). Such phrases as **the weak** and **defiled conscience** reflect the perspective of those who insist that belief in the one God authorizes participation in these meals.

8:10–12. Paul uses the danger to the faith of those weak brothers and sisters to conclude that Christians should not participate in the banquets held in some temple precinct (8:10). Rather than bring others closer to Christ, such activities could lead them back into idolatry. Once more the cross becomes the norm. Christians cannot permit convictions to bring about the loss of **the brother for whom Christ died** (8:11). Suddenly Paul springs a rhetorical trap on his audience. Throughout this section of the argument, he has affirmed the theological position that eating sacrificial food is an indifferent matter. He merely asks caution around the weak. If the cryptic phrases represent hotly contested issues, then the question of conscience may have been raised by Christians who would never go near a temple banquet. They may have accused those who ate of sinning against God. Though Paul agrees that the food as such is indifferent, he asserts that in destroying the faith of the weak **you sin against Christ** (8:12).

8:13. At this point one expects Paul to provide either a rule or general advice about eating sacrificial food. The section on marriage included advice that sometimes left believers with a choice between options. Instead Paul presents a more extreme option than the situation demands: **I would never eat meat again, so as not to cause my brother to fall away** (8:13b). Paul is not proposing vegetarianism as a policy. Rhetorically this suggestion will make his final argument against any participation in "the cup of demons" (10:14–22) more persuasive (P. D. Gooch 1993, 83–84). It will turn out that Christians can consume idol meat only in contexts where it has no religious or symbolic significance whatsoever.

Paul as Example of Christian Freedom (9:1–27)

Following the model of his treatment of marriage, in which Paul compiles a number of related questions, one would expect further discussion of idol meat or related issues. Paul meets those expectations in 10:1–11:1. The generalizing conclusion to the previous section shifted from the second-person plural (8:12) to the first-person singular (8:13). But the defensive outburst, **Am I not free? Am I not an apostle?** (9:1), does not follow from the statement that Paul would never eat any kind of meat if doing so caused a fellow believer to stumble. If that were the context for the questions that open this section, then the response is of course that he is free to do as he chooses. But why underline that individual freedom with a strong statement of Paul's authority as an apostolic witness to the risen Lord? Why does Paul insert this **apology to those who interrogate me** (9:3)?

Paul alternates between first-person singular (9:1, 2, 3, 8) and first-person plural (9:6, 10, 11, 12) before settling into first-person singular at 9:15. Though the first-person plural also refers to Paul's own conduct, he associates Barnabas with that style of ministry in 9:6. The defensive posture appears to be elicited by comparisons between Paul (and Barnabas?) and other known apostles, Peter, and the brothers of Jesus. Curiously, Apollos, the focus of an earlier comparison (3:4–5; 4:6), is not named here. In that case, the comparison was associated with a false estimation of rhetorical skill, human wisdom, and status. In this section, the questions focus on patronage relationships. Apostles who teach spiritual things should receive material support from the churches, an obligation confirmed by Mosaic Torah (9:9), Jesus's teaching (9:14), and general custom (9:13). Has Paul's refusal to enter into such a relationship with them (9:12b) offended some of the more affluent Corinthians?

Questions about the financing of Paul's ministry were raised in connection with the collection for Jerusalem (2 Cor. 11:5–13) when his ministry was under attack from traveling "superapostles." Rather than consider this digression as the response to accusations against Paul such as those he confronts in 2 Cor. 10:1–13:10, most interpreters treat this section as an example offered in support of the recommendations Paul makes (Schrage 1995, 277–79; Mitchell 1993, 130–37). Certainly the policy of adaptability presented in 1 Cor. 9:19–23 suits

> **An Outline
> of 1 Corinthians 9:1–27**
>
> **Paul as example of Christian freedom (9:1–27)**
>
> > **Apostle's rights to material support (9:1–18)**
> >
> > > The apostolic office (9:1–2)
> > >
> > > Agricultural examples (9:3–12)
> > >
> > > Priests and evangelists (9:13–15)
> > >
> > > Renouncing the right to payment (9:16–18)
> >
> > **Apostle's strategy to win as many as possible for the gospel (9:19–23)**
> >
> > **Comparison to runners in the stadium (9:24–27)**

Paul's argument that Christians must consider how their behavior influences others. But the strident tone of 9:1–18 still seems out of place. Two rhetorical questions link the apostle's freedom to the previous topics in a general way: (a) **the right to eat and drink** (9:4) and (b) **the right to be accompanied by a Christian wife like the other apostles** (9:5; Cook 2008). But no one is challenging those rights. Paul presented celibacy as his preferred exercise of a God-given gift (7:6–7).

9:1. This section opens with four rhetorical questions. Each begins with the word **not** (*ou, ouk, ouchi*). Each provides a further specification of the prior category. Freedom is that enjoyed by an apostle. Apostles are a group of persons called by the risen Lord, a criterion that Paul uses to support his claim to the same status as Peter and the others (15:9–11). The evidence for Paul's apostleship is narrowed further: the existence of the Corinthian church that he fathered (4:15). **Freedom** is not that superiority to vice and social conventions claimed by Stoic and Cynic philosophers but the conduct of an **apostle**. The "apostle of Christ Jesus" (1:1) has been called by the risen Lord: **Have I not seen Jesus our Lord?** Even that call does not confer an authority to make demands on other Christians. Rather the truth of Paul's apostolic claim must be demonstrated in the communities of faith that resulted from his ministry.

9:2. A statement follows the set of four questions in 9:1. It repeats the claim that Paul's audience proves the truth of his claim to be an apostle: **You are the seal of my apostleship.** Though Paul does not make the point directly, the letter asking Paul to resolve a number of questions is evidence of the apostle's authority within the Corinthian church.

9:3–12. Before Paul can use his own conduct as an example of the principle that those who have authority, insight, or advantages might choose not to act on them, he must establish the rights of an apostle. He opens with a long string of rhetorical questions (9:4–7), a demonstration from Scripture (9:8–10), and concluding questions (9:11–12a). The expression **if others** (9:12) in the final verse in this section matches that found in 9:2: **if to others.**

The formal pattern of analogies stated in rhetorical questions in 9:4–7 is interrupted by the citation of Torah (9:9–10). To match the interrogative style, these quotations are also introduced with questions. Thus Paul's direct statement about his own conduct in 9:12b–c is highlighted by the contrast.

Initial questions point out that the apostles routinely expect support for themselves and their families: **the right to eat and drink** and to **have a sister [believer] as wife** (9:4–6; Cook 2008). He presumes that his audience knows of the important role played by **Cephas [Peter] [and the] brothers of the Lord** [especially James] in early Christianity (9:5–6; cf. Gal. 1:18–19; 2:1–14; Acts 10:1–11:18; 15:1–35). Patronage relationships in which local elites supported orators, philosophers, artists, and authors were routine in antiquity. Patrons also provided the material support for various associations, civic events, and religious activities. Therefore the apostles both expected and received material support from the communities in which they preached.

Paul and his earlier associate Barnabas (Gal. 2:1, 9, 13; Acts 13–15) broke with that convention by working at a trade. Such independence may have provoked the criticisms Paul levels at elite members of the church, but turning down such patronage had risks. In addition to the personal hardship that Paul had to endure, the apostle has also undermined his own public status. Paul adopted a mode of preaching that he insists fits its content (1 Cor. 2:1–13).

Three commonplace examples—serving in the army, cultivating a vineyard, and shepherding sheep—show that individuals are entitled to food in exchange for their labor (9:7). Paul then shifts to demonstrate the same point from the Mosaic law. **You shall not muzzle the ox while it is threshing** (Deut. 25:4) does not specify animal rights. Paul contends that it indicates what is owed to the laborer. **The one who plows and the one who threshes ought to anticipate sharing [in the harvest]** (1 Cor. 9:9–10). Two rhetorical questions apply the agricultural imagery to the work of apostles. The first could be using the plural **we** to refer to apostles as a class: **We have sown spiritual things . . . harvest your material things** (9:11). The second statement employs an argument from a lesser to a greater case: **If others share . . . not more the case [that] we?** (9:12a). Consequently, the plural **we** refers to the two apostles who do not demand the support they could claim, Paul and Barnabas. Paul provides a reason for not requiring material support from the community: **But we endure all things so that we might not create an obstacle to the gospel** (9:12b). It is not clear how closely Barnabas modeled his own conduct on Paul's, since he is no longer one of Paul's missionary associates (Acts 15:36–40). Nor are the Corinthians likely to be in a position to judge the matter for themselves. Since Paul is pressing toward a conclusion he wishes his audience to adopt, he needs to show that he is not alone in choosing this strategy.

9:13–15. First Corinthians 9:13 opens with the familiar **do you not know?** The example of priests and those engaged in sacrifices dividing the offerings brings the discussion closer to the problem of sacrificial meat posed in the previous chapter. Paul, however, takes the argument in a different direction. The **Lord [himself] commanded those who preach the gospel to live from the gospel** (9:14; cf. Matt. 10:10; Luke 10:7).

Paul employs slogans from a stock philosophical debate to justify setting

A Cynic Philosopher's Freedom

"I sleep on the ground; I have neither wife nor children, . . . only earth and sky and one rough cloak. Yet what do I lack? Am I not free from pain and fear, am I not free? . . . And how do I face those before whom you stand in awe and fear? Do I not face them as slaves? Who, upon seeing me, does not feel that he is seeing his king and master?" (Epictetus, *Diatribai* 3.48–49 AT)

119

aside the Lord's command (Malherbe 1995, 240–52). He has no need for the material support that others require.

Paul admits that the vigorous defense of those apostolic rights to material support could be misinterpreted as a rhetorical ploy to inaugurate a shift in his relationship to the Corinthian church. So Paul interjects a caveat that he is not attempting to secure any kind of patronage from them: **I would rather die than [that]—no one will nullify my boast** (9:15b).

9:16–18. Paul distinguishes between activity performed under compulsion and that freely undertaken. He insists that preaching the gospel belongs to the former category: **a necessity is imposed on me** (9:16b). Since he has no choice in the matter, Paul cannot claim any credit for doing his work (9:17). He can, however, go beyond what is required by **presenting the gospel without charge** (9:18). In so doing, Paul follows a principle of Stoic philosophy. The wise recognize that they have no control over the external ordering of everything that occurs. The wise adapt their own conduct to accord with what cannot be changed (Malherbe 1995, 245–50). Paul implies that Jesus's instructions about accepting support from those who hear the gospel is not a requirement. It is an authority or right that lies within an individual's power. That leaves the apostle free to **not make use of my right in the gospel** (9:18c).

9:19–23. The phrase **being free** (9:19; from 9:1) introduces a long sentence of balanced clauses that explain the use Paul makes of this freedom: **so that I will certainly save some** (9:22). Though his behavior might be interpreted as **enslaving himself** to those who lack his knowledge, Paul insists that he is serving the gospel by adapting to those among whom he works: **Jews, those who observe the Mosaic law, those without [that] law**, and **the weak** (9:20–22; Schrage 1995, 338–40).

Rather than employ the binary category "Jew and Greek" (1:22–24; 10:32; 12:13), Paul uses the contrast between **under the law** and **lawless** (9:20–21). Paul uses a string of words based on the *nomos* (law) stem in 9:20b–21 that are difficult to capture in translation: 9:20b substitutes a string of **under the**

Paul's Cultural Strategy

"1 Cor 9:20–21 is revealing: he can afford to live sometimes ['as under Torah'] and sometimes ['as Torah-less'], since his true position is neither . . . but ['under law of Christ']. . . . It clearly cannot contain the cultural commitment of submission to the Jewish law, nor the absence of moral obligation which Paul associates with Gentile 'lawlessness.' This culturally adaptable morality is evoked as the paradigm for Paul's converts in 1 Cor 10:31–11:1 where their dietary practices are left deliberately undetermined, so long as they represent giving glory to God." (Barclay 1995, 154–55)

law phrases in a pattern that parallels 9:20a on the Jews; and 9:21a repeats the pattern a third time, substituting those who are *anomos*. The term **lawless** (*anomos*) not only reflects the Jewish view of gentiles but also can refer to nonobservant Jews (Fredriksen 2010). It could raise suspicions that the Christian movement subverted the moral standards of society. Paul counters by qualifying the statement that he is willing to be one of the **lawless**: **not being lawless [before] God, but subject to the law of Christ** (9:21). First Corinthians 9:22 repeats this set of phrases for a fourth time, substituting **the weak**, as those to whom the apostle conforms his behavior. That final term brings the audience back to the caveat in 8:11: **The one who is weak will perish by your knowledge**. Paul concludes by insisting that his choices serve to spread the gospel (9:23). Although it is possible to treat this strategy of accommodating oneself to diverse audiences as simple pragmatism, early Christian writers recognized that Paul was referring to the condescension of God in becoming human (e.g., Phil. 2:6–11; Mitchell 2001; Glad 2003).

9:24–27. By comparing himself to athletes in the Isthmian Games, Paul distinguishes himself from famous orators or philosophers who enjoyed the leisure provided by wealthy patrons. The apostle is comparable to the runners or boxers who must follow a rigorous training schedule and diet to compete for the victor's crown. The stakes are much higher for the apostle than for athletes, who **receive a perishable crown** (9:25). Without rigorous training, Paul would risk being as foolish as the runner who strays from his lane on the course (i.e., **runs aimlessly**) or a boxer **punching at air** (9:26–27a). Though the Corinthian elite considered Paul's way of life demeaning, he invites them to consider it a form of self-discipline. No one can suspect him of preaching the gospel for personal advantage (Winter 2002, 169–72).

Philosophers were expected to provide students with a living embodiment of their teaching. If the apostle is not careful to see that his way of life conforms to the gospel he preaches (2:1–5), he may fail to attain the salvation that he preaches to others (9:27b).

On Participation in Cult Meals and Banquets (10:1–11:1)

The initial discussion dealt with eating what had been sacrificed to idols, who are not really divine beings (8:4). Paul concedes that meat from a sacrifice to those gods has no sacred character for believers. Eating it becomes an ethical question for believers only if their conduct risks leading other Christians back to old habits of venerating gods and goddesses. The

---

An Outline of 1 Corinthians 10:1–11:1

On participation in cult meals and banquets (10:1–11:1)

Cautionary *exemplum*: Israel in the desert (10:1–13)

Ruling against participation in temple banquets (10:14–22)

Concern for the faith of others at private dinners (10:23–31)

Imitating the apostle's example (10:32–11:1)

excursus concludes with Paul's own example of shifting lifestyles in order to preach the gospel effectively (9:19–23). This apostolic flexibility could, however, be viewed as a license to join celebrations that honor the gods as long as no one would be offended (8:10; P. D. Gooch 1993, 84).

To guard against such a misreading, Paul sets further limits on consuming sacrificial meat. Paul introduces this return to the topic with the phrase **I do not wish you to be ignorant** (10:1a). After presenting the story of Israel's wilderness apostasy as instruction for believers (10:1b–13), Paul applies the lesson to his audience (10:14–22). The application opens with yet another imperative: **Flee from idolatry** (10:14). Any meal within sacred precincts or in a context that is dedicated to honoring one of the gods or goddesses is off limits. The meat in itself may be indifferent (8:13), but participating in the meal is equivalent to entering into a partnership with demons (10:20; Murphy-O'Connor 2009, 83).

The argument that Paul gives for this position opens with an example from Scripture. God punished the Israelites in the wilderness for worshiping idols (10:1–13; Num. 25:1–9). Paul applies that story to the Corinthian situation. Their participation in the Christian meal fellowship excludes joining any other association honoring gods or goddesses (1 Cor. 10:14–22). This conclusion appears more restrictive than what was suggested in 8:1–13. Attempts have been made to distinguish the two cases by treating **reclining at an idol's table** (8:10) as meals in temple precincts that were not dedicated to the deity and **drink the cup of a demon . . . share the table of a demon** (10:21) as those involving cult. Evidence that a first-century audience would have made such careful distinctions is, however, dubious (P. D. Gooch 1993, 47–52). It is easier to treat 10:1–11:1 as resuming and completing the argument initiated in 8:1–13. Initially Paul accepts the premise that eating idol food is morally neutral but concludes that the impact on fellow believers is not. Therefore refraining is preferable. Now an argument grounded in the authority of Scripture finds a situation in which any participation in a cult banquet offends God. Therefore refraining is necessary. This argument draws a stricter conclusion: one is not simply avoiding offense to the weak; one also risks participating in idolatry (Fitzmyer 2008, 377). Paul concludes the discussion in the form of rhetorical questions with warnings against provoking God's wrath (10:22).

The familiar slogan **all things are permitted but not all are helpful** (10:23a; 6:12a) opens the final section in this part of the letter. It is followed by a brief statement of the principle that governs all cases in which one is choosing between options that appear equally acceptable: **Let no one seek his own [advantage] but that of another** (10:24). Paul analyzes yet another situation, invitations to a meal in a private home where sacrificial food is served (10:23–11:1). On the one hand, everything sold in the market (10:25) or served by one's host (10:27) is acceptable food, so one need not refuse an invitation to dine with unbelievers. On the other hand, a situation could arise in which another's conscience is at stake. Then it is morally preferable to refrain from eating (10:28–29). Paul concludes this division of his letter with the exhortation to imitate his example in these matters (11:1; cf. 4:16).

10:1–5. Paul concluded the previous section with the hypothetical possibility that even he could miss out on salvation if his conduct failed to match his preaching (9:27). He invokes Israel's story to warn his audience: **God was not pleased with most of them** (10:5). The comparison between those led by Moses and believers depends on analogies between Israel's experiences and Christian practices: **All were baptized into Moses** (10:2), and **all ate the same spiritual food and . . . drank the same spiritual drink** (10:3–4). By referring to the wilderness generation as **all our fathers** (10:1), Paul invites his audience to consider themselves part of God's people even though most are not Jewish Christians (Schrage 1995, 388). **Baptized into Moses** corresponds to "baptized into Christ" as participants in the group that experienced God's saving acts. Without commenting on a specific text, Paul highlights key motifs in the wilderness story.

Table 11
Exodus Motifs in 1 Corinthians 10:1–5

cloud	"in front of them in a pillar of cloud" (Exod. 13:21–22)
sea	"into the sea on dry ground, the waters forming a wall . . . on their right and on their left" (Exod. 14:22, 29)
manna and quail	"the LORD gives you meat to eat in the evening and your fill of bread in the morning" (Exod. 16:4, 8, 12)
spring	"water will come out of it so that the people may drink" (Exod. 17:6)
apostasy	"the people sat down to eat and drink, and rose up to revel. . . . about 3,000 people fell that day" (Exod. 32:6, 28)

By speaking of **spiritual food** and **spiritual drink** Paul equates the wilderness sustenance with the bread and wine of the Christian meal. One should not attribute the apostasy of the Israelite ancestors to some inferiority in God's presence, in Moses, or in the food. Paul contrasts the privileges that Israel had enjoyed: (a) under the cloud and through the sea (baptism), (b) eating and drinking spiritual food, and (c) accompanied by the spiritual rock (10:1b–4). That sharpens the tragedy of the desert veneration (10:5). Instances in which the Israelites angered God follow: (a) idolatry, (b) sexual immorality, (c) challenging the Lord, and (d) grumbling (10:6–10).

Lest his audience fall into the trap of thinking that being in Christ renders them immune to divine judgment, Paul discovers the presence of Christ with the Israelites: **Now the rock was Christ** (10:4). Philo's allegorical interpretation of the water and the manna distinguishes between souls that turn to God and are freed from domination by the passions and those that are not. The latter are destroyed. Though some in Corinth might have thought themselves to be such "God-loving souls," drinking from the fountain of God's Wisdom,

Paul continues to challenge any pretensions to wisdom as he did in the opening sections of the letter.

The word *pantes* (**all**) runs through these verses as a drumbeat as it opens each clause. The Israelites' experience of being saved was just as comprehensive as that of the Corinthian believers. The conclusion bursts into this litany of saving experiences: **With most of them God was not pleased; they were struck down** (10:5).

10:6–10. As Paul begins to apply the lesson to the situation of his audience—**these things happened as models [***typoi***] of us**—he combines the idea that the story is a warning about being carried away by passions (10:6) with the case at hand in Corinth: **that you not become idol worshipers** (10:7a). Paul cites the description of the Israelites' celebrating a festival before the golden calf (10:7b; Exod. 32:6b LXX). Such feasting and merrymaking also described the banquets in honor of local deities and civic religious holidays that some in his audience continued to attend (Smith 2002, 80–85).

When Paul develops the story of Israel's defection in the wilderness, he introduces further cases: **Let us not engage in sexual immorality** (1 Cor. 10:8), **put the Christ to the test** (10:9), and **grumble rebelliously** (10:10). Each incident concluded with swift and wide-ranging divine punishment. Sexual relations with Moabite women led to participation in the sacrifices offered to their gods. Thousands of idolatrous Israelites were killed to avert God's anger (Num. 25:1–9). The second example involved God's response to the people's complaints against Moses for bringing them from Egypt and subjecting them to the horrid diet of manna and water. The attack of poisonous snakes elicited repentance, Moses's intercession, and healing (Num. 21:5–9). Just as Paul identified Christ with the water-giving rock, so Christ rather than Moses is the one being tested. The third member of the triad could be a repetition of the second, but the Greek verb for complaining in Num. 21 LXX is *katalalein*, while Paul employs *gongyzein*, a verb stem that appears in Num. 14:1–38, where a fearful people rebel against Moses and Aaron and a generation is condemned to die in the wilderness.

10:11–13. Paul's rhetoric requires an audience able to retrieve the larger story of Israel in the wilderness from memory. Taken at face value, the stories appear to support the position of those earlier considered to be "weak" in their conversion to the one God (8:7–13). Don't touch any meat remotely connected with an idol sacrifice lest God lash out with similar violence. Although Paul inserted "the Christ" for Moses in alluding to Num. 21:5–9, the caution not to rebel verbally against God's servant could transfer to the apostle-founder just as easily. Paul expects the Corinthians to accept his authority, just as the Israelites had to follow Moses and Aaron. Paul does not, however, draw the harsh conclusion his punishment list suggests.

Instead he expands the claim that the OT stories provide examples that apply to Christian believers (1 Cor. 10:6). Unlike Philo's distinction between literal events and allegorical teaching about the soul's need for wisdom to rein in the passions, Paul distinguishes between the Israelites and Christians, **for whom the end of the age has arrived** (10:11b). What does it mean to have these stories **recorded in Scripture for our instruction** (10:11a)? Though the apocalyptic scenario is not yet complete (15:20–28), believers already experience the presence of the new age in part (Dunn 1998, 461–72). The cycle of sin, punishment, repentance, and forgiveness repeated in Israel's history ends with Christ.

Paul's answer makes a subtle shift that moves his audience from identifying with the majority who perished to identifying with those who came through the trials in the desert to become God's people. Throughout the letter, Paul steps in to correct overconfident claims about salvation and Christian freedom in Corinth. So he initially presents the stories as a warning: **Let the person who thinks he stands secure watch out lest he fall** (10:12). Does that mean those God has called in Christ could suffer devastating losses? Some apocalyptic scenarios imagine that the evils of the last days will leave very few righteous people standing.

Paul concludes on a different note. Any **testing** (*peirasmos*) faced by believers is not of that sort. It is **merely human** (10:13a). Instead, by identifying with those who perished in these wilderness trials (Fitzmyer 2008, 388), his audience learns that **God is faithful, who will not permit you to be tested beyond what you are able [to endure]** (10:13b). God does not shield the elect from circumstances that test their faith. In a somewhat cryptic shorthand, the sentence concludes: **but he will provide with the testing the way out, the ability to endure** (10:13c). Looking back to the examples given, the Corinthians could see that God had provided for his people in the wilderness. Those who rebelled and complained were rejecting the means of survival and salvation that God offered them.

Evil at the End of Days

"Days are coming when those who inhabit the earth shall be seized with great terror, and the way of truth shall be hidden.... Unrighteousness shall be increased beyond what you yourself see." (2 Esd. [*4 Ezra*] 5:1–2 NRSV)

"And if the Lord had not cut short those days, no one would be saved; but for the sake of the elect, whom he chose, he has cut short those days." (Mark 13:20 NRSV)

125

Figure 11. Persons Assembled at an Altar for a Sacrifice.

10:14–15. Paul invites his audience to join him in working out the implications of the general principle: **Flee idolatry** (10:14). He credits them with sufficient practical intelligence to make a judgment about what he is going to propose (10:15). Even though the various cases treated in this division of the letter include some definitive prohibitions, the deliberative tone continues. After considering the examples and arguments that Paul proposes, believers should have sufficient insight to resolve many diverse situations.

10:16–18. The decisive factor in determining proper conduct is the *koinōnia* ("fellowship, association") created by participating in the Christian meal. In 10:16 Paul inverts the order of the traditional eucharistic blessing (11:23–25; cf. *Didache* 9.1–2; Fitzmyer 2008, 390–91)—**cup . . . partnership in the blood of Christ . . . bread . . . partnership in the body of Christ**—to permit an expansion on the bread word in 1 Cor. 10:17. Paul hammers home the unity created by the Christian meal, employing the word **one** in each of the three clauses that make up this sentence: **one loaf, one body,** and **the one loaf.** This emphasis serves the larger agenda of the letter, establishing concord in the divided church. It could draw on the social conviction that participation in common rituals identifies fellow citizens, fellow tribesmen, members of a particular trade group, or the like (Mitchell 1993, 141).

For the Corinthian believers who thought that participating in cult banquets was not detrimental to their faith, such social ties could, however, have been the motive for doing so (Murphy-O'Connor 2009, 96). After all, Paul does not insist on breaking one's ties to nonbelievers (5:10; 7:12–14). Paul must still persuade his audience that participation in the festive meal associated with a sacrifice offered by someone else counts as idol worship. For Jews like Paul, the distinction may have felt obvious. Participation in their common rites excluded adopting idolatrous sacrifices from or even intermarriage with the Moabite women in the episode alluded to. Paul's churches are not, however, Jewish proselytes. So his move to convince them that the Christian meal excludes participation in other cult meals cannot appeal to Israel's exclusive covenant with God. Instead 10:18 makes a rather general connection between the unity of Israel in the biblical account, **historical Israel** (*Israēl kata sarka*), and the people's participation in shared sacrifices. Eating what has been sacrificed makes them **participants [*koinōnoi*] of the altar**. Paul leaves the logical conclusion incomplete at this point. Even if one is not part of the small group that actually participated in the sacrificial rite itself, one becomes a participant in what occurred there by sharing the meal.

10:19–22. Paul acknowledges that someone in his audience might object that this line of reasoning assumes that pagan gods and goddesses are real, something we know is not true (10:19; 8:4–6). He skirts that apparent contradiction by identifying the recipients of such sacrifices as demons: **what they offer to demons and not to God** (10:20a). Believers would not wish to enter into a **partnership with demons** (10:20b). First Corinthians 10:21 reformulates the cup-and-loaf formulation from 10:16 by substituting **dining table [*trapeza*] of the Lord . . . dining table of demons** in place of the loaf. This shift calls to mind the group reclining at the banquet table, perhaps even pouring out some wine as a libation to the deity being honored. Thus Paul has come back around to the very sight that horrified those he spoke of as having a "weak conscience, being built up to eating idol sacrifices" (8:10). There the danger that participating in cult meals posed to fellow Christians who felt themselves drawn back into idolatry dictated avoiding such conduct. Here Paul appears to have sharpened the restriction. Even if there were no scandalized believer to witness one's participation, a Christian should not join in the cult festivities (P. D. Gooch 1993, 103–5). In suggesting that the idols are demons Paul also departs from his earlier argument: "An idol is nothing in the world" (8:4).

Scholars suggest various solutions to the contradictions between Paul's opening position and the one he reaches here. The series of arguments is less problematic if one treats this section as the climax of a rhetorical argument, not a logical one (R. Collins 1999, 375–78). Having conceded points to those who had joined in such cult meals, Paul actually wishes to convince them not to do so under any circumstances. The initial argument against participation, practical concern for fellow believers, came to a dramatic conclusion with Paul's first-person exclamation: "If food scandalizes my brother, I would never eat meat" (8:13). Drawing its premises from Scripture, the final argument warns against repeating the rebellion of the Israelites in the wilderness. The dramatic conclusion assumes that similar punishments might befall Christian idolaters: **Or are we going to provoke the Lord's jealousy? Are we stronger than he?** (10:22). In this context **the Lord** refers to God rather than to Christ.

10:23–31. Paul returns to principles of discernment for situations that are neutral on the face of it: **Not all things are beneficial . . . not all things build up** (10:23; 6:12). One must judge appropriate actions by their impact on the community as a whole (10:24). Paul qualified the application of knowledge (*gnōsis*) to the question of sacrificial meat with the counterphrase "love builds up" (8:1). He returns to these principles of love and building up the community in discussing appropriate conduct in the worshiping assembly (13:1–3; 14:26).

Any situation that involves public honor paid to gods and goddesses is considered idolatry. Christians cannot participate. But Paul allows for individual discretion in situations that are not of this sort. The first case concerns meat sold in the market. Evidence does not allow scholars to determine how much of what was for sale came from sacrificial offerings or how often such animals were sacrificed in contrast to other types of offering such as incense, grain, or wine. The **market** (*macellum*; Paul uses a Latin term; 10:25) was near the main temples in Pompeii, which suggests that a fair supply of meat on sale came from temple sacrifices (Beard 2008, 293). Jewish communities had their own meat market in order to comply with kosher rules. Pompeii even provides evidence for a dealer in kosher *garum*, the popular Roman fish sauce. So Paul himself may never have confronted the questions facing his non-Jewish converts. Whether a purchaser would have known the source of meat being sold is unclear. In any case, Paul once again returns to Scripture, citing in 10:26 a familiar phrase from the Psalms: **The earth is the Lord's and its bounty** (Pss. 24:1; 50:12; 89:11).

The second case concerned only the wealthier members of the church. Could they accept invitations to a dinner from non-Christian friends, associates, or patrons? If so, should they avoid some of the food items on offer? Paul's initial response would have elicited sighs of relief. It follows the **all things are permitted** principle: go and eat anything without worrying about it (10:27). But he then considers a possible complication: suppose someone else points out that meat being served was **offered in sacrifice** (10:28a). Suddenly the rule of not eating because of the conscience of the informant comes into play (10:28b–29a). This situation remains ambiguous. Who is the informant? A nonbeliever, perhaps even the host boasting about the superior quality of his meat because it came from a sacrificial animal? Or a fellow Christian who happens to know its source, perhaps one of the slaves or entertainers serving at the banquet? While either scenario is possible, the social consequences of not eating are more serious in the first instance. A host desiring to impress his guests with the dish being presented would be insulted. A quiet word in the ear from a fellow diner or servant that led one to decline a particular dish would be less problematic.

The remark **why should my freedom be determined by another's conscience?** (10:29b–30) is a hypothetical objection to

---

Table Manners at a Banquet

"We must avoid all boorish manners and excess, and touch what is set before us politely, keeping the hand, the dining couch, and the chin free of stains, preserving a dignified face that is undisturbed, and make no loud noises when swallowing." (Clement of Alexandria, *Paedagogus* 2.1.13 AT)

Paul's determination. Whether it represents his rhetorical imagining of what the Corinthians might object to or something they actually had written, we cannot tell. The somewhat awkward sequence of objections appears to be Paul's own attempt to formulate the sort of protest the Corinthians might give (P. D. Gooch 1993, 86–92). Therefore **why am I treated as a blasphemer over something for which I give thanks [to God]?** (10:30b) does not refer to some actual accusations (against Murphy-O'Connor 2009, 91). It is another example of heightened rhetoric intended to dispose the audience to accept Paul's conclusion. This kind of nasty recrimination, one Christian accusing another of blasphemy, hardly serves to build up the community. In the end, Paul concludes that the choice is not about personal freedom or its restraint but about honoring God: **Whatever you do, do all things for the glory of God** (10:31).

10:32–11:1. The conclusion to this section of the letter applies the principle of seeking what benefits others to every situation. Paul invokes the familiar baptismal affirmation "no Jew or Greek . . . you are one in Christ" (Gal. 3:28; 1 Cor. 12:13) against the Corinthian tendencies toward making distinctions between believers (10:32). He then reminds the audience of his own example in adapting his conduct to others, Jew and non-Jew alike (9:19–23): **not seeking my own benefit but that of the majority so that they may be saved** (10:33). But Paul does not leave the question as one of missionary strategy. As he does repeatedly in the letter, he calls his audience back to consider the example of Christ himself. Earlier he said of his own arrival in the city, "I determined to know nothing among you except Jesus Christ and him crucified" (2:2). So he now asks them to **imitate me as I [imitate] Christ** (11:1).

Theological Issues

Many of the specific issues raised by the Corinthians are alien to Christians in today's urban, industrialized societies, but quite familiar to missionaries working among indigenous peoples (Newton 1998). Religious practices associated with spirits, out-of-body journeys by shaman healers, praying at temples honoring local divinities, and wedding and funeral customs might call on Christians to participate in meals or other rituals along with family members. The most common situation of Christians engaging in rituals that involve "other gods" involves marriage ceremonies. One may have the Hindu-Christian case in which the couple goes through two ceremonies, Christian and Hindu.

Paul has not sided with either the more educated elite or the weak, though the elite often have more to lose in breaking with the standard cultural norms (Murphy-O'Connor 2009, 106). Cult banquets and religious festivals provided places of honor for the local elite. All benefits, including food distribution in an ancient city, were greater for the "haves," so that those at the bottom received little or nothing. Consequently it could be considered unpatriotic for a prominent person to withdraw from participating in festivities honoring the city's gods (Beard 2008, 292). What the weak did concerned no one except immediate family, perhaps. Consequently, the picture of Christ as one who let go of equality with God to identify with the lowest in dying on a cross (Phil. 2:6–11) inverts the basic values of a Roman colony (Reumann 2008, 370–71). Paul's own life embodied an analogous surrender of status markers (Phil. 3:4–11; 2 Cor. 11:16–29). He expects his audience to copy that pattern (1 Cor. 11:1; Phil. 2:5).

Questions about sexuality, marriage, and divorce continue to arise in the churches. Many Christians think that the church has no business putting restrictions on their freedom in any of these areas. Whatever civil law permits should be acceptable to the church. Since Paul felt guided by the Spirit in modifying the Lord's words about divorce in the case of Christians with unbelieving partners, most churches have adopted a similar line in the case of divorced Christians. Paul's two criteria were possible reconciliation between Christian parties (1 Cor. 7:10–11) and the harmony of the household in the Christian/non-Christian situation (7:12–16). A couple that has reached the point of divorce is rarely amenable to reconciliation, even if only one party wishes to end the marriage. Marriages today carry a burden of personal fulfillment, isolation from larger family units, economic complexity, and temporal duration far beyond anything imagined in the first century. Therefore it appears reasonable for churches to allow divorce between Christians when the marriage relationship is irretrievably broken (Hays 1996, 347–78; Meilaender 1997).

Paul's preference for celibacy often leads to the conclusion that he is hostile to the passions generally or to the pleasure involved in sexuality—as D. Martin (1995, 215–17) describes it, "the ideal of sex without desire." If that is what Paul meant, then Christians today would be right to challenge his advice on sexuality. Most people find the proper management of the body and its desires expressed by ancient medical writers to be a better guide to sexual behavior (D. Martin 1995, 217). Christians find it easier to agree with Paul's view that God intended sexual relations between married persons as the way in which such desire is expressed. Such random sexual encounters as those provided by the sex trade or through hookup dating are either immoral exploitation or evidence of immaturity and lack of self-control.

Paul does not deal with all the other "what ifs" of marriage and sexuality in his own day or ours. But the conclusion to the section on marriage does place his "celibacy preferred" option squarely within the principle of considering what is beneficial for others. Paul considers the urgency of evangelization in the end time. Those unencumbered by family obligations are free to concern themselves only with the Lord (7:29–35). He did not intend to undermine the

Christian witness of married couples. Several, such as Prisca and Aquila (Rom. 16:3–5), had worked alongside the apostle in missionary efforts.

Rather than press Paul for a set of marriage rules or even a theory about sexuality equivalent to that of his (or our) medical experts, Christians should consider how his approach to particular problems can shape our ethics. Both the marriage and sexuality questions and the subsequent problems linked to meat from sacrifices and sacrificial banquets are complicated because Paul insists that believers remain part of the larger society. Non-Jews are not to become Jews. Marriages to nonbelievers are not dissolved. Even some situations that involve eating sacrificed meat are not a problem. This openness to the other provides a foundation for the global, multicultural situation in which twenty-first-century churches find themselves. But Paul is careful to insist that just as he is not a "lawless" person but one "governed by the rule of Christ" (9:21), so Christians cannot adopt the "everything is permitted" slogan of the Corinthians. They must ask what sort of conduct "gives glory to God" (10:31). Putting the needs of others ahead of self-interest, building up the community, and loving service as well as concern for the weakest among us are all good principles. Paul also rejects the nasty name-calling that can break out when Christians come to different conclusions on complicated moral questions (10:29–30). Part of the complexity or even seeming contradictions in these chapters results from Paul's attempt to find consensus where the church is divided. Rhetorically he states as consensus positions that will require the Corinthians to modify their views (P. D. Gooch 1993, 110).

1 Corinthians 11:2–14:40

Problems in the Community Assembled
for Worship

Introductory Matters

Paul shifts to a new set of concerns—conduct when believers assemble as a
group. It is not clear how the three situations mentioned are related to one
another or where Paul obtained his information. He introduces two situations
with a statement that the church claims to hold on to traditions Paul had
taught them (11:2) but does not deserve praise in these cases (11:22c). Their
worship does not conform to that in the other Pauline churches (11:16). The
first two—(1) appropriate hairstyle or covering for men and women prophesying (11:3–16) and (2) distinctions between rich and poor at the Lord's Supper
(11:17–34)—are clearly identified as traditions that the apostle established
in his churches (11:2, 16, 17a, 23a). Paul returns to the introductory formula
"now concerning" (12:1) to introduce the question of spiritual gifts, which
will take up the next three chapters of the letter. The macrostructure of this
section of the letter is comparable to that in the previous one. The second
major topic will be interrupted by an excursus that opens with a sharp shift
into the first-person and could stand on its own. Indeed the celebration of
love in 13:1–13 has become a popular choice for weddings. But Paul expects
readers to apply that example to the topic within which it is embedded. Here
Paul returns to questions surrounding spiritual gifts with the exhortation to
"pursue love" (14:1a).

The problem of gatherings involving speaking-in-tongues and prophecy
(14:1–40) might have occasioned a Corinthian question about spiritual gifts

(12:1). That issue forms the leitmotif for what follows. After establishing the principle that all believers possess the Spirit (12:2–3), Paul turns to the diversity of gifts bestowed on individuals (12:4–11). He combines a familiar political image of the community as a body whose parts must function harmoniously with the Christian church as the body of Christ (12:12–31a).

Evidently just as wealthy Christians had dishonored the body of Christ—that is, poor believers—at the Lord's Supper, so claims to superior spiritual gifts were dividing the church. As in the previous section of the letter, Paul inserts a digression before establishing rules to deal with the immediate difficulty. He crafts a speech in praise of love (13:1–13). The verses that frame this encomium remind readers of its specific purpose to persuade his audience that the love described is the highest form of spiritual expression.

Though 12:4–11 mentioned a longer list of gifts necessary to the community, the final section (14:1–40) focuses on only two of them, praying in tongues and prophecy. The latter may take the form of interpreting what has been expressed by someone speaking in tongues, but it also involves other words spoken to admonish, instruct, or inspire. Paul wishes to persuade his audience that because prophecy benefits the entire community, it should be preferred to unintelligible tongues-speaking. He lays down rules to impose order on both types of speech. Just as Paul insists on correcting the order of worship in the cases of women prophets and the conduct of the Lord's Supper, he concludes the discussion of tongues and prophecy in an equally authoritative manner: "What I am writing to you is a command of the Lord" (14:37).

The sequence of topics in 11:2–14:40 is disjointed. Some scholars think that it contains sections copied into the original letter by a later scribe. For example, the speech in praise of love can be applied to the situation of a divided church, but it also stands on its own. Its reference to speaking in tongues undoubtedly gives the positive valuation that the Corinthians attached to the experience, joining in the language of worshiping angels (13:1). Other scholars take a less radical view. Paul has crafted this digression as a key part of his argument. First Corinthians 13:1–3 and 13:8–13 fit into the larger concerns of these chapters very well. The middle section (13:4–7), however, employs a different style and vocabulary. Paul may have taken that poetic prose from earlier teaching already well known in Corinth (Patterson 2009).

The contradiction between instructions on the attire of men and women prophesying (11:3–16; D. Gill 1990) and the prohibition against women speaking in the assembly (14:33b–36) is glaring. Both are characterized as authoritative for all the churches (11:16; 14:33b). Although some have advanced arguments to treat 11:3–16 as an interpolation (Walker 1989), most exegetes alleviate the difficulty by treating 14:33b–36 as a later interpolation. It had become the customary teaching in Pauline churches by the time 1 Timothy was composed (1 Tim. 2:11–13; Conzelmann 1975, 246; Schrage 1999, 443). A marginal note to that effect in a copy of Paul's letters could have found its way into the text without scribes feeling the need to correct the apostle by omitting what he had said earlier about women prophets. The tensions between the two passages are not limited to the role of women prophets. Once Paul proposes rules about how the assembly is conducted, and not simply appropriate dress for those prophesying, he places severe limits on everyone's speech (Thiselton 2000, 1154–56). The awkwardness in this particular passage could reflect an echo of some comment about women prophets made in the Corinthians' letter. First Corinthians 14:36 provides Paul's general response to issues raised by Corinthian men, since the concluding plural "you" is modified by a masculine plural "only" (Fitzmyer 2008, 533). Both 11:7 and 14:34–35 take it for granted that Gen. 3:16 requires women to defer to their husbands. If Paul is concerned for ordering the worshiping assembly to reflect dignified, public behavior, then excluding women from the limited number of speakers would be expected.

Another solution to the complicated argument in this section assumes that Paul is speaking of three distinct gatherings for worship. The first, in which men or women are praying, might be one of the individual house-churches in a gathering comparable to that of a Roman household at the family altar (for a description of the latter, see Beard 2008, 295–98). That setting did not involve competitive jockeying for position or even public speech. There may have been only one or two persons capable of leading the group.

Both the Lord's Supper (1 Cor. 11:17–18) and the gathering at which tongues-speaking and prophecy occur (14:26) assume that the whole community has gathered. Even nonbelievers could happen to witness tongues-speaking and prophecy (14:23–25). Paul also mentions psalms and teaching in that setting (14:26). How are we to relate these two settings? Although one might think of two distinct occasions—one for prayer, prophecy, and teaching, and another for the Lord's Supper—they could have been the same. If the churches adopted the order of a formal dinner, then the meal would be followed by wine and conversation (Smith 2002, 173–217; Horrell 1996, 104). Paul certainly assumed that the Lord's Supper was an occasion comparable to the banquets his audience once celebrated in honor of pagan gods (10:14–22). The banquet setting was not, however, the only occasion for teaching in Corinth. When Paul imagines the nonbeliever's reaction to a gathering in which all are speaking in tongues, he does not speak of drunkenness as if from too much wine (contrast Acts 2:13–15) but of being in a form of prophetic ecstasy (1 Cor. 14:23). Admittedly, in the case of the Dionysus cult, the two were not distinguished. In addition Paul concludes the meal directives by stating that he will deal with other questions when he returns to Corinth (11:33–34). He comes to an equally authoritative conclusion at the end of the section on tongues-speaking and prophecy (14:37–40). Though Paul could be referring to a single worship assembly in all three cases, concluding each with an assertion of authority suggests that three distinct situations are involved.

Tracing the Train of Thought

Paul opens these chapters with words of praise (11:2), only to take them back a few verses later (11:17). He insists that the Corinthians retain the traditions and customs known in other churches (11:16; 14:33b). The overarching appeal for harmony and concern for the whole community sounded in the letter takes on a particular urgency in this section (Mitchell 1993, 149–56). Divisions and discord when the church assembles for worship strike at the very heart of its identity. Paul employs both the high poetry in praise of love and the sharp tone of command that tolerates no dissent. Inspired by the former, most readers today bristle at the latter. Shifting one's tone from gentle encouragement to harsh rebuke was a standard tactic in moral pedagogy. Philosophers in the first century observed that wise teachers know how to use both types of speech. The philosopher tries to instill virtue in individuals and adapt his style to the situation. Paul has a harder task than that of a philosopher. He is struggling to keep diverse individuals united in a new form of community.

> ### 1 Corinthians 11:2–14:40 in the Rhetorical Flow
>
> **The letter opening (1:1–9)**
>
> **Against divisions: God's wisdom (1:10–2:16)**
>
> **Against divisions: Paul and Apollos as *exempla* (3:1–4:21)**
>
> **Reports about unholy conduct among believers (5:1–6:20)**
>
> **Questions in a letter from Corinth (7:1–11:1)**
>
> ▶ **Problems in the community assembled for worship (11:2–14:40)**
>
> > On the dress of women prophesying in the assembly (11:2–16)
> >
> > Against dishonoring the poor at the Lord's Supper (11:17–34)
> >
> > On spiritual gifts in the one community (12:1–31a)
> >
> > On *agapē* as the greatest gift (12:31b–13:13)
> >
> > On speech in the worshiping assembly (14:1–40)

Paul deals with a specific set of topics, then introduces another issue that is discussed in two rounds. The excursus that divides the long discussion of spiritual gifts takes the pressure off momentarily. It also provides the listener with another reason for coming around to Paul's point of view. Paul may not get high marks in a formal contest with trained orators, as he admitted early on (2:1), but he exhibits a natural ability to orchestrate a complex argument in his letters (Anderson 1998, 113–19, 278–80). Just as the previous section encouraged listeners to seek what is best for the larger group, not what suits them as individuals (10:33), so this appeal for unity promotes the welfare of the church as a whole (12:12–26).

On the Dress of Women Prophesying in the Assembly (11:2–16)

11:2–5. Paul steps back from the catalogue of corrections briefly. On the whole, the Corinthians **are keeping up the traditions** (11:2) that Paul gave them. Confusion over sacrificial meat and cult banquets did not mean that believers were falling away from Christ into old habits of idol worship. At the same time, this note of praise signals a shift from deliberation about whether particular actions are expedient to cultural codes of honor and shame (J. Thompson 2003, 240–43). Paul indirectly challenges his audience to show themselves worthy of praise. The overall point is clear enough. Men or women leading the community in prayer or instructing it by prophesying must dress as a respectable man or woman would.

Because Paul never indicates how or why the Corinthians deviate from honorable dress, scholars have advanced many hypotheses over the years. The focus of attention concerns whether the head is covered and whether the hair is long, short, or (worst case) shaven. Before speaking to the issue, Paul proposes a hierarchy using the word **head** (*kephalē*) as a metaphor for the guiding authority, leader, or ruler (Fitzmyer 2008, 410–11): **Of every man the head is Christ, and the head of a woman, the man, and the head of Christ, God** (11:3). That principle would have seemed obvious to his audience. It sets a framework for what follows.

The next two verses take up the specifics of **every man praying and prophesying** (11:4) and **every woman praying and prophesying** (11:5) respectively. Throughout the section Paul will emphasize cultural distinctions between the two genders. Figuring out the coded terminology that Paul is using generates heated debate. Paul says that a man **having [what?] down from his head disgraces [*kataischynein*] his head** (11:4b; Massey 2007). The first use of **head** is taken literally, and the second metaphorically (i.e., he disgraces Christ). But what is hanging down from a man's head? Artistic representations of Roman sacrifices show the priest or civic official presenting the offering with the toga up over his head (Oster 1988). After a section on sacrificial meals, that would seem to be the most natural image for Paul's audience. But why is copying a familiar ritual gesture a disgrace to Christ? Perhaps, though he does not say so, because it suggests that the man praying or prophesying is claiming an authority that belongs only to Christ. The elite whose claims to wisdom Paul shot down earlier in the letter would be candidates for such attempts. Other scholars avoid the difficulty by assuming that Paul is using **head** in the second case as a stand-in for the whole person. On that reading the individual in question is disgracing himself, not Christ.

Following the lead of a seminal article by Jerome Murphy-O'Connor written in 1980 and later reprinted (2009, 142–58), other scholars, however, point to the complex cultural codes associated with male hair. As far back as fifth-century BC Athens, the wealthy, aristocratic young men flouted the mores of their elders with long locks, elaborately coiffed. Accusations of effeminacy or homosexual proclivities were directed at those who wore their hair in that fashion, along with jewelry and fancy clothing. In Paul's day Jewish moralists (Pseudo-Phocylides 210–14; Philo, *De specialibus legibus* 3.37), Roman moralists (Musonius Rufus, frag. 21), and satirists (Horace, *Epistulae* 11.28; Juvenal, *Satirae* 2.96) attacked elaborate hairstyling, pulling out male body hair, and using cosmetics to create a smooth (i.e., feminine) appearance. A philosophical diatribe in which the philosopher Epictetus dresses down a young man who shows up for instruction coiffed, bejeweled, and dressed up like a popular orator provides a suggestive comparison to the Corinthian situation (Epictetus, *Diatribai* 3.1; Winter 2002, 113–15, 222). The philosopher rejects alterations of the external appearances provided by nature, including the male and female differences in bodily hair (*Diatribai* 3.1.26–29). Those who think that "cleaning up" a male's appearance makes him more attractive might as well try to deprive the lion of his mane or the cock of his comb (*Diatribai* 3.1.43–45).

For the woman praying or prophesying, an **uncovered head disgraces her head** (11:5a). As in the previous case, the disgraced **head** could be the husband mentioned in 11:3 or the woman herself. Of course, Roman sculpture, portraiture, and tomb reliefs all depict respectable women without anything covering the head. Therefore some scholars suggest that Paul is referring only to the carefully coiffed and bound hair of such figures (Murphy-O'Connor 2009, 147–48). A seated female figure with two children on the Ara Pacis in Rome, however, has a cloak or veil loosely draped over her head, as do the wives in other family portraits of enfranchised slaves from Rome (Kleiner 2005,

> ## Goals of Rhetoric Described by Aristotle
>
> "The goal of deliberative rhetoric is what is expedient [sympheron] or harmful; a speaker may exhort (the audience) to adopt (a course of action) as the better one... for those in court cases (the goal is) the just and unjust ... for those speaking to praise or blame (someone, the goal is) what is honorable [kalon] or disgraceful [aischron]." (*Rhetorica* 1.3, 5 AT)

Figure 12. Roman Woman's Hairstyle.

Giovanni Dall'Orto. Wikimedia Commons

137

Figure 13. Woman with Head Covering on the Ara Pacis. The woman (or goddess) depicted in this detail from the Ara Pacis has a cloak or veil loosely draped over her head.

228, 263, 276). Nothing obscures the woman's face or obstructs her speech. Hence the tendency of some commentaries and translations to refer to the Corinthian women prophets as **veiled** or **unveiled** (NRSV) gives the wrong impression to modern readers.

In one of the family portraits, there is little difference between how the cloth is draped over the head of a male offering sacrifice and over a female. Kleiner's examples of ex-slaves copying hairstyles popular among Rome's elite demonstrate that status did not dictate women's coiffure; popular images of the emperor did: "The portraits of these freedmen, the style in which their likenesses are carved, and the dress and hairstyles they wear are very informative. The men look like Caesar and the women resemble Cleopatra" (2005, 274). If Roman Corinth copied the fashions of the capital, then Paul's initial distinction may have puzzled his audience as much as it does us. Paul adds a phrase to explain the disgrace: **It is just the same as if she had been shaved** (11:5b).

11:6–9. Paul must be aware that his example does not elicit the feelings of disgrace that the argument requires. Hence he shifts to shaven-headed women (11:5b–6). This bit of sarcasm, similar to Epictetus's remark about trying to take the mane off the lion, shifts from the world of elite and working women to the slave market or brothel. Paul has no intention of presenting the shaved head as an alternative to draping the cloak over the head for women prophets. He expects his audience to respond to the scenario of patching the shaven-headed male onto a female with one of a number of reactions: incredulity, pity, contempt, or comic laughter. Though residents of Roman Corinth might react negatively toward a shaven-headed female, that gut reaction does not secure the sharp line between male and female dress that Paul's argument requires.

Paul returns to the hierarchical scheme introduced in 11:3. Without citing scriptural authority, he fills it out in 11:7–9 by alluding to the creation stories of Gen. 1–2. On his reading, **the image of God** in Gen. 1:27 refers only to the male Adam, not to humanity as a species of males and females as in Genesis. Eve's subsequent creation from Adam's rib (Gen. 2:21–23) places her below Adam: **For the man was not created through the woman but the woman through the man** (1 Cor. 11:9).

Examples of Shaved Heads in Antiquity

As an Omen in Dreams

"To dream one's whole head has been shaved is good for priests of the Egyptian gods, for buffoons and those whose custom it is. But for all others it is unlucky.... The evils it indicates will be more violent and abrupt." (Artemidorus, *Onirocritica* 1.22, trans. R. White 1975)

By Shipwrecked Sailors

"The captain nursed his lame vessel through.... The crew with shaven heads, safe home at last, kept telling the tale." (Juvenal, *Satirae* 12.81, trans. Beard, North, and Price 1998)

Of Slaves

"Let him shave your heads right now and your eyebrows too. Then I will mark your foreheads ... so you will look like slaves punished by branding. These letters will divert ... suspicion and hide your faces with the shadow of punishment." (Petronius, *Satyricon* 103 AT)

By Priests of Isis

"Having a beard and wearing a coarse cloak does not make philosophers, nor does dressing in linen and shaving the hair make devotees of Isis." (Plutarch, *De Iside et Osiride* 352c AT)

Upon Giving Up Philosophy

"You'll soon see me without my long, shaggy beard and ascetic lifestyle ... to show the world I've given up that trash.... I could even shave my head like men safe after a shipwreck, as a thank offering.... If I ever meet a philosopher again even by accident ... I'll turn and avoid him like a mad dog." (Lucian, *Hermotimus* 86 AT)

11:10–12. Paul adds another even more puzzling reason for the dress required of females engaged in praying or prophesying: **an authority [*exousia*] on her head because of the angels** (11:10). What is he talking about? The preposition *epi* with the genitive also means "over" in expressions that refer to persons in charge of something. In that case the woman is being told to "take charge of her head" or exercise authority over it (R. Collins 1999, 410–11).

Most translators assume that the cloth draped over the head is a sign of authority, so the NRSV's "symbol of authority." For whom is this sign required? Apparently not the assembled believers but angels. Paul's cryptic remark could refer to angels in a variety of capacities: angels who lusted after human women

Angels in 1 Corinthians 11:10

Fallen Angels of Genesis 6:4

"Order your wives and daughters not to adorn their heads or appearances in order to deceive men.... For thus they charmed the Watchers before the flood. As they continued looking at the women, they were filled with lust for them." (Testament of Reuben 5.5–6, trans. H. C. Kee in OTP 1:784)

Guardians of Created Order

"Lieutenants of the Ruler of all things, like eyes and ears of the great king, ... these other philosophers call 'demons' but the holy word customarily calls them 'angels'... for they convey the Father's orders to his offspring and report the needs of the offspring to the Father." (Philo, De somniis 1.140–41 AT)

Worshiping God, Joined by the Righteous

"I thank you Lord, because you saved my life from the pit.... The depraved spirit you have purified ... so that he can stand with the host of the holy ones.... You cast an eternal destiny for man with the spirits of knowledge to praise your name in the community of jubilation." (1QH 11.19–23, trans. García Martínez and Tigchelaar 1997, 165)

in Gen. 6:4, angels as guardians of the created order similar to the Satan of Job 1:6–7, or heavenly angels worshiping God.

In each example, the ritual gesture that Paul requires compensates for a defective female nature that would otherwise endanger her or the holiness of the angelic assembly. She could be attacked by lustful angels (demons), or be subject to divine punishment for violating the order of creation, or be considered a source of contamination if angels were thought to be present as the Christian assembly gathered in worship. An Essene rule excluding defective persons appeals to a similar view (1QSa 2.3–9; 1QM 7.4–6; Fitzmyer 2008, 419).

Rather than complete the argument, Paul steps away from the asymmetry between the male as image and glory of God and the female as glory of the male to affirm that men and women are necessary to each other (11:11–12). Rather than base that mutual need in the creation of Eve (Gen. 2:18), he bases it on their relationship **in the Lord** (1 Cor. 11:11) and to the Creator: **all things [are] from God** (11:12b). This interruption of the logical conclusion to Paul's argument reflects the baptismal confession that ethnic, status, and gender distinctions have no bearing on one's salvation in Christ (Gal. 3:28; 1 Cor. 12:13). Some interpreters hypothesize that the female prophets in Corinth employed the semantic code of an "uncovered head" to symbolize their new being in Christ, much as Paul will contrast the "uncovered face" of Christian believers with the veiled Mosaic Torah in 2 Cor. 3:18 (Meeks 1974, 199–203). Any scenario constructed to represent the ideology and behavior of women praying and prophesying in Corinth remains speculative because the apostle offers no specific details such as slogans being employed or activities apart from the uncovered head.

11:13–16. Paul continues to waver between assuming that the audience will agree with him—**judge for yourselves: is it fitting for a woman . . .** (11:13)—and the need to insist on conformity in this matter regardless of objections: **we do not have such a custom, nor do the churches of God** (11:16). Between these two statements he trots out a version of the conventional argument that nature employs hair to distinguish between male and female (11:14–15). Paul is speaking in shorthand, assuming an audience that knows the drill on that one. The Epictetus example shows that even though hair lengths and styles were matters of convention, one could presume that established custom was both natural and honorable. Paul ignores the obvious objection that if nature has provided females with **hair as a covering** (11:15), then a woman need not employ her cloak in that capacity. Murphy-O'Connor's hypothesis that the issue for women prophets is coiffed rather than the loose hair of a mantic prophet resolves this problem by removing covering the head as a question. Paul's information about this aspect of Corinthian worship could have been minimal. Murphy-O'Connor suggests that the word *angeloi* be taken as a reference to humans who were messengers between churches, rather than to angels (2009, 158). Such persons would be more aware of departures from custom in a given church than local members may have been.

Against Dishonoring the Poor at the Lord's Supper (11:17–34)

Paul did not identify a source for his information about women and men prophesying and praying. The second topic, divisive behavior at the Lord's Supper, must be a response to what he has heard about their behavior on such occasions (11:17–18). Although Paul concludes with two rules for the Lord's Supper—**wait for one another** (11:33b) and **if someone is hungry let him eat at home** (11:34a)—he indicates that unresolved issues remain to be settled (11:34b).

11:17–22. This section is framed by the category of praise, or in this case, Paul's inability to do so: **I do not praise** (11:17a), and **Will I praise you? In this I do not praise [you]** (11:22b). At this point in the letter, the audience could hardly be surprised to hear Paul challenging yet

> **An Outline of 1 Corinthians 11:17–34**
>
> **Against dishonoring the poor at the Lord's Supper (11:17–34)**
>
> Divisive behavior at the Lord's Supper (11:17–22)
>
> Received tradition, the Lord's words (11:23–26)
>
> Warnings against participating in the meal unworthily (11:27–34)

another form of division within the church (11:18a). These divisions reflect an attitude that treats the communal meal as though it were **one's own** (11:21a), the ordinary banquet in which the social distinctions of rich friends and poorer associates or clients were expressed in food offered and seating arrangements (Horrell 1996, 102–3). Contrary to the previous case, which confirms routine cultural categories of honor and shame, such a business-as-usual approach cannot be tolerated at the Lord's Supper.

The sequence is interrupted by a digression, as Paul introduces an item from apocalyptic speculation, the eruption of turmoil and divisions in the last days. Such outbreaks serve to test God's elect (Schrage 1999, 21–22): **There must be divisions among you so that it becomes clear who the genuine among you are** (11:19). Such testing anticipates the divine judgment. Paul will pick up that note in warning the community that elements of their present experience are signs of God's judgment against the community (11:30–31; Fitzmyer 2008, 433).

The initial details are fairly sparse. Despite the communal gathering, **each goes ahead to eat his own supper; one is hungry while another is drunk** (11:21). For the entire church to assemble, apparently weekly (16:2), required the generosity of its wealthier members. It is less clear whether the person who supplied the physical space also provided the food. Nor is the archeological data adequate to indicate what spatial arrangements were possible in average households (Fitzmyer 2008, 428; Horrell 1996, 91–101; 2006). Few houses in Pompeii had specialized dining rooms, so the proposed division whereby a wealthy host and friends reclined in the triclinium while the rest of the community was relegated to the atrium seems implausible. Triclinia at Pompeii are quite small; allowing space for couches, tables, servers, and the like permits at most six to nine guests (Beard 2008, 94–96, 221–22). Literary and painted representations of elaborate banqueting seem more fiction than reality. Some Pompeian wall paintings show guests just arriving while others are already drunk (Beard 2008, 218–19). So the hungry-versus-drunk distinction does not necessarily correlate with the rich elite over against a poor majority. It does correlate with Paul's rule that the entire community is to be present before the banquet begins.

A second question concerns the phrase **eat his own supper**. Is that a preliminary supper that the host provides for his personal friends as distinct from the bread and wine of the Lord's Supper provided for the entire community? Some ancient cult associations have rules specifying what is to be provided for a group's meals. Or do individuals come bringing their own food (as at some public banquets; see Tyldesley 2008, 85–86), which they refuse to share with the group as a whole? Rulers or victorious generals might claim to have instituted a major public feast while providing only for their own circle. Lesser handouts might be made to the populace, or a crowd might consume whatever wine and food they brought with them (Athenaeus, *Deipnosophistae* 7.2–3).

Paul seeks to distinguish between the sort of dining that occurs in private houses and the Lord's Supper: **Don't you have homes for eating and drinking? Or do you despise the church of God and humiliate those who have nothing?** (11:22). This case demonstrates that in some situations the ethos of household must be distinguished from that of the church that meets there (Barton 1986, 234–38). Paul's critique is directed against some elite members whom he does not wish to castigate directly (Barton 1986, 237). The phrase **humiliate those who have nothing** points to the sort of social behavior Pliny observed in his host. The routine pattern of dominance and subordination enacted at such meals reinforced the status hierarchy. Pliny's argument that all guests should receive the same quality food and drink incorporated a redefinition of his relationship to invited freedmen. For the duration of the banquet, they are guests and not ex-slaves. Paul must engage the more privileged Christians in making a similar shift when participating in the Lord's Supper with their poor brothers and sisters.

11:23–26. Paul turns to the tradition at the heart of the Lord's Supper. Unlike the meals of a private association, whose sponsors and menu may be stipulated in the group's bylaws, this meal rests on a received tradition that goes back to Jesus himself (11:23). Since the introduction refers to **the night on which he was betrayed,** the bread and cup sayings must have included a longer narrative about the meal and events leading to Jesus's crucifixion (R. Collins 1999, 427).

Paul alluded to this tradition in his argument against participation in cultic banquets (10:16). Participating in the blood and body of Christ excludes even social participation in rites honoring other deities. Paul refers to blessing the cup and bread in that setting. Therefore some scholars propose that the brief tradition about the Lord's words at the supper were not yet being employed as a ritual act. They do not turn up in either *Didache* 8–9 or Justin Martyr's *Apologia* 1.65 (McGowan 1999, 75–79).

> **Menu for an Association in Lanuvium**
>
> "Presidents of the dinner in the order of the member list, appointed in turn four at a time, shall be required to provide one amphora of good wine each ... bread costing two asses, four sardines, a setting and warm water." (*CIL* 14:2112, trans. Kloppenborg 2006, 334)

Table 12
Versions of Jesus's Words over the Bread and Cup

1 Cor. 11:23–25	Luke 22:19–20	Mark 14:22–24	Matt. 26:26–28
taking bread	taking bread	while they were eating taking bread	while they were eating Jesus taking bread
and having given thanks he broke and said	having given thanks he broke and gave to them saying	having said a blessing he broke and gave to them and said	having said a blessing he broke and giving it to his disciples he said
this is my body for you	this is my body given for you	take, this is my body	take, eat, this is my body
do this in memory of me	do this in memory of me	—	—
likewise the cup after they had eaten saying	and the cup likewise after they had eaten saying	and taking a cup having given thanks he gave it to them	and taking a cup and having given thanks he gave it to them saying
—	—	and they all drank from it, and he said to them	all of you drink from it
this cup is the new covenant in my blood	this cup (is) the new covenant in my blood	this is my blood of the covenant	for this is my blood of the covenant
—	which is shed for you	which is shed for many	which is shed on account of many
do this as often as you drink in memory of me	—	—	for forgiveness of sins

The institution narrative explains what the Christian meal commemorates and the significance of Jesus's death for the community. It does not necessarily indicate what words were employed in blessing the bread and cup. Nor does Paul's version refer to all sharing one loaf or one cup. Depending on the size of the gathering, individual groups could bless their own bread and cup—yet another occasion for distinctions in the amount and quality of what was offered.

Paul concludes with a reminder: **As often as you eat this bread and drink this cup, you proclaim the Lord's death until he comes** (11:26). This phrase interprets the *anamnēsis* phrase attached to the bread and cup sayings (Fitzmyer 2008, 426). The Corinthians might have understood the remembrance as the institution of a cultic meal honoring the Lord. Paul focuses their attention on the symbolic code that ties the bread and cup to Jesus's death on the cross. That has been the center of Paul's preaching since he founded the community (2:2, 7–8). Indirectly Paul reminds readers that they live between the times. Their present experiences of salvation in renewed community, healing, and spiritual gifts anticipate fulfillment at the parousia (13:8–13; 15:20–28).

11:27–34. For those who are unfaithful the return of the Lord will mean condemnation. So Paul issues a warning against becoming **guilty of the body and blood of the Lord** (11:27–28). The expression might have perplexed his readers. The rituals of sacrifice in the city's temples demanded that words and actions be performed with precision. Deviations could require repetition from the beginning or even canceling the proceedings. But the festal banquet that followed was much less restrained. Private associations included rules governing the conduct of members at banquets, sometimes imposing fines for violations (Kloppenborg 2006, 335).

> ### Fines for Misbehavior by Members
>
> *"If a member gets drunk and misbehaves, let him be fined whatever the association determines. . . . If a member ignores someone in distress and does not assist . . . 8 drachmae. Whoever shoves in front of another at the banquets shall pay an extra 3 obols to sit in his own place."* (Papyrus Michigan Tebtunis 243, trans. Ascough 2003, 86)

While the gods might retaliate against ritual violations, they had no interest in the behavior of those who belonged to private associations. Paul is asking his audience to treat behavior toward fellow believers at the supper as though it occurred during a ritual. How are they to make that transfer? It requires identifying the body of Christ formed by the believing community (12:12–26), the individual member of the church (6:19–20), and the bread shared at the meal (11:25), with the result that one could be **eating and drinking a judgment against himself . . . not discerning the body** (11:29).

In the earlier treatment of eating sacrificial meat, Paul acknowledged the objection that one's relationship to God is not determined by what one does or does not eat (10:30–31). He insisted that one consider the impact of one's behavior on fellow believers (10:29). Rhetorically, Paul counters those who might assert that bread and wine are just food, not sacred ritual objects. He does so by claiming that cases of illness and death in the community are not from mere natural causes but are divine punishment: **For this reason many among you are weak, sick, and dying. . . . Being judged by the Lord, we are being educated so that we will not be condemned with the world, my brothers** (11:30–32). This transition makes modern readers uncomfortable as evidence of religious superstition. A lethal bout of food poisoning caused by the popular fish sauce *opson* that might have done-in some of the elite whose conduct Paul decries (11:20–22) is one scholarly attempt to ground Paul's comment in local experience (Bach and Glancy 2003, 454–58). D. Martin invokes the ancient concept of *pharmakon*, a drug that is poisonous in large doses but curative in small ones or combined with other substances. Consumed with proper respect for the weakest members of the community, the Eucharist is beneficial. Employed as yet another occasion for divisions, it is deadly (1995, 190–97). Exegetes generally take the issue from the opposite direction. Paul is not attributing some sort of magical protection against illness to the elements of bread and wine when consumed under the proper conditions (Fitzmyer 2008, 447).

A rhetorical solution is simpler than these proposals. Paul is employing ordinary convictions about divine reaction to ritual infractions. Things go badly for persons who fail to show the gods proper respect. Christians had to be reassured that the city's gods had no reality (8:4–6) or were "demons" (10:20), lest misfortunes lead them to revert to former rituals. Rates of illness and mortality are so high at all levels of society that Paul does not need to have any particular examples in mind. He does modify the paradigm slightly. Proper response—correcting disregard for the body of Christ—ends the matter. Misfortunes are not evidence of divine wrath or rejection any more than disciplining a child is evidence of rejection. Paul's initial rules are much less complicated than those of other private associations. Perhaps **the rest I will give instructions for when I come** (11:34) included a more formal ordering for the communal meal.

On Spiritual Gifts in the One Community (12:1–31a)

By introducing this section with the phrase **now concerning** (*peri de*), Paul indicates a shift of topic. What follows is not the **remaining matters** associated with the gathering to celebrate the Lord's Supper that Paul promises he will deal with when he visits (11:34b). Socioeconomic distinctions at the meal celebration were not the only source of division in the worshiping community. Spiritual gifts such as speaking in tongues and prophecy provided some with claims to a higher status than fellow believers (D. Martin 1991). Paul devotes several chapters to these problems. The term *glōssa* ("tongues") occurs twenty-one times in 1 Cor. 12–14 and not elsewhere in the Pauline corpus with reference to the spiritual gift. "Prophecy," introduced at 11:4–5, returns twenty times. Although Paul will refer to other spiritual gifts that are necessary for the community, his focus is the proper ordering of speaking in tongues and prophecy (Thiselton 2000, 913–15). If the meetings in which speaking in tongues and prophecy occurred followed the Lord's Supper, as some interpreters suggest, then this sequence may represent two stages

---

**An Outline
of 1 Corinthians 12:1–31a**

On spiritual gifts in the one community (12:1–31a)

The diversity of gifts from one Spirit (12:1–11)

Comparison of the community to a human body (12:12–31a)

  Incorporation through baptism (12:12–14)

  Fable of revolt by body parts (12:15–17)

  Harmonious coordination of the body's parts (12:18–26)

  Spiritual gifts in the body of Christ (12:27–31a)

in a single event. The break in introducing the topic and the discussion of other spiritual gifts necessary for the church as a Spirit-driven community (11:4–11, 28–31) indicate, however, a shift to the larger context of Christian life (Zeller 2010, 381). After the excursus on love, Paul returns in 14:1 to the specifics of gatherings for worship with the exhortation to **be zealous for spiritual gifts** [*pneumatika*].

12:1–3. Paul praised the church for its endowments in the opening of the letter: "You are not lacking in any charism [*charisma*]" (1:7). In 7:7 the Greek word *charisma* refers to a God-given calling to celibacy or marriage, not to a spiritual gift as it is used in 12:4, 9, 28, 30, 31. The topic of spiritual gifts (*pneumatika*; 12:1) may have been sparked by a question from the Corinthians. Substitution of the word *pneumatika* for *charismata* in the introductory phrases (12:1; 14:1) allows Paul to highlight the relationship between these gifts and the Spirit of God (12:4, 9, 11), who dwells in the believer (6:17, 19) and the community (3:16). *Charisma* appears to be the word ordinarily used for the gifts in question.

> ### Cursing Jesus as Apostasy
>
> As governor of Bithynia (AD 110), Pliny used this tactic to ferret out Christians:
>
> *"Others . . . denied it. . . . All these also both paid homage to your [Emperor Trajan's] statue and to the cult images of the gods and cursed Christ." (Epistulae 10.96.6 AT)*

Paul's opening gambit points out that every believer is a "spiritual person" as evidenced by their confession: **no one can say "Jesus is Lord" except in the Holy Spirit** (12:3). By contrasting this situation with the Corinthians' past as idol worshipers (12:2), Paul fits this topic into the larger set of religious questions that began in 1 Cor. 8. Jewish authors often speak of idols as mute. Unable to see, hear, or speak, these gods cannot aid those who believe in them (Ps. 115:5–6). But Paul's comment that **no one speaking in the Spirit of God says "Anathema Jesus"** (1 Cor. 12:3a) remains puzzling.

Is Paul simply making up a rhetorical antithesis to the Christian confession in the second part of the verse? Or were persons engaged in such speech? The phrase **no one speaking in the Spirit** appears to rule out treating the anathema phrase as pagan speech hurled against Christians. Some scholars, however, consider that the only plausible explanation for the phrase. The awkward expression follows from an equally clumsy statement about the audience's past experience of idols in 12:2. The idols to which the gentiles were being led are incapable of speech, so it is unlikely that Paul imagines some sort of Bacchic frenzy in which participants are unknowingly cursing Christ. The peculiar qualifying clause, **as you were led**, using the imperfect tense with the particle *an*, is grammatically odd. It is possibly a way of indicating repetitive action (Fitzmyer 2008, 457).

With the particle *dio* introducing the next sentence, one expects an explanation. But of what? The standard conversion pattern of phrases—"once you were . . . but now you are . . ."—leads one to expect some description of the believer's present experience that contrasts it with what has been said in 12:2. Paul's elegant parallelism with **in the Spirit** as its frame generates verbal awkwardness in 12:3:

> A no one speaking [*lalōn*]
>   B in the Spirit of God says [*legei*]
>   C anathema Jesus
> A′ no one is able to say [*eipein*]
>   C′ Lord Jesus
>   B′ except in the Holy Spirit

The phrase **anathema Jesus** is a curse formula intelligible to both non-Jewish and Jewish audiences. Perhaps the latter group employed it to refer to death on the cross as evidence that the victim was under God's curse according to Deut. 21:23 (Gal. 3:13; Fitzmyer 2008, 459).

12:4–6. A rhythmic pattern—**different sorts of . . . but the same**—in 12:4–6 reminds readers of the unity served by diverse spiritual endowments. The terms **gifts** (*charismata*), **ministries** (*diakoniai*), and **tasks** (*energēmata*) serve as generic descriptions for the type of activities carried out by believers. Paul employs a triadic set of phrases to refer to the one divine spirit behind the diversity: **Spirit**, **Lord**, and **God**.

12:7–11. Since all believers have been given the Spirit, the generic categories of gifts, ministries, and tasks suggest that every member of the church has something to contribute. The general principle **to each . . . for the benefit [of the community]** (12:7) dictates how such activities are to be evaluated. The list that follows opens with the displays of rhetorical sophistication and knowledge—**speech of wisdom and speech of knowledge**, which dominated the opening of the letter (1:5, 17; 2:1)—and concludes with the manifestations of the Spirit that are in question in this section: **to another prophecy, to another discernment of spirits, to another kinds of speaking in tongues, to another interpretation of tongues** (12:8–10). Separating each item in the list with **to another** limits the possibility that any single individual could claim to embody the entire catalogue of spiritual gifts. Paul himself, however, must possess a number of the charisms listed, even tongues and prophecy (14:14–19). First Corinthians 12:11 picks up the unity motif **one and the same Spirit** from 12:4. Paul insists that gifts of the Spirit are not under human control. The Spirit determines how they are distributed to members of the community (12:11b). Paul has situated spiritual gifts firmly on the ground. They foster Christian life in this world. Christians who exercise them do not gain some form of access to the heavenly realms (Schrage 1999, 165).

12:12–21. Paul adopts an image frequently used in political rhetoric to urge harmony in a divided community, that of diverse members united in a single body (Mitchell 1993, 157–58). *Stasis*, or civic discord, is often depicted as a disease that must be cured (D. Martin 1995, 39).

When Paul identifies the basis for membership in the **one body . . . the Christ** (12:12), he introduces an important distinction. The citizenship conferred by baptism transcends those divisions that separate humans into distinct political, ethnic, and social groups, because whether **Jew or Greek, slave or freeborn, we all drank of one Spirit** (12:13). The phrase **drank of one Spirit** takes readers back to the example of their Israelite ancestors baptized in

> ### Citizens as Part of a Body
>
> *"What then is the promise of a citizen? Not to take what is advantageous [sympheron] for him as a private individual, not planning so as to be released from anything, but rather like a hand or foot if it had rational abilities and could understand the natural constitution, would never be eager or stirred up to do anything other than referring to the whole."* (Epictetus, *Diatribai* 2.4 AT)

passing through the sea and drinking the spiritual drink from the rock, Christ (10:1–4). Ancient cities guarded their citizenship rolls jealously. Slaves, former slaves, persons born to noncitizen parents, foreigners, and the like need not apply. So this open-ended inclusion points up the difference between the body of Christ and a civic body.

Initially Paul's development of the image follows the usual rhetorical pattern. God has ordered each part of the body to function harmoniously with the others: **each one of them in the body as he pleased** (12:18). It would be absurd for individual members to rebel because they were not created as some other part: **If the foot should say, "I am not a hand so I am not part of the body," is it not part of the body on that account?** (12:15). It would be equally insane for the entire body to be eye or hearing: **If it were entirely one member, where is the body?** (12:19). All these diverse parts are necessary. For one to tell another that it is not needed would be equally insane (12:21).

12:22–26. Paul's first run through the members and body image fits ordinary rhetorical conventions. In the second, he picks up another familiar topic, the distinction between respectable, uncovered parts of the body and the disgraceful parts connected to sexuality and bodily waste. Ordinary political discourse treats the civic elite as the head, face, or other respectable body parts. The masses of urban poor or rustic farmers correspond to the ugly, disgraceful ones. The inferior parts should accept their lot and accept the direction and superiority of the head.

Paul's treatment shifts those expectations (D. Martin 1995, 94–96). He has warned the elite against humiliating the poor at the Lord's Supper (11:22). So he treats clothing as more than the cover for what is dishonorable: **We drape the parts of the body that we consider dishonorable with greater honor . . . the elegant parts have no need of it** (12:23–24a). Where Cicero spoke of nature making this arrangement, Paul substitutes **God**. God has not just arranged to keep the ugly parts out of sight. God actually **arranged the body, giving greater honor to the inferior part** (12:24b).

In a subtle way Paul has endowed those weaker members of the community with more honor than the elite. As he concludes this analogy, Paul provides a further argument against divisions within the body of Christ. Each part of the body is linked to all the others: **If one member suffers, all the members suffer together; if a member is honored, all the members rejoice** (12:26).

12:27–31a. Paul now applies this image to **the body of Christ** (12:27). He provides what begins as a numerically ordered list: **God placed in the church first apostles, second prophets, third teachers, then powerful deeds, then gifts of healing, helping actions, acts of steering, types of speaking in tongues** (12:28). When the list is repeated following **not all are/have**, some items from the earlier list are omitted (helping, steering), and **interpret** follows the reference to tongues (12:29–30). The first three correspond to established ministries in all the churches. The apostles are not permanent residents in a particular community but are key in founding new churches and linking the network of churches together (3:10). Prophesying and teaching provide for the ongoing life of local churches. Paul has already regulated dress for men and women engaged in praying and prophesying (11:2–16). The other items in the list may have been more transitory. Different individuals could have undertaken them as need or opportunity arose. Some exegetes see this catalogue as evidence that eventually Paul will respond to the discord in Corinth by establishing structures to govern communal life (Mitchell 1993, 164).

After repeatedly insisting that distribution of spiritual gifts is God's work rather than that of individuals, the phrase **seek the greater spiritual gifts** (12:31a) strikes a discordant note. Some exegetes avoid the difficulty by treating *zēloute* not as an imperative ("strive for" by NRSV) but as a present indicative verb and reading the sentence as an ironic question, thus continuing the series of questions in 12:29–30 through 12:31a: **Are you striving for the greater gifts?** (Fitzmyer 2008, 484). However one parses the sentence, Paul appears to have opened the door for the elite whose disdain for the "dishonorable" poor members of the church was evident at the Lord's Supper. Of course they will go for the greater or more honorable spiritual endowments. Now that he has their attention, Paul will pull the rug out from under them in the excursus on love.

Disgraceful Body Parts Are Clothed

"Nature seems to have had a great design in our bodies. Our face and figure generally, insofar as it is good-looking, she places in full view; while the parts ... that serve the needs of nature and have an ugly and unpleasant appearance, she has covered and hidden from view." (Cicero, De officiis 1.35 AT)

On Agapē *as the Greatest Gift
(12:31b–13:13)*

12:31b. And I will show you a still higher way (12:31b) leads into that challenge. On either translation of *zēloute* in 12:31a, Paul promises a far superior way. If the elite thought Paul was finally going to let them in on the secret of how to attain visions of the heavenly world (2 Cor. 12:1–10) or some form of special knowledge, a "wisdom for the mature" about which Paul spoke in 1 Cor. 2:6–16, they would be disappointed once

> **An Outline
> of 1 Corinthians 12:31b–13:13**
>
> **On *agapē* as the greatest gift
> (12:31b–13:13)**
>
> Love's superiority to all other spiritual gifts (12:31b–13:3)
>
> *Encomium* celebrating love (13:4–7)
>
> Love's eternity (13:8–13)

again. In the previous section of the letter, Paul used an excursus to provide an example of the desired behavior. His freedom as an apostle lies in giving up rights that he could claim in order to win as many as possible for Christ (1 Cor. 9). The shift from the second-person plural to the first-person singular that opens this excursus suggests that it will present another such example (Holladay 1990, 84–87).

The speech in praise of love (*agapē*) falls into three sections. The first makes it the necessary accompaniment to an impressive catalogue of spiritual gifts or heroic deeds (13:1–3). It employs the first-person singular throughout. The second provides an equally impressive list of character traits that flow from love (13:4–7). This series personifies love. The final section contrasts the enduring character of love with the eventual failure of spiritual gifts prized by the Corinthians: **prophecies, tongues, knowledge** (13:8–13). Paul returns to the image of childish immaturity he employed earlier (3:1–3) to undercut Corinthian presumptions about wisdom. These gifts themselves are for believers as long as their knowledge of God remains immature. The last word of the encomium is **love**. The final section begins with the third-person singular (13:8), shifts to the first-person plural (13:9, 12a) and first-person singular (13:11, 12b), before concluding with the theological virtues: **faith, hope, love** (13:13).

13:1–3. A series of parallel phrases listing spiritual gifts negates their significance without love. The first four in the catalogue refer directly to items Paul has already addressed in the letter: **ability to speak in tongues, prophecy, knowledge of mysteries,** and **other sorts of knowledge**. The final three heighten the stakes: **faith capable of moving mountains, giving away all one's possessions,** and **handing over one's body to boast.**

Since Paul is about to take up tongues and prophecy as practiced in the Corinthian assembly, one might hope for insight into how they understood the phenomenon being referred to as *glōssa*. But there appears to be a disconnect between the **of human beings and angels** here and the insistence in what follows that tongues-speaking is inherently unintelligible except to God (14:2, 6–19). The phrase could be poetic hyperbole on Paul's part, a way of saying

Orators out of Control

"If someone should ask the smallest thing beyond what they have said, like bronzes [chalkia] *that have been struck sound with a great racket and will not stop until someone puts a hand on them, so these orators when asked the smallest thing produce a marathon distance speech* [logos]." (Plato, *Protagoras* 329a, trans. Lombardo and Bell 1997, 762)

that no speech, human or heavenly, counts for anything without love (Fitzmyer 2008, 492). Or it could be an allusion to Jewish mystical traditions in which a visionary ascends into the heavens and hears or participates in angelic worship. Paul claims a comparable experience but refuses to (or cannot) disclose its content in 2 Cor. 12:1–4: "I heard the unutterable words that human beings are not permitted to utter" (12:4). The comparison of speech without love to a *chalkos ēchōn* (**noisy bronze**) is not necessarily referring to a particular instrument (often translated "gong," so NRSV). Bronze plates often served as sounding boards or amplification for various instruments in theaters (Vitruvius, *De architectura* 5.3.8; Fitzmyer 2008, 492). Corinth was famous for the manufacture of bronze vessels. Those fascinated with oratory might have recognized in the metaphor a classical allusion to the pompous rhetorician with nothing important to say.

Paul does not explicitly link faith that moves mountains and giving away possessions with the Jesus tradition. A similar indirect reference, however, appeared in Paul's comment on lawsuits (6:6–8). Specific references to Jesus's teaching (7:10–11; 9:14) and words at the Last Supper (11:23–25) make it possible that these two additional items are derived from Jesus tradition: the rich man who fails to give up his possessions (Mark 10:17–22) or the disciples who have done so (10:28–30) and Jesus's saying on faith moving mountains (11:22–23). The third item in the series, **handing over one's body to boast**, is puzzling. Some ancient manuscripts substitute the verb **burn**. Giving up one's body to be burned suggests martyrdom to Christians familiar with stories of those Nero used as human torches. It also provides a more dramatic climax for the series of really extraordinary actions. Perhaps the early manuscripts that have **boast** refer back to Paul's own physical hardships (9:15–16; 2 Cor. 11:16–28). Other translations and commentators retain the reading **to be burned**, even though **boast** is found in the earliest witnesses and is clearly the more difficult reading (Fitzmyer 2008, 494). Paul speaks of the bodily tribulations that attended his apostolic efforts as handing himself over to death in order to manifest the life of Jesus (2 Cor. 4:7–11). Holladay detects references to Paul's apostolic biography in all of the items listed (1990, 88–92).

Each of the three examples ends with a statement indicating that the activities described have no value. They form a graded series: producing nothing

Patterns in 1 Corinthians 13:4–7

1 Corinthians 13:4a

The first portion of this catalogue forms a chiasm with an A-B-B'-A' pattern:

"love is patient"	*hē agapē makrothymei*
"kind is love"	*chrēsteuetai hē agapē*

1 Corinthians 13:4b–6a

This portion consists of two groups of four lines. The opening seven-syllable line of each group has a similar sounding verb (following NA[27] in including *hē agapē* after *zēloi* in 13:4b):

"love is not jealous"	*ou zēloi hē agapē*
"it is not conceited"	*ou perpereuetai*
"not arrogant"	*ou physioutai*
"does not behave improperly"	*ouk aschēmonei*
"does not seek its own advantage"	*ou zētei ta heautēs*
"is not irritable"	*ou paroxynetai*
"does not calculate evil"	*ou logizetai to kakon*
"does not take joy in injustice"	*ou chairei epi tē adikia*

1 Corinthians 13:5b–6

This portion, which uses some lines from the preceding example, displays antithetical parallelism, rejecting vice and promoting good:

"does not calculate evil"	*ou logizetai to kakon*
"does not take joy in injustice"	*ou chairei epi tē adikia*
"but rejoices in the truth"	*synchairei de tē alētheia*

1 Corinthians 13:7

This portion consists of four staccato phrases opening with "all things" (*panta*):

"puts up with all things"	*panta stegei*
"believes all things"	*panta pisteuei*
"hopes all things"	*panta elpizei*
"endures all things"	*panta hypomenei*

of value (1 Cor. 13:1), the actor being of no value (**I am nothing** in 13:2), and gaining nothing (13:3; Fitzmyer 2008, 494).

13:4–7. Paul shifts to a catalogue listing the virtues of love (*agapē*), which may have been a set piece familiar to his audience since it lacks the direct links

In Praise of Love

"Love fills us with togetherness and drains all our divisiveness away. . . . Love moves us to mildness, removes from us wildness. He is giver of kindness, never of meanness . . . father of elegance, luxury, delicacy, grace, yearning, desire. Love cares well for good men, cares not for bad ones. In pain, in fear, in desire, or speech, Love is our best guide and guard; he is our comrade and our savior. Ornament of all gods and men. Every man should follow Love, sing beautifully his hymns." (Plato, *Symposium* 197d–e, trans. Nehamas and Woodruff 1989, 37)

to the larger context evident in 13:1–3 and 13:8–13 (Patterson 2009, 89–90). The linguistic shape of its phrases gives these verses a poetic or raplike sound.

Some scholars compare this brief speech in praise of *agapē* to a somewhat longer one celebrating the beneficent effects of Eros in Plato's *Symposium* (R. Collins 1999, 479). Though there is some overlap between the beneficent effects of Eros and the virtues that flow from *agapē*, *agapē* lacks those notes of sexual passion, attraction to what is fine or beautiful, elegance, and luxury. One can imagine the city's wealthy elite charmed by poetic celebrations of Eros. It has no place for the ugly, unsophisticated, lowborn, or impoverished—in short, for those members of Christ's body whom Paul has endowed with greater honor (12:24). By adopting a little-used noun, *agapē*, Christians could reorchestrate the cultural discourse about love as a divine gift. This small passage of ornamental prose, whether composed by the apostle or taken from familiar tradition, replaces the praises of love familiar to his audience from their childhood.

13:8–13. Paul returns to the issue at hand in his own voice. Instead of the sequence of four characteristics (13:7), the section on *agapē* concludes with a familiar Christian triad: **faith, hope, love** (13:13; 1 Thess. 1:3; 5:8; Col. 1:4–5). The opening sentence, **love never fails** (1 Cor. 13:8a), could be heard as yet another piece in the list of praises celebrating the eternity of love. But Paul has a different rhetorical agenda. The immortality of love highlights the temporality and imperfection of the other spiritual gifts: **prophecy, speaking in tongues, knowledge** (13:8b). Someone might protest that Paul mentioned the **tongues of angels** (13:1), and **knowledge** similarly requires a grasp of what is always the case. Though he does not articulate such objections, Paul skirts the problem by returning to the first-person. Certainly whatever language angels use to praise God is eternal as is truth, but we humans do not have a secure grasp on either: **We know partially** (13:9a). Though he does not explicitly point forward to the end time, Paul's quasi-logion, **when what is perfect**

comes, what is partial passes away (13:10), anticipates the final transformation of believers into the image of the risen Christ (15:49).

Paul reinforces the distinction between all our gifts and knowledge and the perfect reality to come using two analogies, childhood and mirrors. No one in antiquity had the romantic view of children common among modern readers. The transition from child to adult came sharply when the father introduced his son to fellow citizens (Gal. 4:1–2) or arranged his daughter's marriage (Dixon 1992, 98–116): **When I became an adult, I did away with childish things** (1 Cor. 13:11b). It is hardly an accident that the **things** put aside are not the protective amulets, games, dress, or playmates of the child, as in the ordinary case, but attributes generally associated with adulthood: **speech, thinking,** and **reasoning** (13:11a). Children were hardly capable of exercising practical wisdom or reasoning. Even their speech was subject to scrutiny and disciplined correction. Since being adult and exercising these capacities are linked, the audience would have been surprised by this compressed argument. Paul mentions speaking and reasoning by name only in connection with their childish use. Consequently, they are the **childish things** now discarded. The elite's preoccupation with rhetorical sophistication and misplaced claims to wisdom earned a sharp rebuke in the opening section of the letter: "I cannot speak to you as spiritual people but as fleshly, as children in Christ" (3:1; Nasrallah 2003, 62–82). The pedagogical intent of the entire letter is to move its recipients away from the various forms of childish speech, thought, and reasoning toward Christian maturity.

At the same time, Paul retains a tension between what believers can achieve in this world and the perfection that will be realized when God's reign is fully realized. The Corinthians may have treated such gifts as speaking in tongues and prophecy as evidence that those who exercised them were already perfect. Paul's second example, looking at one's own image in a mirror, underlines the imperfection in our self-knowledge. By inserting the contrast between **now . . . see dimly . . . know partially** and **then face to face, know as I am known [by God]** (13:12), Paul indicates that no corrective measure transcends the limitations of this life. Contrary to Corinthian expectations, spiritual gifts do not provide direct access to heavenly immortality (Schrage 1999, 305). That emphasis on spiritual gifts as aids in a time of imperfection explains a puzzle posed by the **faith, hope, love remain** expression (13:13a). If Paul were speaking only about our eschatological transformation or seeing the glory of God in Christ (2 Cor. 3:18), then one would expect Paul to have said that only love remains. One might invoke later traditions of apophatic mysticism that hold that God is permanently beyond any human understanding. From that perspective faith always remains part of the relationship between Creator and creature. But that solution cannot apply to hope. It cannot be said to remain once the full experience of God's salvation arrives in the eschaton. Paul probably did not consider such nuances. In this letter he has no intention of encouraging the Corinthians to seek a mystical knowledge of God or an apocalyptic revelation of things to come. He wishes to show that their relationships with one another are at stake (van Unnik 1993). These three virtues are essential for every believer. And as he promised to show a more excellent spirituality, **the greatest of these is love** (1 Cor. 13:13b).

On Speech in the Worshiping Assembly (14:1–40)

Paul returns to the topic of spiritual gifts (*pneumatika*). Love would heal the multiple sources of division within the church that have been discussed in the letter. So Paul generalizes the encomium on love by encouraging the audience to **pursue love** (14:1). As he moves into the concrete stipulations that will govern speech in the assembly, Paul retrieves a specific manifestation of love introduced earlier in treating the question of idol meat (8:1; 10:23). Love seeks to build up (*oikodomein*; 14:3, 4, 12, 17, 26).

But that general principle does not resolve the questions concerning spiritual gifts introduced at 12:1. The discussion began in 1 Cor. 12 with additional principles about the diversity of gifts necessary in the church. All of them have been bestowed as God chooses, to unify the church (12:4–11). No one, not even an apostle, can claim superiority over other members of the community based on the spiritual gift God has given. Every part of the body plays an important role in the well-being of the whole (12:27–31a). Paul finally identifies the specific problem in Corinth: factionalism created by those speaking in tongues and prophesying. The two activities, **speaking in tongues** (*lalōn glōssē*) and **prophesying** (*prophēteuōn*), are compared (14:2–5, 20–25), with prophecy receiving higher marks as a community-building activity (Zeller 2010, 421; Smit 1994).

> **An Outline of 1 Corinthians 14:1–40**
>
> **On speech in the worshiping assembly (14:1–40)**
>
> Superiority of prophecy to tongues (14:1–5)
>
> Principle of building up the community (14:6–12)
>
> Using intelligible speech in worship (14:13–19)
>
> Believers and unbelievers in the assembly (14:20–25)
>
> Types of speech in the assembly (14:26–33a)
>
> Rule silencing women (14:33b–36)
>
> Principle of orderly and dignified behavior (14:37–40)

The elaborate rhetorical patterns and repetitions with which Paul builds his case suggest that he anticipates resistance to that conclusion from his audience. The two comparative sections frame an extended argument against the communal value of speaking in tongues based on its character as sounds that are unintelligible to auditors (14:6–19). In the process, Paul extends an olive branch to those who value tongues-speaking. God might give another the gift of interpreting those noises so that they could serve as community-building communication (14:5, 13, 26). But how likely is that option? When Paul presents himself as exemplar (14:18–19), he implies that one can choose between tongues and rational speech. Specific instructions for speech in the worshiping assembly follow (14:26–40). Paul concludes the discussion by insisting that a **command of the Lord** (14:37–38) prohibits disruptive speech (Vos 1993, 262–63).

14:1–5. The numerical list at 12:28—apostles, prophets, teachers—should have prepared the audience for the direction Paul takes. Speaking in tongues and even interpretation of such speech bring up the rear (12:28, 30). This section opens by identifying prophecy as the spiritual gift one should desire most—**that you may prophesy** (14:1c)—and concludes with its communal impact—**that the church may receive building up** (14:5d). The central verses (14:2–4) create a hypnotic effect with parallel repetitions:

> A   for one speaking in tongues [*ho gar lalōn glōssē*]
> > B speaks not to human beings but to God [*ouk anthrōpois lalei alla theō*]
> > > C   for no one hears; in the Spirit he speaks mysteries [*oudeis gar akouei, pneumati de lalei mystēria*]
> A′ and one prophesying [*ho de prophēteuōn*]
> > B′ speaks to human beings [*anthrōpois lalei*]
> > > C′ building up and encouragement and comfort [*oikodomēn kai paraklēsin kai paramythian*]
> A″ one speaking in tongues [*ho lalōn glōssē*]
> > > C″ builds up himself [*heauton oikodomei*]
> A‴ and one prophesying [*ho de prophēteuōn*]
> > > C‴ builds up [the] church [*ekklēsian oikodomei*]

Paul shifts to the first-person (**I wish**) and uses a chiastic formulation in the concluding verse:

> A all of you to speak in tongues [*de pantas hymas lalein glōssais*]
> > B or rather that you prophesy [*mallon de hina prophēteuēte*]
> > B′ as the one prophesying is greater [*meizōn de ho prophēteuōn*]
> A′ than the one speaking in tongues [*ē ho lalōn glōssais*]

This arrangement permits him to tack on the exception, an interpretation, which would shift tongues-speaking into the category of activities that build up the church.

Paul makes the superiority of prophecy to speaking in tongues depend on its contribution to communal life: **The one prophesying to people speaks [a word that is] building up, exhorting, and encouraging** (14:3). Speaking in tongues may seem to represent greater spirituality because it is inspired speech representing heavenly mysteries. But only the Spirit and God know what it is about (14:2, 4). Clearly Paul does not consider tongues the capacity to be speaking different languages as in Acts 2:8–11, an experience familiar to residents of a major east-west sea-lane like Corinth. Whatever their mother tongues may have been, most could communicate in Greek.

Paul's arguments will build on the premise that not even the speaker knows what the sounds that he or she utters mean. Any value to the experience is purely subjective: **The one speaking in tongues builds up only himself** (1 Cor. 14:4a). There is, however, an exception. If God gives another the ability to interpret tongues, the community could benefit (14:5, 13, 26). Since Paul mentions that exception at several points, it appears to be an open possibility. When Paul establishes rules to order the assembly, lack of such interpretation requires that those moved to speak in tongues remain silent (14:28). Although tongues appears to be nearly on equal footing with prophecy, the upshot of the argument as a whole is to suppress tongues-speaking in communal worship.

14:6–12. Paul presses the point by asking the audience to imagine what would have been the case if he had arrived preaching the gospel by speaking in tongues. He lists the types of intelligible speech that were part of his efforts: **revelation, knowledge, prophecy,** and **teaching** (14:6). Two images of incoherent or unintelligible sound support this evaluation of speaking in tongues. Sounds from badly tuned instruments, **flutes or lyres,** make no sense (14:7). Even more important for a Roman audience, a **trumpet** incapable of the appropriate notes cannot direct soldiers on the battlefield (14:8). Similarly, speaking in tongues is **speaking into [thin] air** (14:9). Though Paul had presented tongues as speech directed to God (14:2), this suggestion that such noises simply vanish in the air constitutes a humorous challenge to that understanding (Fitzmyer 2008, 512). Speaking in tongues neither entertains and soothes, as in the case of the flute or lyre, nor summons the group to effective action, as in the case of the trumpet.

Despite the negative overtones associated with speaking in tongues in 14:6 and 14:9, Paul's audience could easily retain their positive view of that spiritual gift. Paul has employed lists of gifts in 1 Cor. 12–14, which either begin or end with tongues.

If Paul cannot deny the powerful experience of tongues-speaking, he can challenge its efficacy. Communication is the purpose of speech. A busy commercial crossroads like Corinth provided occasion for the polyglot sounds of unfamiliar tongues among sailors, traders, and immigrant artisans. The turn in 14:6 to address this audience of **brothers [and sisters]** as **you** shifts from a hypothetical question about what Paul's ministry would have been if he had spoken in tongues to their own speaking (14:9). Paul uses the common term for a person unable to speak Greek, *barbaros*, to describe the relationship between other members of the church and those speaking in tongues (14:10–11). He may also expect hearers to link the alienation created by humanity's linguistic diversity to the story in Gen. 11:1 (Fitzmyer 2008, 514). There is no communal solidarity between persons who lack a language in which they can

Table 13
Spiritual Gifts of Speech and Knowledge in 1 Corinthians

Beginning	14:6	13:1–2	12:8–10	1:5
	tongues	tongues	word of wisdom	word
	revelation	prophecy	word of knowledge	knowledge
	knowledge	know all mysteries	prophecy	—
	prophecy	all knowledge	tongues	—
	teaching	—	interpretation of tongues	—
Ending	**14:26**	**13:8**	**12:28–29**	**8:1, 7, 11**
	teaching	prophecy	prophets	knowledge
	revelation	tongues	teachers	—
	tongues	knowledge	tongues	—
	interpretation	—	tongues-speaking	—
	—	—	interpreting	—

communicate. Paul draws this set of examples to a close with an imperative. Christians pursuing spiritual gifts should **seek to build up the community** (14:12). This principle has a purpose: **that you may excel** [*perisseuein*]. What is the abundance Christians can anticipate if they adopt Paul's principle? The audience may supply any or all of the spiritual gifts listed. First Corinthians 1:5 gives God thanks for enriching the Corinthians **in every way, in him** [Christ], **in all speech** [*logos*] **and all knowledge.**

14:13–19. Speaking in tongues is so much a part of Corinthian worship that Paul cannot exclude it from Christian prayer altogether. Rather **let him pray that he can interpret** (14:13). Interpretation was tightly bound to tongues in earlier lists. It is distinct from prophecy and not one of the community-founding modes of speech employed by the apostle.

First Corinthians 14:13 serves as a transition between the previous section and a new line of argument that once again opens with the hypothetical first-person singular, **if I am praying in tongues** (14:14–15), and shifts to the second-person. But instead of speaking directly to the audience with plural "you," Paul employs the second-person singular (14:16–17). That shift creates a rhetorical situation in which the apostle addresses an imagined individual who is speaking in tongues. Paul returns to plural "you" at the conclusion of this section, which once again holds up his own modes of speech as the example to be emulated (14:18–19).

Terms for prayer are threaded through this section: **pray** (14:13, 14 [2x], 15 [2x]), **recite a psalm** (14:15 [2x]), **bless** (14:16), **amen** (14:16), and **give thanks** (14:16, 17). Since tongues-speaking occurs during worship, it must be related to the forms of speech that Christians use in prayer and praise.

Paul continues the argument in favor of speech that is intelligible to those who hear what is being said. He introduces a new antithesis between **spirit** and **mind**. The spirit of the person praying is active, but there is no benefit to the mind (14:14). Though modern readers tend to think of the antithesis as inferior, irrational speech contrasted with rational speech, ancient readers would have a different reaction. Philosophers going back to Plato (*Phaedrus* 244) recognized that the inspired speech of a prophet or famous oracle is different from the raving of an insane person. Its divine origin makes such speech important when it is properly interpreted. During the process the mind is suspended (D. Martin 1995, 96–101). Therefore the hypothetical individual who favors speaking in tongues might interpret the experience as divinely inspired.

Rather than treat spirit and mind as antithetical, Paul proposes a harmonious relationship between spirit and mind in Christian prayer: **I will pray in the spirit and I will also pray in the mind** (14:15). D. Martin applies this advice to Paul's larger project of persuading the elite to defer to the needs of weaker members of the community. Spirit may be a divine endowment, but it should be subordinate to the mind (1995, 101–2). In the process of listing types of prayer that a speaker may utter—**psalm, blessing, thanksgiving** (14:15–16)— Paul indicates that others responded with **amen**. No one can engage with the prayer of someone speaking in tongues in that fashion. Therefore such prayer does not benefit the community (14:17). Indeed, if the proper liturgical response **amen** becomes impossible, then such speech has no part to play in public worship (Thiselton 2000, 1118). Having said as much, Paul does not discredit tongues altogether. He allows the hypothetical speaker the possibility of addressing God: **You [singular] are giving thanks appropriately** (14:17a).

As he has done so often in this letter, Paul presents himself as an example for believers (14:18–19). He has made it clear from the beginning of the letter that his own example is not an optional illustration. Believers are to pattern their own conduct on the model that the apostle presents. Since Paul cannot be present, he has sent Timothy to serve as a living reminder to the recipients of this letter (4:14–17). Now Paul asserts that he is abler to speak in tongues than anyone in his churches (14:18). But because he can, that does not mean that he should. Because such speech does not benefit the community, he comments: **In the church I would rather speak five words that are intelligible [literally "in my mind"] . . . than thousands of words in tongues** (14:19). Interpreters face the difficulty of deciding how to read this example. Does Paul mean that he has the gift of tongues-speaking to a greater degree, but would never use it? The Corinthians know that he never spoke in tongues when he was among them (14:6a). Or did he himself pray in tongues on occasion? If that were the case, his awkward arguments could reflect embarrassment over curtailing a form of prayer that he once approved. Or is the entire example to be read as a highly sarcastic put-down of those who advocate this form of prayer in public worship? Paul used the expression **I thank God** to introduce an ironic rejection of the Corinthian view of relationships between the baptized and those who baptized them in 1:14, so it could have that tone in 14:18 (Fitzmyer 2008, 518).

14:20–25. Echoes of the opening section of the letter continue to sound in the final treatment of the principles at stake. It is time for Paul's audience to prove that they belong among the spiritually **mature** (*teleioi*; 14:20; 2:6). Before proceeding with another argument that uncontrolled speaking in tongues actually hinders the mission of the community, Paul evokes the encomium on love: it is time to put childish ways of thinking aside (14:20; 13:11; also 3:1–2). He phrases this injunction in a neatly turned chiasm:

A do not be little children [*paidia*]
  B in thinking [*tais phresin*]
    C but be infants [*nēpiazete*] as regards wickedness [*kakia*]
  B′ and in thinking [*tais de phresin*]
A′ be mature [*teleioi*]

Paul inaugurates a new line of argument with a citation of Scripture. Though introduced as Torah—**in the law it is written**—the passage is taken from

Table 14
Scripture Citations in 1 Corinthians 14:21

1 Cor. 14:21 AT		Isa. 28:11–12 NETS		Deut. 28:49 NETS [altered]	
In other tongues	*en heteroglōssois*	Because of contempt from lips,	*dia phaulismon cheileōn*	The Lord will bring upon you	*epaxei kyrios epi se*
and with other lips	*kai en cheilesin heterōn*	through a different tongue,	*dia glōssēs heteras*	a nation from far away,	*ethnos makrothen*
I will speak to this people,	*lalēsō tō laō toutō*	because they will speak to this people,	*hoti lalēsousin tō laō toutō*	from the end of the earth,	*ap' eschatou tēs gēs*
—	—	saying to them, "This is the rest for the hungry, and this is the destruction";	*legontes autō, touto to anapauma tō peinōnti kai touto to syntrimma*	like the swoop of an eagle,	*hōsei hormēma aetou*
and not even [thus] will they hear [me]	*kai oud' [houtōs] eisakousontai [mou]*	yet they would not hear.	*kai ouk ēthelēsan akouein*	a nation that you will not hear	*ethnos ho ouk akousē*
[says the Lord].	[*legei kyrios*]	—	—	its speech.	*tēs phōnēs autou*

The Danger of Divine Mania

According to myth, Cybele-Demeter drove a frenzied Attis to castrate himself. Catullus concludes a long Latin poem recounting the story with an appeal to the goddess:

"Great Goddess, Goddess who guards Mount Dindymus, may your furies all fall far from my house. Make other men mad, but have mercy on me!" (Catullus, Ode 63.2.90–92, trans. Beard, North, and Price 1998, 1:165)

Isa. 28:11–12 LXX, which could be associated with Deut. 28:49, justifying the attribution.

Paul ignores the context of Isaiah: Assyrian invaders speaking a foreign tongue and the message about rest that is rejected. The judgment oracle from Isaiah warns that the leaders of Judah will not listen to the word from God that would have meant salvation (Fitzmyer 2008, 509–10). Paul assumes that they do not listen to the Lord because of the foreign tongues. He may be suggesting a parallel between his words to the Corinthians and those God directed at Israel. If they refuse his teaching, it will be as if he had spoken to them in tongues (Fitzmyer 2008, 520). The antithesis that Paul draws from the biblical text associates a negative tone with speaking in tongues—**tongues are a sign not for believers but for unbelievers** (1 Cor. 14:22)—while the opposite is true for prophecy (Smit 1994).

Paul's antithesis between tongues and prophecy cannot be drawn from the citation directly. It might be deduced from Israel's having rejected God's word through the prophet with the result that a faithless people is addressed in foreign tongues. Paul returns to the specifics of the Corinthian situation by formulating another hypothetical scenario. He asks the audience to envisage the impact on nonbelievers who happen to witness the proceedings: **If . . . all are speaking in tongues . . . will they not say that you are frenzied?** (14:23). Paul treats this case as a gathering of **the whole church at the same place**, rather than in smaller household groups. That stipulation magnifies the distance between this rhetorical fiction and reality. He is challenging the audience to generalize the alleged spiritual value of tongues. If, as they suppose, tongues are the most important gift, then a spirit-filled community (3:16) should expect every member to be speaking in tongues. Outsiders coming upon such an ideal assembly would naturally interpret their behavior as similar to the wild ecstasy that seizes devotees of such gods as Cybele-Demeter or Dionysus. Such an interpretation would not draw the nonbeliever to worship Israel's God.

Paul continues this hypothetical case by asking his audience to imagine an alternate scenario, generalizing prophetic speech as the preferred option. Suppose an outsider came into an assembly in which **all were prophesying . . . he is convicted by all, he is called to account by all, the things hidden in his heart are revealed** (14:24–25a). Earlier Paul reminded the Corinthians that all the hidden secrets and plans of the heart will be laid bare at the judgment: neither he nor anyone else can judge the apostle's fidelity to his God-given mission until "the Lord comes, who will illuminate things hidden in darkness and will make manifest the plans of hearts" (4:5). So this alternate description of the community—where all prophesy—is ideal, not real. This vision of prophetic speech requires participation in God's knowledge of the human heart.

The hypothetical outsider who stumbled into a church where everyone could expose what lies hidden in the heart would have to conclude that such prophetic words of judgment could come only from God. Unlike the unintelligible sounds of a community speaking in tongues, the testimony of a community prophesying would have a dramatic effect on outsiders. One would see these nonbelievers prostrating themselves in **worship of God** (14:25b) and confessing: **certainly God is among you** (14:25c = Isa. 45:14). Thus the community would be built up as the place in which the nations come to worship God, as Isaiah had predicted. It would display its core reality as God's Spirit-filled temple (1 Cor. 3:16) before the world. If the audience has followed Paul's rhetorical logic, comparing the two outcomes makes the choice obvious. If they are to ask God to endow all believers with one of the two spiritual gifts, they should opt for prophecy.

Since Paul presents this scenario as an imaginative one, one should not infer that everyone in the community was expected to speak in tongues or to prophesy. Given that conclusion, one cannot conclude from this passage that outsiders were present when the community was engaged in prayer either. To be an effective conclusion for the argument that prophecy is to be preferred to speaking in tongues, it must have been possible for outsiders to be present. The Christian assembly is not that of initiates into a mystery cult shrouding its rites in secrecy.

14:26–33a. Paul concludes this treatment of spiritual gifts with rules for speech in the assembly under the general principle of building up the community. The initial list of types of speech—**psalm, teaching, revelation, tongues, interpretation** (14:26)—omits the term "prophecy," which returns in the detailed rules that follow. Perhaps **teaching** and **revelation** cover the kind of speech that Christian prophets engaged in. The earlier treatment of how women prophets are to dress (11:3–16) indicates that prophecy was not restricted to interpretation of tongues. Teachers are third after apostles and prophets in the list at 12:28 (Zeller 2010, 440). The rules that follow mention persons who speak in tongues, who interpret, who prophecy, and who receive revelations (14:27–31).

Paul limits the number of speakers in each instance, **two or three**, stipulates what others should do instead of clamoring to speak, and imposes silence in several cases (14:28, 30). A person moved to speak in tongues is to **be silent in the assembly** [*ekklēsia*] **but speak to himself and to God** (14:28) if there is no interpreter. Similarly, someone prophesying is to **sit down** and **be silent** if someone else receives a revelation (14:30). Paul explains that insisting on prophets speaking **one at a time** permits **all to learn and all to be exhorted**

(14:31). There is a possible objection. Rules for taking speakers one at a time are all well and good for the philosophical discussion that accompanies after-dinner wine at a well-run symposium (Smith 2002). Similar rules apply when a Jewish group like the Essenes assemble for study of Torah. Such situations involve application of human reason to the questions at hand. With the exception, however, of reciting psalms or teaching, the activities Paul refers to—tongues, their interpretation, prophecy, and revelations—all depend on God's inspiration. Therefore someone in the audience might protest that inspired speech cannot be regulated in the same fashion that permission to speak is granted or withheld in other forums.

Two points made earlier in the argument support Paul's position that the various forms of speech in the Christian assembly can be regulated. First, the Spirit works within the diversity of the ecclesial body to promote unity, not discord (12:4–11). Second, Paul equates prophecy with rational speech, "through my mind," because it is intelligible, unlike tongues (14:18–19). Therefore Paul concludes that **spirits of prophets are controlled by prophets** (14:32). The intelligibility of prophetic speech correlates with its effectiveness in building up the church. The hypothetical case of outsiders wandering in when everyone is speaking in tongues and that of their presence in a group engaged in prophecy supports this view of prophetic discourse. The tongues-speaking assembly appears to be a bunch of crazed maenads. The prophetic assembly testifies to God's presence. Paul wraps up this set of rules with the reminder that **God is not [one] of discord but of peace** (14:33a). The term **discord** (*akatastasia*) recalls the political metaphor of the civic body torn apart by strife that Paul employed earlier (Mitchell 1993, 173). Thus Paul evokes the two popular images of discord most feared in antiquity: religious and political. If he has succeeded in persuading the audience that their gatherings could be mistaken for either or both of these types of disorder, then Paul has made a powerful case for reforming the order of worship.

14:33b–36. Because an earlier set of rules about dress assumed that women did prophesy in the assembly (11:3–16) and because Pauline churches barred women from teaching men at a somewhat later period (1 Tim. 2:11–12), many exegetes treat these verses as a later updating of the regulations. However, if the rules in this section of the letter represent a gathering of the whole church—perhaps following the weekly celebration of the Lord's Supper—then the audience may infer that the rules given apply to a different situation. For example, the earlier passage could reflect a smaller, less formal gathering for prayer comparable to the household offerings to its deities. In either case, the rule that women are not to speak in a public assembly but should be taught at home by their husbands reflects social convention in antiquity.

The protests of modern readers that the community included women whose husbands were not believers (1 Cor. 7:13) and that the women involved in Paul's wider missionary efforts must have instructed males (Phil. 4:2–3; Rom. 16:1–3) challenge those twenty-first-century churches that still silence women. It is less obvious that a first-century AD audience would have found anything amiss in the regulations (Fitzmyer 2008, 530–31). These rules address the general case of a well-ordered worshiping assembly that applies **in all the churches** (1 Cor. 14:33b, 34). As in the situation of how women praying and prophesying should dress, the accepted social code of honor and disgrace determines the decision: **it is a disgrace for a woman to speak in an assembly** (14:35b). Clearly that same social code does not apply today, as women have public roles as leaders of nations, corporations, educational institutions, and so forth. The sharp tone of 14:36 is a puzzle: **Has the word of God gone out from you or has it reached only you?** Is Paul picking on women prophets whom he expects to be opposed to his authority in particular (Wire 1990, 14–17)? Or is this simply a rhetorical way of insisting on Paul's authority to implement rules in Corinth that will bring their communal worship into line with the practice in churches generally? Because the adjective **only** is masculine plural, a direct challenge to women prophets seems unlikely. Also unlikely is the counterproposal that treats 14:36 as a challenge to men who wish to deny women the right to speak in the assembly (R. Collins 1999, 522). Therefore the expression is best considered a general reinforcement of Paul's authority to introduce rules. The masculine plural adjective indirectly indicates that the apostle envisages male leaders as responsible for administering church affairs (Fitzmyer 2008, 533).

14:37–40. The authoritative tone of 14:36 continues into the verses that conclude this long discussion of spiritual gifts, which began at 12:1 (Fitzmyer 2008, 536). If anyone considers himself **a prophet or spirit-led person [*pneumatikos*], he [or she] should acknowledge the things I am writing to you are command of the Lord** (14:37; cf. 14:36; 11:16). How does Paul reach that level of conviction without reference to any Jesus tradition? Since the apostle outranks prophets and teachers, he may assume the model of early Christian prophets speaking in the name of Jesus. Nothing they can say in Jesus's name could contradict the apostle's teaching (Thiselton 2000, 1162–65). The next verse reinforces that authority by invoking God's judgment against anyone who refuses to accept this teaching (14:38). The passive verb in the second clause, **he is not recognized,** is the "divine passive," an indirect way of speaking about God (Fitzmyer 2008, 537). An alternative interpretation takes the verb as a directive to the community not to acknowledge such persons. The apostle states it as a fact. No person whose prophecy or teaching contradicts what the apostle has written can be accepted by the Christian community (Thiselton 2000, 1166).

Although Paul's rules might appear to be hostile to speaking in tongues, since speaking in tongues is not permitted where no interpreter is present, he defuses that impression: **Seek to prophesy and do not prohibit speaking in tongues** (14:39). In concluding, the apostle reminds readers of the purpose for these diverse rules: **Let everything happen in a dignified and orderly way** (14:40).

Theological Issues

As Paul grapples with concrete problems in Corinth, he formulates important insights into the nature of the church. The model of a community as a body whose diverse parts must function harmoniously to ensure its health was well known to a first-century audience. That metaphor ordinarily served the interests of the governing elite seeking to quell turmoil among the populace. Although we do not know the particulars of the situation in Corinth, the dangers of division in small house-churches are no less serious than those of rebellion in cities. The church crosses boundaries of gender since it incorporates men and women, of social status and class since it includes rich and poor and slave and free, and of ethnic origins since it incorporates Jews and non-Jews. This Spirit-filled temple of God is being built up from the diverse mix of peoples in ancient Corinth. Therefore the natural bonds that individuals form with their own kind are not correlated with membership in the church. Its very diversity could be responsible for the divisions.

Some of the private associations studied by scholars cross one or two of the normal boundaries, but they ordinarily employ other ethnic, socioeconomic, or cultural ties to motivate group solidarity. Such groups do not challenge an individual's relationship to the deities and religious customs of family and city as Christianity did. Measuring the task at hand against the social setting is crucial to evaluating Paul's rhetoric. His authoritarian tone should not be misconstrued as intolerant or domineering. The appeals to conform with standards that apply to churches elsewhere are necessary to create boundaries for the new group. Nor does Paul presume that there is a single mold into which every church fits. He acknowledges that preaching the gospel often required that he adapt to cultural differences of those to whom he preached (9:19–23).

Sociocultural analysis does not tell the whole story. Paul repeatedly brings his audience back to theological considerations. What makes the church different from the political and social models of community that Paul employs to awaken listeners to the seriousness of disorder in their church life? The most important theological characteristic of Christian community sounds throughout the letter from its opening words (1:1–9). Its members have been called by God, have responded in faith, and can rely on God's faithfulness to be with them. Unlike the many deities they had worshiped, who must be appeased with complex rites, this God sacrificed his own Son for the sake of humanity. The Christian meal celebration recalls Jesus's self-offering. So Paul consistently asks the more privileged members of the community to imitate that sacrificial attitude. They must show a consideration for the poorest and weakest members, which runs against the grain of a deeply competitive social system. Another's gain meant the individual's loss. As Paul's own example demonstrates, servant leadership does not mean loss of honor or failed authority. Believers today can point to thousands of heroes past and present who stepped off the ladder of success to found major initiatives in lifting up suffering humanity, such as Albert Schweitzer, Mother Teresa, or Dr. Paul Farmer. Local media often feature stories of teens who come up with initiatives to help others. Some are sponsored by churches, synagogues, or mosques. Others have no directly religious tie, but demonstrate the power of compassion over teenage self-absorption.

Paul provides an example of how Christian insights can transform culture. He applied the message of the cross to a familiar political trope, that of society as a body. An image that once justified elite rule of the lower orders of society has been turned on its head. We clothe those lesser parts of the body. Noticing the importance of other parts of the social body does not constitute a revolution. Feet, bellies, and the like do not take over the job of heads and hands. Honoring the parts of the body that are socially despised does what the political speakers never do—it acknowledges that they are just as important as the head, hands, eyes, or feet. In Paul's theological perspective every part of the body has a responsibility for the whole.

Because ancient medicine often analyzed the operation of spirit in bodily health, Paul can introduce another theological translation by treating the physiological spirit that designates the vital forces in the human body as an image of God's own Spirit at work in the church. Consequently, the Spirit distributes charismatic gifts in the community in a harmonious manner. Individuals do not choose the roles in which they are to build up the body of Christ; the roles are God's gift. Even though Paul speaks of preferring prophecy and the like, the Spirit must enable individuals to do so. The longer lists of necessary gifts set such less glamorous tasks as administration, service, and healing alongside others. His emphasis on speaking in tongues and prophecy does not necessarily represent all the Spirit-inspired functions necessary for a healthy church. It happens that the Corinthians misinterpreted tongues as evidence of a higher spirituality than that attained by those performing other equally needed functions. It would certainly strike Paul as peculiar to make a dramatic experience of "tongues-speaking" or "being slain in the Spirit" the condition of full membership in the church, a practice followed in some Pentecostal communities (Zeller 2010, 437).

In addition to including as spiritual gifts some more general categories such as administration—activities that would not require the same level of education as the ability to speak, teach, or lead psalms—Paul insists that everyone in the community has been gifted with the Spirit. Everyone who has been baptized into Christ receives the Spirit of God. Though the wealthier members who provided the space, food, and other resources for the Lord's Supper probably never considered going ahead with their own meal an affront to the poor, Paul objects. The church is not the place to reinforce one's dominance over others. However, Paul does not tell Christians to break off their ties to non-believers. His comment, "if someone is hungry, let him eat at home" (11:34), points out that the apostle does not imagine transforming the larger society. Unlike Jesus's parable of the great banquet (Luke 14:15–24; Matt. 22:1–10), for example, Paul is not asking believers to shake up social conventions. In some cases, such as the dress for men and women praying in the assembly (1 Cor. 11:3–16) and the hypothetical case of outsiders who might witness the church at prayer (14:20–25), Paul indicates that ordinary cultural conventions concerning what is dignified behavior apply to believers. Augustine concludes that because members of the heavenly city are drawn from all nations and tongues, they should continue to follow the diverse customs, laws, and institutions that promote earthly peace so long as these do not prevent worship of the true God (*De civitate Dei* 19.17). Today many Christians would expand the task of promoting earthly peace to issues of social justice and human rights.

Many of the divisions within congregations and denominations today arise from social and cultural shifts in understanding what is respectable or helpful in worship services, in leadership by men and women, in supporting families, and in engagement with the larger society. Christians must work hard to deal with these problems without dividing the church. Some conduct individual services in different languages or combine multiple languages and forms of music in a single service. Paul's efforts to create harmony in Corinth remain focused on the way in which Christian believers relate to one another. His insistence that there be an interpreter or limited instances of tongues-speaking might be transferred to this setting. New patterns of worship should enable all those present to participate and understand what is going on. It may require interpreters or simple hymn refrains and prayer formulas that those who do not speak the language can learn. As Paul puts it, the goal is good order, not chaos.

These chapters in 1 Corinthians provide glimpses into Christian worship that leave many questions unanswered. Consequently churches with very different orders for worship and celebration of the Lord's Supper can find their life anticipated here. Since Paul employs the traditional words of the Lord about the bread and the wine in a rhetorical argument intended to remind the audience of what the meal commemorates, some exegetes even doubt that those words functioned as a ritual formula. If they were a set formula, there is no indication of whether a specific person was charged with pronouncing them in the manner of an officiating priest at a pagan sacrifice, for example. Nor is it clear whether the bread and cup words occurred together prior to a distribution of bread and wine to the assembly or were spoken at separate points during the meal as in the blessings at a Jewish Passover meal.

Another question concerns the praying, prophesying, and tongues-speaking activities. Some scholars appeal to the custom of discussions accompanied by wine after the dinner at banquets. They suggest that these spiritual activities occurred at the same gathering as the meal. This sequence reverses the order of service of the Word preceding the Eucharist familiar to many Christians. But this interpretation assumes that when the community gathered for formal worship, celebration of the Lord's death was included. Other scholars are equally convinced that the activities that involve teaching, praying, prophesying, and tongues-speaking refer to gatherings that were not necessarily connected with the Lord's Supper (Zeller 2010, 431). Some of the disagreements mentioned earlier in the letter, especially the partisanship that Paul criticizes in 1 Cor. 1–4, suggest that the church in Corinth also gathered in smaller groups. Those groups probably engaged in praying and prophesying as well. Paul presumes that his audience is familiar with parts of the Scripture. Hearing Scripture must have been part of the teaching ministry mentioned in the list of spiritual gifts. With literacy rates in the general population no higher than 10–20 percent, reciting psalms required leaders who had learned them by heart and could teach verses to others. Worshipers were not flipping to the appropriate page in a Bible or prayer book.

Additional spiritual gifts involve activities that are less directly connected with the worshiping assembly, such as healing. Paul provides no indication about the context within which healing of the sick occurred or whether it was accompanied by prayer and anointing as was later the case (James 5:14–15). Many congregations today seek to move beyond the simple listing of sick members in prayers to rituals of healing either as separate healing services or as an altar call for those who wish to come forward for laying on of hands.

Though these chapters do not mention any charitable distributions beyond the insistence on common food being shared at the Lord's Supper, Paul proposes that contributions for the poor in Jerusalem be taken up at the weekly gathering (1 Cor. 16:1–2). Someone must have been custodian for the funds. Private associations often specified how much members were to contribute to common activities such as sacrifices, meals, and the burial expenses of members. Those groups also had officers in charge of activities and finances. Paul does not mention such officers in Corinth. Teachers may have been a stable ministry in the church. As Paul describes them, the gifts of prophecy, tongues, and the like might be given to anyone in the church as the Spirit chooses. Therefore one cannot extract authorization for a particular form of church order from 1 Corinthians. Perhaps the anticipation of repeated visits by the apostle himself or his representatives like Timothy made it unnecessary to craft the kind of bylaws typical of other associations. We know that Paul intends to make additional arrangements for the Lord's Supper on his next visit (11:34b).

Paul never lets his readers forget that the church is more than its human dimensions. God has called this assembly into being with no small tasks at hand, bringing all humans into the body of Christ. The self-sacrificing example of the Son of God who died on the cross is the basic paradigm for Christian life. Though we may be tempted to view disagreements and misunderstandings between Paul and the Corinthians as a series of power struggles, the apostle does not. The Corinthians remain his beloved children. He has a parental concern for their welfare and that of all the other churches he has founded. Paul also has another conviction expressed in the body-of-Christ analogy. Every member of the community has been gifted with the Spirit. Those gifts are not divisive but coordinated to promote the health of the entire body. An effective pastor today is something like the general manager/head coach of a sports team, able to fit the diverse gifts in the congregation together and coax the best from everyone—even the three-year-old bringing up a can of tuna or soup for the food pantry!

1 Corinthians 15:1–58

Reports That Some Deny the Resurrection

Introductory Matters

Paul having mentioned that he will provide further instructions for the Lord's Supper when he comes (11:34) and having concluded with a reminder to do everything in an orderly way (14:40), one might expect the standard letter conclusion, winding up any loose ends, travel plans, and greetings as in 1 Cor. 16. Paul delays to treat a topic that is central to Christian faith, resurrection (15:1–5; Zeller 2010, 454). In 15:1 he introduces this new section with a phrase heard earlier at 12:3: "I am informing you, brothers" (assuming "brothers" from 12:1). In both cases, what follows is not new information but an injunction to pay attention to something they presumably know. Unlike the earlier case in which the brief confessional statement "Lord [is] Jesus" follows in the same sentence, here Paul defers the creedal statement to 15:3b–5. In the interim, a series of short phrases hammer home the point that what follows is the basis for salvation (15:1b–3a). By expanding the list of witnesses to the resurrection from Peter and the Twelve to others and finally to himself (15:6–11), Paul indicates that resurrection is the problem (Gerhardson 2003).

Paul has heard that some people in Corinth deny that the dead are raised (15:12). That assertion is phrased as a generic statement about the fate of deceased humans. It was not necessarily applied to the figure of the exalted Christ by those who held that view (Zeller 2010, 459). Paul's opening gambit—believing (as you must) *x* about Christ implies that *y* must be true of the (Christian) dead—may well have come as a surprise to listeners. Attempts to discern populist views about death by studying the gravestone inscriptions of merchants, craftsmen, entertainers, and the like show a diversity of possibilities. Some may have believed in a personal deification, inferred from depictions of the deceased in poses characteristic of gods, particularly Mercury and Hercules. Others imagined an afterlife as comparable to the earthly household. Still others held a more fatalistic "dead and gone" point of view (Toner 2009, 43). Whatever individuals thought about post-mortem existence, many belonged to associations that provided funeral rites for their members (Toner 2009, 39). If Paul's earlier warnings against "sharing the cup . . . sharing the table of demons" (10:21) applied to burial and commemoration of the dead, then the Christian fellowship would have to provide burial benefits as well. Perhaps such questions arose in that context. Paul does not say anything about the practical questions of burial. Instead he elevates the discussion to a theological plane. What does the gospel of Christ's death and resurrection imply about the final destiny of believers?

Although some interpreters attempt to correlate denial of bodily resurrection with an elite philosophical perspective that privileges an immortal, nonmaterial soul over the body, that distinction does not appear in 1 Cor. 15 (Engberg-Pedersen 2010, 8–32). There is no indication that this question is associated with the various conflicts addressed earlier in the letter. Paul uses a number of rhetorical tactics to present his case, including the hypothetical opponent "someone" to whom he responds in second-person singular "you" (15:35–36). That objection permits him to turn to the question of how resurrection can be understood as bodily. Paul does not appear to be responding to a spiritualizing, gnostic, or Platonic ideology, views often attributed to the opponent. Having learned of uncertainty about the fate of the dead at Corinth (cf. 1 Thess. 4:13–18), he formulates this coda on resurrection eschatology. By concluding with this topic, Paul takes his audience out of their individual conflicts and even their immediate concerns over various sorts of spirituality. God's plan of salvation goes well beyond the earthly, human dimensions of our experience (Mitchell 1993, 137). All things will be transformed at the end time. Believers are raised to participate in the glory of the risen Christ. Death is abolished. Through Christ everything will be subject to God's rule (1 Cor. 15:20–28, 50–57).

Resurrection of the Dead and the God of Israel

The scenario that Paul lays out in 1 Cor. 15 modifies common Jewish beliefs to accommodate the Christian conviction that God has raised Jesus from the dead as "firstfruits of those who have fallen asleep" (15:20). The standard model held that at the end of days, God would revive faithful Israel (Ezek. 37; Levenson 2006, 142–200). This new exercise of God's creative power would restore a bodily existence in which all of God's promises to save his people would be fulfilled (Isa. 25:8). Stories of the Maccabean martyrs, who died

---

Resurrection in Jewish Sources

"And he will destroy on this mountain
the shroud that is cast over all peoples . . . ;
he will swallow up death forever.
Then the Lord God will wipe away the tears from all faces,
and the disgrace of his people he will take away from all the earth."
(Isa. 25:7–8 NRSV)

"Thus says the Lord God: I am going to open your graves, and bring you up from your graves, O my people; and I will bring you back to the land of Israel. . . . I will put my spirit within you, and you shall live, and I will place you on your own soil; then you shall know that I, the Lord, have spoken and will act, says the Lord." (Ezek. 37:12–14 NRSV)

"Be gracious to me, O Lord.
See what I suffer from those who hate me;
you are the one who lifts me up from the gates of death,
so that I may recount your praises. . . .
The wicked shall depart to Sheol,
all the nations that forget God.
For the needy shall not always be forgotten,
nor the hope of the poor perish forever.
Rise up, O Lord! Do not let mortals prevail;
let the nations be judged before you."
(Ps. 9:13–19 NRSV)

"At that time Michael, the great prince, the protector of your people, shall arise. . . . Your people shall be delivered, everyone who is found written in the book. Many of those who sleep in the dust of the earth shall awake, some to everlasting life, and some to shame and everlasting contempt. Those who are wise shall shine like the brightness of the sky, and those who lead many to righteousness, like the stars forever and ever." (Dan. 12:1–3 NRSV)

"When he was at his last breath, he said, 'You accursed wretch, you dismiss us from this present life, but the King of the universe will raise us up to an everlasting renewal of life, because we have died for his laws.'" (2 Macc. 7:9 NRSV)

The Talmud on Those Who Deny Resurrection

"A Tanna taught: He denied the resurrection of the dead. Therefore he shall have no share in the resurrection of the dead. For all the measures [of retribution] of the Holy One (blessed be He!) operate on the principle that the consequences fit the deed." (Babylonian Talmud, tractate *Sanhedrin* 90a; Levenson 2006, 25)

rather than renounce Judaism, included dramatic confessions to this effect thrown in the face of their tormentors (2 Macc. 7). Other Jewish authors picture the righteous raised to angelic, starlike glory (Dan. 12:1–3). Passages from the lament psalms in which God delivers the sufferer from the powers of death of Sheol provided additional confirmation for this belief (Pss. 9:13–14; 40:2; 61:1–4; 88:1–9; Levenson 2006, 36–39). Jonah's deliverance from the belly of the fish (Jon. 2:2–7; Levenson 2006, 42) found its way into early Christian tradition as confirmation that God had raised Jesus (Matt. 12:39–41).

Modern readers often come to the question of resurrection from the perspective of an isolated individual asking the question about what happens to that person after death. The biblical tradition does not put the question that way. It speaks of the larger group to which individuals belong, such as the nation of Israel, the righteous of Israel (as opposed to the wicked), or, as Paul put it in the previous chapter, "the body of Christ" (Engberg-Pedersen 2010, 142). One does not have to puzzle over what happens to the individuals between death and bodily resurrection as long as they continue to be remembered by God or are "written in the book of life." Levenson coined a lovely description for this God who promises ultimate victory and life to the faithful: "He keeps faith with those who sleep in the dust" (2006, 181).

Though many Jews today have forgotten this tradition and ignore its presence in the prayer books, it was taught as orthodox belief by the rabbis (Levenson 2006, 1–22). They employed various arguments to show that even the Mosaic Torah taught resurrection. As the midrash put it, "No passage lacks the resurrection of the dead, but we lack the capacity to interpret properly" (*Sifre Deuteronomy* 32; Levenson 2006, 23). Christians will be familiar with a gospel depiction of Jesus's entry into this debate, finding evidence for resurrection of the dead in Exod. 3:2–6 and 15:16 (Mark 12:18–27). Ask one of the early rabbis what would happen to "some who say there is no resurrection of the dead" (1 Cor. 15:12), and he would have replied that such people have no share in the age to come. Paul agrees with this framework with the additional proviso that incorporation into the body of Christ defines those who participate in the age to come (Engberg-Pedersen 2010, 12).

Corinth was not the only church puzzled by resurrection of the dead. Paul confronted confusion over the fate of believers in Thessalonica who died before the parousia (1 Thess. 4:13–18). Somewhat later false teachers turn up claiming that the resurrection has occurred already (2 Tim. 2:17–18). Evidently non-Jewish converts had as much difficulty assimilating the symbolic and theological framework necessary to make resurrection of the dead intelligible as believers, both Jewish and Christian, do today.

Afterlife and the First-Century Corinthians

What assumptions did the first-century believer bring to the topic of post-mortem existence? Most of the religious activity devoted to the gods and goddesses sought protection, prosperity, and success for individuals, families, and the civic community. Religious festivals were also holidays, occasions for feasting and celebration. They had nothing to say about any future life for the dead or the existence of an immortal soul (Beard 2008, 302). Some religious cults, like the popular Egyptian goddess Isis, provided elaborate rituals of initiation. The devotee might be conducted to the underworld, experience a vision of its gods, and reemerge transformed. Initiates claimed immortality. Even so, scholars remain hesitant to claim that the desire to assure immortality or secure a pleasant afterlife motivated most participants in such mystery cults (Beard, North, and Price 1998, 1:287–90).

Some philosophical schools posited immortality of that part of the human soul or mind capable of grasping eternal truths. Plato invents philosophical myths in which the virtuous philosophical soul comes close to identifying with the divine that it beholds. Other souls eventually reincarnate in lives that are somehow correlated with the wicked or immature character they possessed upon dying (*Phaedrus* 245c–50c; *Respublica* 614b–21d). Cicero's "Dream of Scipio" imagines a glorious astral immortality for the great men of the Roman Republic. Immortality presumes a soul or mind that is separable from the mortal body that it governs. Contemplation of the eternal order of the heavens as well as pursuit of philosophic truth facilitates the transition to immortality (Cicero, *De republica* 6.26–29).

Isis Promises a Devotee Blessings in This Life and the Next

"Know that for the rest of your life until its end you will be obligated to serve me; do not consider that an injury. . . . You will live blessed, you will live gloriously by my tutelage; and when after your allotted life span you descend to the infernal regions, there you will see me in that subterranean firmament shining in the darkness of Acheron and reigning . . . and you will worship me. . . . And if you are obedient to my commands . . . know that I have the power to prolong your life span beyond what the fates ordained for you." (Apuleius, *Metamorphoses* 11.6 AT)

Other philosophical schools disagreed with the Platonic account of soul or mind. A number of variants on the human being as a psychological and physical unity were circulating in Hellenistic philosophy (C. Gill 2006). Some interpreters suggest that the Corinthians would have taken Paul's talk of the spirit (*pneuma*) operating in the body quite literally. For Stoic philosophy, "spirit" is a kind of substance that pervades the entire cosmos. It is "reason" and "mind" as well as what we think of as "matter" in various forms. Hence the question "what sort of body?" do the resurrected have (15:35–40) stems from that point of view. Engberg-Pedersen (2010, 8–32) argues that Paul envisaged the material transformation from a physical to spiritual body in Stoic terms. The divine spirit at work within believers effects what Aristotle would call a substantive change.

These examples show that there is no single understanding of the soul or mind, its relationship to the body, its immortality, or its transition through a postmortem period back to another incarnation. Individual members of the church probably had very different opinions on the subject (Segal 2004, 70–246). Some scholars argue that the more educated, whose views Paul has been correcting throughout the letter, probably accepted some form of Platonism. Their immortal soul invigorated by God's Spirit possesses eternal life. It's the bodily character of resurrection that they deny. To some degree Paul both misunderstands and misrepresents their argument (Wedderburn 1981). But the arguments Paul presents do not appear to be directed at a particular group within the community. Given the considerable evidence for diverse images and concepts concerning the afterlife in the first century AD, Paul's audience probably interpreted resurrection language in diverse ways that do not fall into an elite-versus-populist dichotomy.

How Humans Become Divine: Heroes and Emperors

The triadic formulas that Paul employs in 1 Corinthians recognize Christ as an expression of God, not simply the wise philosopher or the noble Roman of Cicero's dream. However, the tradition associated with the Lord's Supper (11:23–26) points to the human story that ended in a degrading death on the cross. Since their liturgy also called for Christ's speedy return at the end time (16:22b), the Corinthians must have understood the phrase "God raised Jesus from the dead" to mean that Jesus was still alive. What were the options in the religious world of first-century Corinth?

Our closest examples involve divine honors paid to humans after their death. A mythical figure like Hercules died an excruciatingly painful death but was taken up into the heavens as a semidivine being and honored in various cult centers. Similar legends and honors attached to other heroes such as Aeneas (Klauck 2000, 261–66). Certainly the most famous, as well as notorious, examples stem from the divine honors attached to members of the Roman imperial family (Klauck 2000, 288–314). Legend had it that the comet visible for seven days during the games Augustus held in honor of Julius Caesar proved that the emperor's soul had been taken into heaven (Suetonius, *Julius Caesar* 88). Ovid somewhat ironically comments that neither his triumphs nor his comet made Julius Caesar divine; that honor goes to Augustus (*Metamorphoses* 15.745–51). Clearly people were not naïve about the political value of the emperor cult. Jews would soon find themselves embroiled in conflict over an emperor's demand that his statue be erected in the sacred precincts of the Jerusalem temple. And within a few decades Christians could be executed for refusing to offer incense before the emperor's statue. But Paul still considers imperial authority benign, permitted by God to order human society (Rom. 13:1–7). It would be easy enough for his converts in these romanized cities to imagine the risen Christ as a divinized human comparable to the emperor. By the time Paul brings his eschatological vision to its triumphant climax, the exalted Lord is far above any emperor, having defeated even death itself (1 Cor. 15:51–57).

Paul opens this section of the letter that establishes the resurrection of Jesus as the principle of Christian faith with rhetorical appeals to established tradition, early eyewitnesses, his own experience, and the unanimity of apostolic preaching (15:1–11). Whatever inappropriate distinctions the Corinthians were drawing between apostles (1:10–17), they cannot point to any difference on this principle (15:11). Paul does not indicate the reason for introducing the topic of resurrection until 15:12. It begins a sequence of hypothetical clauses that runs through 15:19: if x is (is not) true, then y is impossible or foolish. Each if-clause picks up from the previous sentence, as with 15:12: "If Christ is preached." First Corinthians 15:19 brings the sequence to a conclusion comparable to the "when you're dead, you're dead" tombstone epitaphs.

A new stage in the argument begins at 15:20, which associates the resurrection of Christ and the fate of deceased Christians. A series of temporal clauses highlights the ordered series of eschatological events from the resurrection of Christ through that of believers to the final subjection of all things under God (15:20, 23–28). A brief digression on Adam and Christ (15:21–22; Dunn 1996, 107–8) has been incorporated into the chain. Paul will return to the Adam/Christ comparison in the subsequent treatment of resurrected bodies (15:45–49). Before continuing with that substantive argument, Paul inserts another collection of absurdities (15:29–32). Neither customs followed by the Corinthians nor his own apostolic hardships make sense if the dead are not raised. Paul rounds off this section with a somewhat disjointed moral exhortation (15:33–34).

A fictional interrogator introduces the next major turn in the argument: what sort of body do the resurrected possess (15:35)? That topic dominates the rest of the chapter (15:35–57), which once again concludes with a brief word of exhortation (15:58). This section falls into two distinct subdivisions.

The first addresses the problem of "what sort of body?" directly, providing distinct arguments for the possibility of a spiritual or heavenly body that is eternal. Creation itself is evidence for distinct types of body, earthly and heavenly (15:35–41). It also supports the transformation of dead bodily material into living plants in the case of seeds. Therefore the hypothetical question is stupid (15:36). Applying that analogy to resurrection of the dead preserves a form of continuity between the earthy body that is buried and the spiritual one that is raised (15:42–49). Paul provides scriptural support for this conclusion by distinguishing the Adam of Gen. 2:7 from Christ, the last Adam, a life-giving spirit (1 Cor. 15:45–47). Finally Paul returns to the place of resurrection in God's eschatological timetable (15:50–57): "I am saying this, brothers" (15:50); "look, I am telling you a mystery" (15:51). In this connection, transformation from mortal flesh to an incorruptible form is required to participate in the kingdom of God and represents the decisive victory over sin and death, which God bestows on the faithful (15:50, 57; Hurtado 2003, 170).

Tracing the Train of Thought

This section of 1 Corinthians is a self-contained sample of deliberative rhetoric (Schrage 2001, 10). Paul begins as though everything the Corinthians have believed, and with that their very salvation, is at risk (15:1–2). Thus the audience has a heightened sense that what follows is of critical importance. Although Paul is able to negotiate the tension between apostolic weakness and future glory with the Lord (4:1–13), his audience is not. Some believers who claim to be "the wise" or "the spiritual ones" need reminding that all the gifts of the Spirit that Christians experience now are not evidence of perfection but support our partial knowledge until the last day (1:7–8; 13:8–13). Therefore Paul incorporates the resurrection into the larger scenario of the end-time resurrection of the dead and the establishment of God's universal rule (Schrage 2001, 9).

It is difficult to tell whether the questions about resurrection involve the entire community or only "some among you" (15:12). As we have seen, there is sufficient evidence to suggest a widespread concern for burial and commemoration of the dead, apart from the more limited mystery cult initiations or philosophical instruction. The latter options are limited to the elite. Citing comparable problems in 1 Thess. 4:13–18, D. Martin suggests that Paul himself is to blame for confusion over the death of believers. He did not treat resurrection of the body in his instruction of new converts (1995, 120). Perhaps the Jewish views of resurrection surveyed above were so ingrained in Paul as a Pharisee that he did not anticipate the problems of non-Jewish converts.

1 Corinthians 15:1–58 in the Rhetorical Flow

The letter opening (1:1–9)

Against divisions: God's wisdom (1:10–2:16)

Against divisions: Paul and Apollos as *exempla* (3:1–4:21)

Reports about unholy conduct among believers (5:1–6:20)

Questions in a letter from Corinth (7:1–11:1)

Problems in the community assembled for worship (11:2–14:40)

▶ **Reports that some deny the resurrection (15:1–58)**

    Resurrection as apostolic preaching and faith (15:1–11)

        Resurrection and the gospel (15:1–3a)

        Resurrection as received tradition (15:3b–5)

        Additional witnesses to the resurrection (15:6–8)

        Resurrection as the basis for apostleship (15:9–11)

    Christ's resurrection and the fate of believers (15:12–19)

    God's plan: From the resurrection of Christ to the end time (15:20–28)

    Absurdity of denying the resurrection (15:29–34)

    Dialogue: Replies to a hypothetical opponent (15:35–49)

        Distinction between resurrected body and material bodies (15:35–41)

        Transformation of material bodies into spiritual ones (15:42–44a)

        Adam and Christ comparison (15:44b–49)

    Resurrection and God's plan for the end time (15:50–58)

        Transformation of all believers, living and dead (15:50–53)

        God's victory over sin and death (15:54–57)

        Concluding exhortation to perseverance (15:58)

Resurrection as Apostolic Preaching and Faith (15:1–11)

15:1–3a. Paul pounds the opening point home with four short phrases: the gospel [*to euangelion*] that I preached [*euēngelisamēn*], and that you received, and in which you stand firm, and through which you are being saved (15:1–2a). He has rallied the audience to his side before engaging the question at hand. But the sentence concludes with a note of uncertainty. Perhaps the reception is not as secure: **unless you believed in vain** (15:2c). Rhetorically one expects the audience to deny that possibility. Paul, then, introduces the first element of his argument, a tradition that he **received** and **passed on** (15:3a, as in 11:23–25).

15:3b–5. As in the case of Jesus's words at the Last Supper, where Paul added a comment to the formula (11:26), the tradition cited will be expanded. A short set of parallel phrases, each set containing an **according to the Scriptures** expression, represents the initial core:

> Christ died for our sins according to the Scriptures
> and was buried

> and he was raised on the third day according to the Scriptures
> and was seen by Cephas, then by the Twelve

Each clause in the formula poses questions. Expressions that use metaphors referring to Christ's death as **for sin** appear frequently in Paul's letters, though the specific phrase appears only here and in Gal. 1:4. When Paul refers to that death as "on behalf of all" (2 Cor. 5:14), as reconciling humanity to God (2 Cor. 5:18–21), as a sacrifice for sin (Rom. 3:25), he understands the cross as God's initiative, removing sin and the punishment (death) it merits (Gal. 4:4–5; Rom. 8:3; Dunn 1998, 207–33). Paul never, however, cites specific passages from Scripture to support that interpretation of Jesus's death. Exegetes sometimes follow the lead of 1 Pet. 2:22–25 and suggest Isa. 53:5–6, 8–9, 12 LXX as the referent. Without any clear evidence that Jews in this period understood that Isaiah text as indicating the death of a righteous person or martyr as expiation for sin, the proposal remains problematic (Fitzmyer 2008, 546).

Even more vigorous debate swirls around the **and was buried** clause. As noted above, a Jewish picture of resurrection implies being raised up from Sheol, the grave, or the dust. The apotheosis of Caesar from the funeral pyre to heavenly existence would not qualify (Wright 2003, 227–28). Consequently, **and was buried** is the logical preliminary to resurrection underlining the finality of Jesus's death. It is not necessarily evidence that Paul had heard about the empty tomb (Mark 16:1–8a) during his visit with Cephas in Jerusalem (Gal. 1:18; Schrage 2001, 35–37). But such a brief formula cannot be used as evidence against the existence of empty-tomb traditions at this early period either (Fitzmyer 2008, 547). Certainly the biblical images of resurrection imply that to claim "x has been raised from the dead" means that there are no bodily remains of x in the tomb.

The passive **he was raised** designates God as the agent (cf. 1 Thess. 1:10; 1 Cor. 6:14; Gal. 1:1). **On the third day** commonly appears as a chronological marker attached to the resurrection of Jesus in the Gospels and Acts (Matt. 16:21; 17:23; 20:19; Luke 9:22; 18:33; Acts 10:40). It matches the sequence of the early passion traditions, which counts the day of arrest and crucifixion as first, the Sabbath as second, and the discovery of the tomb as third (Mark 16:1–2). The formula may refer to the tradition of Jerusalem appearances on that day (Matt. 28:9–10; Luke 24; John 20:11–23). It is not clear whether **according to the Scriptures** refers to the chronological marker or to the resurrection of Jesus. No strong candidates for **on the third day** exist, though Hosea 6:2 LXX is a popular choice. Another possibility is Jon. 1:17 LXX (cf. Matt. 12:39–40; Schrage 2001, 41).

Luke also reports the tradition that Jesus **appeared to Cephas** (Luke 24:34, which uses his proper name "Simon" rather than the Aramaic nickname). The evangelist may have derived that notice from an early formulaic tradition such as this one. He has no narrative details about that appearance. The addition **then by the Twelve** breaks the symmetry of the formula. The series of additional witnesses consists of a list divided into sections by sequential markers (1 Cor. 15:6–8). Therefore the phrase **then by the Twelve** may also be an expansion of the original formula. Paul likely received the list itself from others, as he never refers to "the Twelve" (Mark 3:14–19; Matt. 10:1–4; Luke 6:13–16) elsewhere (Fitzmyer 2008, 549–50).

15:6–8. Paul continues the traditional list, which will culminate in his own vision of the risen Christ (Gal. 1:16): **five hundred brothers at once, James, all the apostles, last of all also to me.** The reference to **James** the brother of the Lord (Gal. 1:19) and **all the apostles** parallels the initial **Peter, then the Twelve.** Although Luke, writing several decades later, assumes that "the Twelve" and "the apostles" are synonymous (Luke 6:13; 24:10; Acts 1:26; 2:37), the term "apostle" was more broadly used in Paul's day (1 Cor. 9:2; 12:28). He presents his own claim to being a divinely authorized messenger of the gospel as grounded in this vision of the Lord (Gal. 1:17–19). Other traveling missionaries would show up in Corinth claiming to be apostles authenticated by other churches. Paul denounces them sharply as "false apostles" or "apostles extraordinaire" (2 Cor. 11:5, 13) because their lives and teaching do not conform to the crucified Savior as his does (1 Cor. 4:9; 2 Cor. 12:11–12).

It is impossible to correlate each item in the list with accounts of resurrection appearances found in the Gospels. The **five hundred brothers at once** are not to be identified with Pentecost. Nor do we possess any clue concerning an appearance to James the brother of the Lord, though the prominence of James, who was initially second to Peter in Jerusalem and later leader of the church there (Gal. 1:19; 2:1–14; Acts 15:13–21), presupposes such a claim. The Gospels present Jesus's relatives as unbelieving during his ministry (Mark 6:1–4; John 7:1–9). Items in the witness list are joined by the word **then**, which functions to mark items in a series. It need not indicate strict chronological order (Schrage 2001, 51).

When Paul attaches his own experience as **last**, he might have the temporal fact in mind that there are no subsequent appearances. Or he could imply a logical series that is to culminate in his calling to take the gospel to the nations (gentiles), unlike Peter and James, whose efforts are directed at fellow Jews. Paul acknowledges that he has come late to the game by comparing himself to an *ektrōma* (NRSV: "one untimely born"). The term can refer to a premature birth, stillborn child, miscarriage, or abortion. In all the medical examples, it clearly refers to what emerges from the womb dead (Hollander and van der Hout 1996, 227–28). Some exegetes speculate that the word *ektrōma* had been hurled at Paul as a term of abuse. The word was probably taken from the LXX's metaphorical use of the term for the most wretched human suffering (Num. 12:12; Job 3:16; Eccles. 6:3; Hollander and van der Hout 1996, 229–32).

15:9–11. Paul explains the demeaning self-designation *ektrōma* by referring to his own initial response to the gospel: **I persecuted the church of God**

(15:9b; also Gal. 1:13–14; Phil. 3:6; Acts 8:3; 22:4–5; 26:9–11). This dramatic turn from zealous persecutor to an apostle who will suffer anything to spread the gospel demonstrates the power of God's grace: **His grace toward me was not wasted, but I have labored harder than all of them, not I but the grace of God** (1 Cor. 15:10). Paul has compared himself to the other apostles on two fronts: he is unmarried, and he has given up legitimate claims of support to make the gospel available to all, treating his body like an athlete in training (1 Cor. 9). The audience should remember that comparison. Paul is not attacking the apostolic work of those who came before him. Such an inference would undercut the rhetorical climax of this section. All the apostles preach the same message (15:11).

Christ's Resurrection and the Fate of Believers (15:12–19)

15:12–15. The Corinthians obviously did not question the truth of Christ's resurrection, though they may have imagined it as similar to the imperial apotheosis described above. **Resurrection of the dead** as the destiny of all humanity or all believers constitutes the difficulty for some (15:12). Paul opens by insisting that it is absurd to believe "God raised Christ" and deny "the dead are raised" at the same time: **If there is no resurrection of the dead, Christ has not been raised** (15:13). Consequently, Paul presents his audience with the stunning inference that by asking whether and how deceased believers are raised from the dead, the Corinthians are denying the core of their faith and turning the apostles who testify to the resurrection into liars (15:14–15).

15:16–19. Paul intensifies the argument by insisting that a faith without resurrection of the dead is **idiotic** (15:17b). He gives three reasons: **you are still in your sins** (15:17c); **those who have died in Christ are destroyed** (15:18); and **if we have placed hope in Christ for this life only, we are most miserable of all people** (15:19). A hypothetical Corinthian debater could challenge each item in the list. The tradition cited associates forgiveness of sin with the sacrificial death of Christ, not resurrection. So why couple salvation with belief in resurrection as the mode of postmortem existence? There are other options for individual immortality that do not require restoring bodily existence, a fictional opponent might retort. Cultural anthropology shows that societies in which most of the population struggles to secure the bare necessities of life on a daily basis have little interest in or ability to conceive a long-term future (Toner 2009, 15). Paul may be asking for a conceptual stretch that is beyond many in his audience. For most devotees in the temples of ancient Corinth, religious rites were performed so that the gods would assure devotees health and prosperity in this life. Therefore, the mocking tone of Paul's conclusion or tomb inscriptions aside, **having hoped in Christ in this life** (15:19a) would be the default religious orientation. An alternate reading of 15:19 avoids that objection. If **we** refers to Paul and not to believers in general, then the point is comparable to what Paul says in 15:30–31. Paul claims that his personal example of self-sacrifice in imitation of Christ makes no sense if he is not convinced that the dead are raised.

God's Plan: From the Resurrection of Christ to the End Time (15:20–28)

Why does Paul hang on to a Jewish image of the afterlife that causes his non-Jewish converts such perplexity? The reason Paul does so emerges in the eschatological sections of the argument that follows (15:20–28, 50–55). Resurrection of the dead belongs to a larger complex of imagery associated with the end of days. The resurrection and exaltation of Christ mark the beginning of the end. That of believers will occur in association with his second coming to bring all things to their divinely ordained conclusion (1 Thess. 4:13–18; Holleman 1996, 49–94).

15:20–22. First Corinthians 15:20 calls the audience back from the chain of absurdities that concluded "we are the most pathetic of all people" (15:19b) to the creed that **Christ has been raised from the dead** (15:20a). Paul then employs a familiar agricultural image, **firstfruits** (15:20), to link the resurrection of Christ with that of the dead, which still remains in the future. Elsewhere Paul uses familial metaphors to make the same point: Christ is "firstborn" of many brothers (Rom. 8:29) or of the dead (Col. 1:18). Paul consistently accents the bond between Christ and believers (Schrage 2001, 161). As further support for this vision of a corporate identity between believers and Christ, Paul draws an analogy between Adam's responsibility for all humans dying (Gen. 3:17–19; Rom. 5:12) and Christ's offering of life to all (1 Cor. 15:21–22; see Rom. 5:12–21). He will return to the Adam-Christ comparison later (1 Cor. 15:45–49).

15:23–24. Paul spells out a series of events that characterize the end time (15:23–24) and are clarified in the following verses (15:25–28; Lambrecht 1990). For Paul's converts who may wonder what the **parousia** and **the end** are about, he specifies in 15:24b–c their significance with two parallel clauses that begin with **when**:

> when he hands over the kingdom to his God and Father
> when every rule, every authority and power is destroyed

In 15:23 Paul does not pick up on the "all humans" of the Adam-Christ example. Only **those who belong to Christ** are made alive at Christ's parousia. At this point, Paul does not envisage the resurrection of all humanity for judgment (Zeller 2010, 488). The ad hominem argument against Christians dragging one another into court before unbelievers, however, referred to the faithful judging angels (6:3). So the apostle clearly presumes that his audience is familiar with a larger apocalyptic scenario that incorporates a universal judgment. In 15:14 the powers to be destroyed are not human authorities but cosmic and demonic forces that are responsible for the present evils in the world. Therefore Paul is not commenting on the fate of nonbelievers here (Schrage 2001, 163–66).

15:25–28a. Paul's explanation of the previous clause incorporates allusions to two psalms in the phrases **he places all enemies under his feet** (Ps. 110:1 in 1 Cor. 15:25b) and **he subjects all things under his feet** (Ps. 8:6 in 1 Cor. 15:27a–b). The expression **all things** dominates these verses (15:25, 27 [3x], 28 [3x]). Paul inserts the brief identification, **the last enemy is death** (15:26), between the two psalm texts. It takes the reader back to the life-giving Christ of 15:22 (Lambrecht 1990, 149).

15:28b. The story of God's plan of salvation does not terminate with Christ reigning over all things. Paul respects the monotheistic core of Jewish belief (8:6). The Son is always obedient to or under God (3:23b; 11:3). At the end he returns all things to God: **the Son will be subject to the one who subjected all things to him so that God will be all things in all** (15:28b–c). This culmination is not simply an eschatology limited to rewarding (and punishing) humans. Nor is it a variant of the Stoic view that at the conclusion of a cosmic cycle all things return to the undifferentiated, divine *pneuma* from which they emerged (Zeller 2010, 493). This expression has all of creation in view: since creation has suffered the impact of sin, the end of sin and death results in a completely new creation (as in Rom. 8:18–39; Schrage 2001, 184–88). To counter the use of this verse to support Christologies that deny the Son's equality with the Father, the Council of Constantinople (AD 381) added the following phrase to the creed: "His [Christ's] kingdom will have no end" (Zeller 2010, 495).

Absurdity of Denying the Resurrection (15:29–34)

Paul breaks into the discussion with another series of ad hominem arguments against denying resurrection (cf. 15:12–19). The first involves a peculiar baptismal custom (15:29), the second, risks taken by the apostle (15:30–32). The section concludes with a proverbial warning to watch out for the company one keeps (15:33–34) that appears off message, unless it refers to the indefinite **some** of 15:12 or the equally vague **those being baptized** in 15:29.

15:29. A peculiar practice of **being baptized on behalf of the dead** is not attributed to the community as a whole but to some indefinite group: **What are they doing?** There are no indications elsewhere in the epistles or Acts that believers would go through the ritual of baptism into Christ on behalf of deceased persons, which is the interpretation of these verses that follows most naturally from the context in 1 Corinthians (R. Collins 1999, 556–57). Had the Corinthians translated a concern to ensure the afterlife of beloved dead from local cults to some new Christian rite (DeMaris 1995)? If such a funerary baptismal rite was being routinely practiced in Corinth, one would expect Paul to treat it as he did the false allegiance to apostles that had been linked with baptism (1:10–17).

Alternative interpretations of this verse are forced to give the words **baptized** or **the dead** metaphorical meanings that are not used elsewhere in the letter. "Baptized" refers to martyrdom in Jesus's words to James and John (Mark 10:39; Luke 12:50). Some interpreters, instead of treating "the dead" as referring to deceased persons, treat it as meaning "dead things," a negative comment on the body. For example, Philo contrasts the athlete's preoccupation with the body and the philosopher's with beauty and truth found within the soul. The body is a dead thing whose harmful effects on the soul must be restrained (*Legum allegoriae* 3.71–74; Murphy-O'Connor 1981, 532–37). The sense of the slogan, which Murphy-O'Connor presumes was lifted from Paul's opponents, is that the body must be disciplined in order to destroy its passions. Despite such ingenious proposals, the plain sense of the passage remains the most plausible. Likely because they seek to benefit deceased relatives, some persons in Corinth engage in this ritual (D. Martin 1995, 107). To do so would be absurd, Paul remarks, if the dead are not raised to new life in Christ.

15:30–32a. Paul returns to his own example of sufferings endured for the gospel: **Why are we risking danger at every moment?** (15:30). The suffering and humiliation endured by Paul and Apollos served as a rebuke to Corinthians who sought superiority over others (4:6–13). Paul insists that he went beyond other apostles by laboring at a trade to make the gospel accessible to all (9:3–18). His extreme physical sufferings, imprisonments, beatings, hunger, cold, and shipwreck are signs that he is a true apostle (2 Cor. 11:16–29). The Corinthians must recognize that Paul and the other apostles who preach the same gospel (1 Cor. 15:11) are completely convinced of its truth.

The puzzle comes at the end of this list, which suggests that Paul was sent into the arena in Ephesus to face wild animals (15:32). Though a popular means for the elite to exhibit wealth and power or as payback for elevation to civic office, such events were expensive and infrequent. Since Paul was not a trained gladiator, survival would be quite unlikely. Paul does not refer to facing death in the arena in the hardship catalogue of 2 Cor. 11, though he does say that the trials he endured in Asia felt like a death sentence (1:8–11). Again, scholars have sought other explanations. One points to the metaphorical phrase in 2 Tim. 4:17 that speaks of Paul "rescued from the lion's mouth" and the bit of folklore transferred to Paul in the third century about being rescued by a baptized lion. A later scribe's note found its way into our manuscripts or misread an ironic comment that Paul made about his imprisonment at Ephesus. In other words, he was not condemned *ad bestias*, but suppose he had been. What then (D. MacDonald 1980)? Another suggestion turns to magical texts and apocalyptic myths in which lions and other wild beasts represent demonic powers (cf. 1 Pet. 5:8). According to this view, Paul did struggle with wild beasts in Ephesus, but of the human and not of the zoological variety. Luke dramatizes the turmoil that Paul's preaching caused in Ephesus, not least by encouraging people to abandon magic and burn the assorted books associated with it (Acts 19:18–19) and to give up worship of the goddess Artemis (19:27). Once Christians faced danger in the arena, Paul's metaphor was taken literally (Williams 2006).

15:32b–34. This ad hominem digression concludes with proverbial instruction on the futility of life without the hope of resurrection. First, Paul quotes Isa. 22:13 LXX: **we eat and drink, for tomorrow we die** (1 Cor. 15:32). Then without identifying the source, he adds a line from the comic poet Menander (*Thais* frag. 187) that probably circulated as an independent proverb: **Bad company corrupts good morals** (1 Cor. 15:33). His conclusion fits standard ethical preaching calling on the audience to **wake up from your drunken slumber** (cf. 1 Thess. 5:5–11). They cannot take the beliefs of their peers as a guide since **some are ignorant of God**. His conclusion—**I say this to your shame** (1 Cor. 15:34)—fits the genre of harsh rhetoric aimed at ethical reform better than the deliberative tone of this section as a whole. Though these verses appear to be a brief hortatory digression before returning to the theme of his discourse, Paul's audience may have been able to identify persons responsible for the confusion as **bad company** (Zeller 2010, 504).

Dialogue: Replies to a Hypothetical Opponent (15:35–49)

15:35–37. Paul shifts to the rhetorical use of a hypothetical questioner in order to get back to the topic of resurrection. The diatribe style presents an objection that the speaker can reject outright or treat as based on an absurd premise. In this case, the pair of questions can be taken as prelude to an argument opposing belief in resurrection of the body: **What sort of body do they have?** (15:35). Paul will first discuss the second question, **What sort of body?**, in 15:36–49 and then return to an eschatological scenario in replying to the first one, **How are the dead raised?** (15:50–57; Fitzmyer 2008, 585–86). The sharp push-back against the questioner—**you ignorant person, [don't you know that] what you sow does not give life unless it dies?** (15:36)—is characteristic of the genre. The apocalyptic setting for Jewish belief in resurrection never raises the "what sort of body?" question. An appeal to God's creative power suffices to support its plausibility (Schrage 2001, 269–72). Paul makes an attempt to explain the continuity and difference between the seed and the eventual crop by distinguishing **the body that will come into existence** from the **bare seed that happens to be wheat or something of the sort** (15:37).

15:38–41. Paul is not claiming to know how plant growth actually occurs (cf. the farmer in Mark 4:26–29). He falls back on the theological axiom that God the Creator is responsible for the process and the design: **God gives it a body as he wills and to each of the seeds its own body** (1 Cor. 15:38). His shorthand lists of diverse types of body echoes Gen. 1:11–12, 20–27 but divides the types into **bodies found on earth,** all of which incorporate distinct types of **flesh** (1 Cor. 15:39–40), and **bodies that belong to the heavens,** all of which have a distinctive type of **glory . . . for star differs from star in glory**

(15:40–41; cf. Sir. 43:1–10). Scholars often point to the Greek philosophers, who made detailed contrasts between the mixture of elements in the mortal, changeable realm below the moon and the eternal spheres, first those carrying the planets, and beyond that, the sphere of the fixed stars. Those regions have a kind of substance, a mix of fire and spirit or ether distinct from what belongs on earth (Aristotle, *De caelo* 290a9; Plutarch, *Moralia* 928a–29a; D. Martin 1995, 120–21). Paul does not, however, require anything more than the ordered creation of Gen. 1 to make his argument (Fee 1987, 782–83; Zeller 2010, 509–10). Attempts to provide a full-blown philosophical explanation grounded in Stoic physics (Engberg-Pedersen 2010, 17–26) require a terminological and conceptual precision that Paul does not employ. The concluding **star differs from star in glory** refers to the three heavenly bodies of sun, moon, and stars. Since a distinction in heavenly glory remains, Christians from the church fathers (Tertullian, *De resurrectione carnis* 52) to Dante's *Divine Comedy* have seen it as evidence for grades of holiness or love of God among the blessed in heaven.

15:42–44a. Some Jewish images for resurrection refer to the righteous shining like stars (Dan. 12:1–3). By presenting the order of created entities as reaching a climax with the glory of stars, Paul prepares for an analogy to resurrected bodies. As he often does, Paul generates a catalogue of antitheses.

Table 15
Contrasting the Physical and Resurrected Body

Body buried (sown)	Body raised
corruptible	incorruptible
dishonor	glory
weakness	power
animated (*psychikos*) body	spiritual (*pneumatikos*) body

Unlike the contrast between "flesh" and "glory," which differentiated the earthly and heavenly creation in 15:39–41, this set differentiates two types of **body** (*sōma*). Though what is buried cannot inhabit the eternal heavenly regions, what is raised has the attributes appropriate to eternal bodies. One should not treat the terms **spiritual** and **incorruptible** as referring to something that is not a substance. But it is a substance with different characteristics than those we know on earth (D. Martin 1995, 127).

15:44b–49. Paul's initial catalogue of substances left the human among those things God created on earth. Although the seed analogy was intended to demonstrate that the buried dead could be transformed into a kind of heavenly body, that was not the process built into creation. Paul recognizes that his seed analogy is flawed. He states the principle that needs to be argued: **If there is an animated body, then there is a spiritual body** (15:44b).

In 15:21–22 Paul turns to exegesis of the two Genesis accounts of Adam's creation and the Adam-Christ typology to prove his point. Scholars point to exegetical traditions found in Philo as conceptual background for the distinction between an eternal Adam, the perfect human made in the image of God (Gen. 1:27), and the earthly Adam, created out of clay and animated by God's Spirit (Gen. 2:7; Tobin 1983; Sterling 1995, 357–67). In equating the image of God with Jesus raised in glory as the firstfruits of a new creation, Paul must, however, reverse the order in which the spiritual is a heavenly pattern that must exist in the mind of God prior to the creation of earthly entities. Paul insists that **the spiritual is not first but the animated, then the spiritual** (1 Cor. 15:46; Sterling 1995, 359).

The type of exegesis represented in the selections from Philo is motivated by philosophical concerns that are not evident in Paul's treatment (Fitzmyer 2008, 592). The numbering of a **first** and **second** Adam in the biblical text and the distinction between the one made of **clay from earth** and the **heavenly one** (15:47, 49) are possible points of contact. Paul's eschatology, however, requires that the **spiritual** or **heavenly one** be **the last** and be associated with the **life-giving spirit** distinct from the **living soul** given the earthly creature of Gen. 2:7 (1 Cor. 15:45–46). The human being made of earthy elements and animating soul is created second, not first in Genesis. Furthermore the exegetical key to a two-Adam rendering in Philo is the distinction between "image of God" in the first and "living soul" in the second. The former is a perfect, eternal entity; the latter, made of earthy elements, is mortal. From a philosophical perspective, Paul mangles the distinctions. He uses the soul-spirit pairing to distinguish the two (15:45b), puts the **last** or **second** as **human being from heaven** (15:47), and then, contrary to the distinction between Gen. 1:27 and 2:7, employs the term **image** for both. His habit of arguing by generating antithetical parallels generates the concluding antithesis: **image of the one made from clay** and **image of the one from heaven** (1 Cor. 15:49; R. Collins 1999, 569).

The final antithesis advances the argument that Paul is making. Just as all human beings participate in the likeness and mortality of the original Adam, so Christians will share the likeness of the final Adam, the risen Christ (15:48–49). The simplicity of Paul's own argument obscures the mess he makes of philosophical exegesis. If he picked up the categories from an antiresurrection argument advanced by the educated elite at Corinth (Pearson 1973; Sterling 1995), then Paul has perhaps deliberately ignored its distinctions as polemic against these opponents (Schrage 2001, 308). Other scholars protect the apostle from charges of philosophical incoherence by insisting that he is not familiar with the traditions found in Philo (Fitzmyer 2008, 592). The apostle has simply employed terms being used at Corinth to formulate his own innovative reading of the Adam story. It provides the scriptural authority to support a point that is derived not from Genesis but from Paul's Christology. The risen Christ is

Table 16
Philo Parallels to 1 Corinthians 15:44b–47

1 Corinthians (AT)	Philo (AT)
"An animated [*psychikon*] body, a spiritual one" (15:44b)	"There are two species [*genē*] of human beings; the one is a heavenly [*ouranios*]; the other an earthly [*gēinos*] one." (*Legum allegoriae* 1.31)
"The first human Adam became a living soul [*psychē*]" (15:45a)	"By this [Gen. 2:7] he clearly shows that there is a great difference between the human being that is now formed and the one that came into existence according to the image [*eikōn*] of God earlier [*proteron*]." (*De opificio mundi* 134)
—	"The body was made through . . . clay . . . and shaping a human form [*morphē*], but the soul from nothing at all created but from the Father and ruler of the universe, who breathed in, it was nothing other than a divine spirit [*pneuma*]." (*De opificio mundi* 135)
"The last [*eschatos*] a life-giving Spirit" (15:45b)	"A divine spirit [*pneuma*] . . . sent here to assist our race so that although mortal [*thnēton*] in its visible part, it may become immortal in the invisible one. . . . He was created at once mortal and immortal, mortal in respect to the body [*sōma*] and in respect to the intellect [*dianoia*] immortal." (*De opificio mundi* 135)
"But the first [*prōtos*] was not spiritual [*pneumatikos*] but animated [*psychikos*]" (15:46)	"The heavenly human that came into being according to the image [*eikōn*] of God has no share in corruptible, earthly substance [*ousia*] . . . but this mind [*nous*] associated with what is earthly [*geōdēs*] would be corruptible had God not breathed into it a true power [*dynamis*] of life; at that point it becomes a soul [*psychē*], . . . capable of intelligence [*noeran*] and living . . . for it says, 'the human became a living soul.'" (*Legum allegoriae* 1.31–32)
"The first [*prōtos*] human, clay from earth, the second [*deuteros*] human from heaven" (15:47)	"The heavenly human . . . no share in corruptible, earthly substance . . . but the earthly [*gēinos*] . . . from matter [*hylē*] scattered about which he [Moses] called 'clay' [*chon*]." (*Legum allegoriae* 1.31)
—	"That first [*prōtos*] human, the ancestor of our entire race, was created as most excellent in each part, soul and body. . . . For this one was truly beautiful [*kalos*] and good [*agathos*]." (*De opificio mundi* 136)

the **firstfruits** of a new act of creation in which the dead are raised to participate in **the image of the heavenly human being.**

Resurrection and God's Plan for the End Time (15:50–58)

15:50. Before moving on to complete the eschatological scenario, Paul stops to avert a possible misunderstanding of the heavenly body. He does not assume that the philosophical distinctions between earthly, corruptible matter and a heavenly, fire-filled *pneuma* that is eternal are familiar to the audience. He simply evokes items from the earlier antitheses to indicate that nothing of the perishable, earthly elements, that is, the **flesh and blood** parts of the human being, **will inherit the kingdom of God**. This qualification does not presume that the risen believers are disembodied (D. Martin 1995, 128). There is a radical disjunction between bodies as we experience them and that future reality.

15:51–53. The disclosure formula **I tell you a mystery** (15:51a) promises another item in God's plan for the end time. The Corinthians apparently thought that persons speaking in tongues were uttering heavenly secrets or "mysteries" (13:2; 14:2). That usage differs from Paul's apocalyptic terminology, in which **mystery** refers to the end-time scenario. Apostles preaching the gospel disclose "mysteries of God" (2:1; 4:1). Paul treats the crucifixion of Christ as a "mystery" hidden from the powers involved, human or demonic (2:7–8). Although Paul does not identify the source for his knowledge of this scenario, a comparison with 1 Thess. 4:15–18 suggests that he may have early Jesus tradition in mind.

Table 17
End-Time Resurrection of the Christian Dead

	1 Thess. 4:15–18	1 Cor. 15:51–53, 58
Introduction	for we are telling you this as a word of the Lord (4:15a)	behold I am telling you a mystery (15:51a)
Basic affirmation	we who remain alive at the coming of the Lord will not be ahead of those who have fallen asleep (4:15b)	we will not all fall asleep, but we will all be changed (15:51b)
Expanding the scenario	at the shout of command, the voice of an archangel, and the trumpet of God (4:16a)	in an instant, in a blink of an eye, at the last trumpet, for the trumpet will sound (15:52a)
	the dead in Christ will be raised first (4:16b)	and the dead will be raised incorruptible (15:52b)
	then we who remain alive will be snatched up along with them on clouds to meet the Lord in the air (4:17a–b)	and we will be changed (15:52c)
Finality for believers	and thus we will be with the Lord always (4:17c)	for this corruptible [body] must put on incorruptibility and this mortal one put on immortality (15:53)
Transition to exhortation	so that you should encourage one another with these words (4:18)	so that ... you become steadfast, immovable, excelling in the work of the Lord, always (15:58)

Jewish depictions of resurrection as "from the grave" presume that "the risen" have emerged from death. The "died ... was buried ... was raised" (1 Cor. 15:3b–4) of the kerygma and Paul's seed analogy (15:35–41) make the same assumption. That view creates another dilemma. Since the resurrection of believers is tightly bound to the return of the Lord (Holleman 1996), what happens to the living, flesh-and-blood animated bodies? One might conclude that they will have to pass through death. Paul's appeal to a prophetic, Jesus tradition in 1 Thess. 4:13–18 rejects that option based on some form of revelation. His conclusion is not a personal, logical deduction from the previous argument. It introduces a new item of information: **we will not all fall asleep [die] but we will all be changed** (1 Cor. 15:51b).

The **mystery** or revelation concerning the end time is represented by 15:52, which highlights the sudden coming of the end and its consequence for the living: **in an instant, in the blink of an eye, at the last trumpet [Zech. 9:14; Isa. 27:13; 1 Thess. 4:16], for the trumpet will sound and the dead will be raised incorruptible and we will all be changed.** The concluding phrase, **and we will all be changed,** may be Paul's addition to an apocalyptic tradition that simply depicted the emergence of all the dead from the grave on the last day as in Ezek. 37:12: "Thus says the Lord GOD: I am going to open your graves, and bring you up from your graves" (NRSV; cf. Matt. 27:51–53).

15:54–57. The argument comes to a triumphant conclusion. The apocalyptic order in 15:20–28 ended with all things subject to God. This variant highlights the defeat of death, the last hostile power in the cosmos (de Boer 1988, 126–32). The opening image of clothing what is **corruptible** and **mortal** with **incorruptibility** and **immortality** (15:54a) serves to introduce the words of Scripture. A combination of Isa. 25:8 LXX in 1 Cor. 15:54b and Hosea 13:14 in 1 Cor. 15:55 announces the end of death.

Paul attaches an exegetical comment to the word **sting** (*kentron*) from the Hosea citation (15:56–57). Death is not the natural consequence of the elements composing the body, as an Epicurean philosopher might argue, or the separation of an immortal soul from its body, as in Plato. For Paul it is the consequence of sin that itself is reckoned by and exploits God's law (Rom. 5:12–21; 7:7–25; Hollander and Holleman 1993). The defeat of death incorporates in its train the end of sin and its fateful association with the law. This shorthand transition from an existence marked by law, sin, and death to God's gift of salvation in Christ structures the extensive meditation on sin, the law, and new life in the Spirit in Rom. 7:7–8:30 (Schrage 2001, 381–84).

15:58. The final verse shifts from the language of topical instruction to that of moral exhortation: **Be steadfast . . . excelling in the work of the Lord . . . knowing that your labor is not empty.** This final word looks back to the whole spectrum of advice that Paul has given in the course of the letter (R. Collins 1999, 578).

Theological Issues

Paul's treatment of resurrection involves a web of interlocking convictions concerning God's creative power and humans as embodied persons and endowed with God's Spirit, about the death, resurrection, exaltation, second coming of Christ—the end of the world as we know it in God's victorious triumph over death. It insists that an individual's destiny is not personal but shaped by the community to which one belongs. For Paul's audience, that means recognizing both their present obligations as "body of Christ" and their future sharing the divine image of the risen Christ. A Christian life "in Christ" stands between the ordinary, mortal, flesh-and-blood existence shared with all the descendants of that first Adam and the glory of the last Adam.

Throughout the letter Paul has been faced with the challenge of correcting disputes and misunderstanding on fundamental issues of Christian practice and belief. The questions surrounding resurrection in this chapter involve the lack of overlap between the Jewish apocalyptic framework of basic Christian beliefs and the popular philosophic views of bodies, persons, and identity known to his audience. It may be that for the uneducated, resurrection as people dead and buried emerging from the tomb as flesh-and-blood, revived corpses (as in stories of Asclepius [Pausanias, *Graeciae descriptio* 2.26.5; 2.27.4]; Glaucus; Apollonius [Philostratus, *Vita Apollonii* 3.1–2]; or Hercules [Euripides, *Hercules furens* 719]; D. Martin 1995, 122) was just fine. For the more educated elite, such ideas were ridiculous. Paul's solution refuses to opt for the nonembodied, eternal soul that simply takes off for its true home at death. But it also acknowledges the impossibility of introducing the embodied soul as we know it into what is heavenly and eternal. If the hypothesis is true that those whose claims to superior spirituality, which Paul rejected, thought their spiritual experiences were direct examples of such heavenly life, then Paul's disjunction between this age and the eschaton has important implications. For Paul, no human has an entry into the age to come or heavenly reality prior to the eschaton, when all the dead are raised.

Since Paul clearly expects the Lord's return within the near term, he has little reason to speculate about the fate of the dead in the interim. Since Paul is engaged in exhorting believers to live as members of the body of Christ, he pays no attention to such obvious questions as whether the last Adam influenced the destiny of humankind as a whole, just as the first had done. His account applies only to believers. It has no concern about the fate of the wicked. Once all things are subject to God and death has been destroyed, they might vanish or never be raised from the dust at all or suffer some form of divinely ordained eternal punishment. Paul never says. He had given an ambiguous comment on the fate of the man excluded from the community, "handed over to Satan." It could be his "spirit" or God's that is saved on the day of the Lord (5:5).

If the apocalyptic eschatology employed to frame Paul's theological argument for resurrection of the dead remains incomplete in its own terms, its conflicts with other ancient views of cosmology or anthropology are not resolved by Paul's method of antithetical argument. If some Corinthians were as schooled in philosophy as Philo, they would not be impressed. Modern believers face comparable difficulties. Though Paul's apocalyptic eschatology represented a picture of reality widely disseminated among Jews that could be correlated with some elements in philosophy and pagan religions, today it appears as dramatic metaphor or myth.

Since Paul highlighted the discontinuity, one can infer that his answer to the question "how are the dead raised?" serves only to defend God's creative power. After all, that each has its own type of "flesh" or "glory" if the item is sun, moon, or stars has been demonstrated to be false. The entire universe open to human investigation follows the same physics and chemistry. So what once seemed plausible, a kind of body different from earthly ones because it is endowed with divine spirit, does not carry the same persuasive power today. Believers today often find themselves confronted with philosophical arguments against the postmortem survival of a distinctive, individual self. Such arguments appeal to both scientific neuropsychology and debates in analytic philosophy concerning selfhood and embodiment (Johnston 2010).

Though Christians continue to repeat the confession that they believe in resurrection of the dead, many do not accept the Pauline picture of the dead sleeping in their tombs until the final trumpet summons. Thanks to the popularity of "crime scene investigation" television, many people are aware that pathologists have a sophisticated scientific analysis of bodily decay (Vass 2010). Although Paul's plant analogy and transformation language make it clear that the "spiritual body" does not require a one-to-one match with the mortal one, modern medicine weakens the power of the image. Christians are asked to put an organ-donor symbol on their driver's license. Advances in transplant surgery create dilemmas for defining death (Henig 2010). At the same time, success in the field makes it much more likely that individuals will know a transplant recipient.

One might conclude that this multifaceted cultural assault on our traditional images of immortality would erode belief in afterlife among Christians at large. Interestingly, a 2003 survey of Americans shows that belief in some form of afterlife is even more common than belief in God. Eighty-one percent of respondents indicated that they believed in a form of afterlife, with an additional 9 percent responding "probably, but not sure." The majority, 79 percent, agreed with a generic statement compatible with traditional Christian language about heaven and hell: "Every person has a soul that will live forever, either in God's presence or absence" (Johnston 2010, 3).

Most respondents do not think the "transformed bodily person" is alive with God. Instead some immaterial form of the individual has taken off for another region or dimension, where its primary activity is either reunion with loved ones and/or worship of God. Death has no power over that immortal core of humans because it is independent of the body or brain through which it was expressed in this life. That "departure for another dimension of reality" model makes Paul's eschatological framework irrelevant to belief in eternal life. It hardly requires the end of the cosmos as we know it or some new form of eternal bodily existence. This self exists at a level of reality that one cannot grasp completely in this life, as Paul recognizes in distinguishing self-awareness from the truth of the individual known to God (4:3–5; 13:12). Both the dissociation of self-awareness from the body in near-death experiences and advanced meditation techniques seem to provide a taste of consciousness that transcends the shifting patterns, fields, and forces that constitute ordinary reality.

Some Christians choose to believe in an alternate eschatology contrary to the revealed mystery presented in Paul's letters. Many embrace a version of repeated reincarnation until the soul attains enlightenment, a view found in Eastern religions and known in antiquity. Others are persuaded by scientific speculation about the end of the earth, the solar system, or the universe often translated into popular movies (Matson 2010). Paul's audience was also familiar with that option in the Stoic view of a cosmic conflagration. Neither alternative eschatology can be adapted to the Christian belief in resurrection. Both dissolve the critical link between body and the individual called by God to a new form of existence. Reincarnation also relaxes the moral seriousness of the biblical summons to holiness. In short, many believers today are as confused about resurrection as their first-century AD ancestors. For them, Paul's words are akin to an inspiring piece of music or an example of theological poetry.

Paul does not agree with efforts to adopt alternative modes of spirituality or beliefs about the fate of the dead. The mystery of God's plan has the death and resurrection of God's Son at the core of his preaching. God calls all humans regardless of their ethnic, cultural, or gender identities into the body of Christ to share a communal life with others proper to that reality. The image of God expressed in the risen Christ is the proper goal of all human spirituality. At the same time, one cannot formulate a complete description of reality from the diverse ways in which Paul expresses his theological insights, because they are not mutually consistent (Dunn 1998, 314–15). In some cases we lack adequate language to express what Paul is getting at. Resurrection is closely tied to another key element in Paul's theology: participation in Christ. But as Dunn (1998, 409) observes, "Our contemporary concepts of personality are quite inadequate to cope with such a range of imagery and form. How can we speak of Christ as a body consisting of human beings, or subsequently as 'head' of the cosmos, or think of him as somehow 'inside' other individuals and still envisage him as a person in recognizable human form who will return on the clouds?" Paul is not making it up as though he invented a Christ myth. As he reminds us, he has seen the risen Lord and staked his life on that reality (9:1; 15:8–11). He invites his audience to imitate his example. And among the consequences for believers: not a spirituality of mystical insight but one governed by the highest spiritual gift—*agapē*.

1 Corinthians 16:1–24

The Letter Closing

Introductory Matters

Ordinary private letters are much shorter than the long, instructional piece that concluded at 15:58. First Corinthians 16 is of a length similar to such routine communications. After the letter opening, a sender deals with the business at hand, conveys relevant information about travel plans or other persons, and concludes with brief instructions or greetings that the recipient is to convey to others. Paul opens with arrangements for the collection of money to benefit Christians in Jerusalem (16:1–4), describes his travel plans (16:5–9), followed by instructions for a likely visit by Timothy and indication that Apollos will not be coming (16:10–12). The conclusion incorporates some additional comments about members of the community (16:13–18) and greetings from others to them (16:19–21). Just as Paul's letter opening was more ornate than that of an ordinary letter, so the farewell has been expanded with liturgical elements (16:22–24).

The density of proper names also distinguishes this chapter from the rest of the letter. A number of places associated with Paul's missionary efforts (Galatia, Macedonia, Ephesus, Asia Minor) are mentioned along with Jerusalem. In addition to the traveling missionaries Timothy and Apollos, Paul includes greetings from Prisca and Aquila and mentions prominent members of the Corinthian church whom he has recently seen in Ephesus: Stephanas, Fortunatus, and Achaicus. These names make visible the extensive network of ties between the apostle and churches spread from Asia Minor to Greece that are part of his missionary efforts.

A Woman to Her Estate Manager

"Thais greetings to her own Tigrios. I wrote to Apolinarios to come to do the measuring in Petne. Apolinarios will tell you how the deposits and public dues stand; what name they are in, he will tell you himself. If you come, take out six artabas of vegetable-seed and seal them in sacks so that they are ready, and if you can, go up to search out the ass. Sarapodora and Sabinos greet you. Do not sell the young pigs without me. Farewell." (*Papyrus Oxyrhynchus* 6.932, trans. Rowlandson 1998, 236)

Paul's account of an accord between those involved in evangelizing non-Jews and the leaders in Jerusalem, which stated that gentile converts will not be required to undergo circumcision or adopt other Jewish customs, concludes with an agreement to take up a collection for the poor in Jerusalem (Gal. 2:10). No reference to that stipulation appears in the version of events presented in Acts 15:1–29. Some scholars read the verb *mnēmoneuōmen* ("we should remember") as an ongoing attitude toward the poor that was well established in Torah and Jewish piety (Deut. 24:10–22; Amos 8:4–6). Acts 11:27–30 associates Saul and Barnabas with famine relief taken to Jerusalem from Antioch (ca. AD 47). Josephus mentions that Queen Helena of Adiabene, a Jewish sympathizer, also sent famine relief at that time (*Antiquitates judaicae* 20.51–53). The collection that Paul is soliciting from his churches, however, is clearly distinct from a local relief effort tendered by the church in Syrian Antioch. The enthusiasm that Paul says that he had for the project from the beginning is borne out by the energy he devotes to soliciting participation from his gentile converts.

Churches in Galatia (Gal. 2:10; 1 Cor. 16:1), Macedonia (Philippi and Thessalonica; 2 Cor. 8:1; 9:2–3), Corinth (1 Cor. 16:1; 2 Cor. 8:1), and Achaia (2 Cor. 9:2) are involved. In his efforts to revive flagging enthusiasm in Corinth, Paul suggests that the poorer Macedonian churches have been much more generous and willing to complete the task. His involvement in raising money for the poor in Jerusalem seems to have provided an opening for opponents to accuse Paul of financial dishonesty, using the monies to support his own activities (2 Cor. 11:7–11; 12:14–18). Some scholars think that at the end of the day the Galatians dropped out of the effort (Georgi 1991). The Macedonian churches have their own highly regarded representatives to accompany Paul when he delivers the money to Jerusalem. These community members can serve as witnesses to the proper disposal of the funds and as representatives of the flourishing gentile churches to Jewish Christians in Jerusalem (2 Cor. 8:18–22; Betz 1985, 72–76).

By the time Paul writes to Christians in Rome, the collection in Corinth and the province of Achaia has been completed. Paul is setting out for Jerusalem to deliver the collection for the poor there. He presents that gift as an appropriate acknowledgment of the spiritual debt that gentile Christians owe to the Jewish Christians (Rom. 15:25–27). That understanding of the collection distinguishes this effort from a charitable outreach from wealthier communities to struggling Christians elsewhere. Only Jerusalem can occupy the symbolic position of the city from which God's word has gone out to the nations: "For a teaching will go out from me, and my justice for a light to the peoples" (Isa. 51:4 NRSV).

Paul also sees this collection as a concrete sign that despite their differences in origins and religious practices, gentile and Jewish believers belong to a single fellowship. Other theological elements from Paul's apocalyptic understanding of God's plan of salvation might have contributed to the urgency with which Paul views the collection. The wealth of the nations was imagined flowing into Jerusalem at the end time (Isa. 45:14; 60:5–17; Mic. 4:13). Perhaps Paul even hoped that when fellow Jews saw the outpouring of gentile concern for their coreligionists, they would be stirred to "jealousy" (Rom. 11:13–27). In that case, Paul considers his entire missionary effort as part of the events that mark the end time (Dunn 1988, 873–76).

The first half of this concluding chapter (1 Cor. 16:1–12) ties up some loose ends. The two topics introduced with the expression "now concerning," namely the collection (16:1–4) and the possibility of a future visit by Apollos (16:12), seem to be replies to questions put to the apostle. Paul's own plans for a visit to Corinth (16:5–9) were mentioned earlier in the letter (4:19–21; 11:34c), as was his intention to dispatch Timothy as a stand-in for his own presence (16:10–11; 4:17). Though Paul had hoped to visit Corinth fairly soon (4:19), other plans will cause some delay (16:8–9). It seems clear that after Paul's founding efforts, Apollos's preaching had the greatest impact on the Corinthians (3:4–9; 4:6). Paul must be aware that his own delays and his inability to assure a visit by Apollos would come as a profound disappointment. He interjects brief words of encouragement that appropriately conclude: "Conduct all your affairs with love" (16:13–14).

Paul has not mentioned the names of any persons associated with Corinth since the first chapter: Chloe (1:11) and those he remembers baptizing, Crispus, Gaius, and the household of Stephanas (1:14–16). In the final greetings, we learn that the "household of Stephanas" had a major role in supporting the church in Corinth, as they were among Paul's first converts (16:15–16). Furthermore, Stephanas and two others, Fortunatus and Achaicus, whose names indicate freedmen, had brought the Corinthians' letter to Paul (16:17–18). Paul commends them as representatives of the community. A series of brief clauses beginning with the verb "greet" follow (16:19–21). The series culminates with words written in Paul's own hand. A series of liturgical phrases bring the letter to an end (16:22–24). The last words that those in Paul's audience have ringing in their ears reassure them of the apostle's love for all of them.

Tracing the Train of Thought

The nuts and bolts of bringing the letter to a close are like the faded photos of an old family homestead generations ago. Some of the people in the picture cannot be identified. A few details grab one's attention for a few minutes until the album is stored away. Similarly these verses provide a few glimpses into the nuts and bolts of Paul's missionary outreach. They demonstrate the extraordinary achievement involved in establishing a faith that many Christians today take for granted. But unlike many other passages in 1 Corinthians, such as the celebration of love in 1 Cor. 13, these final verses are not on permanent display in Christian worship or study. Before closing the book, note how subtly Paul frames even this mundane section. Once the immediate business of the collection and travel plans are out of the way (16:1–12), love frames the second half of the chapter, first as a reminder to the audience—"Let everything you do be in love" (16:14)—and then as the last words of the entire letter: "My love is with all of you" (16:24).

The Collection for the Poor in Jerusalem (16:1–4)

Paul devoted considerable effort to soliciting funds for poor Jewish Christians in Jerusalem. This gesture is not an annual tax comparable to that sent by Jewish communities to support the Jerusalem temple. Nor is it a response to a particular crisis that had hit the city. Though charity toward the poor was a regular part of Jewish piety, the idea that one should aid persons who are not part of one's own family or city would have been strange to non-Jewish believers. Generosity was embedded in a network of relationships through which donors expected to be repaid in some form: prestige, deference, support for a benefactor in civic office, or the like. For the wealthiest, communal gratitude might take the form of statues and inscriptions. Since it turns out

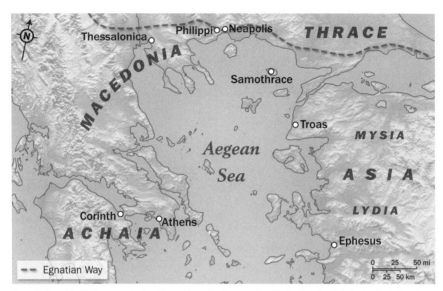

Figure 14. Map of the Mediterranean Region. This map shows the places mentioned by Paul in 1 Cor. 16:5–9, where he indicates his intent to remain at Ephesus until Pentecost and then to pass through Macedonia on his way to Corinth.

that the Corinthians did not respond with enthusiasm, Paul will have to argue the case in subsequent letters (2 Cor. 8–9). He will even engage in some arm-twisting by sending Titus along with representatives from the churches in Macedonia to complete the job. Surely the more affluent Corinthians would not want the embarrassment of a meager offering when poorer churches have been so generous!

16:1–2. All that is in the future. Here Paul sets up a procedure that he has already used **in the churches of Galatia** (16:1). For the final time, he insists on common practices in his widely scattered churches (4:17; 7:17; 11:16; 14:33). Presumably someone whose spiritual gift is "helper" or "administrator" (12:28) would receive the offering that individuals make when the community gathers each week. **On the day after the Sabbath** indicates that the day of the Lord's resurrection is the holy day for Christians. Unlike the Jerusalem temple tax or the dues of private cult associations, which stipulated what members were to pay into the common fund, Paul leaves individuals free to determine the amount (also 2 Cor. 8:11). He would like to have the business wrapped up before he next visits the city (1 Cor. 16:2).

16:3–4. Paul then explains how the money collected will reach Jerusalem. Representatives accredited by the community **through letters** will be sent to convey their **gift [*charis*, a word that also means "grace"] to Jerusalem** (16:3). It is unclear why Paul appears hesitant to state that he will accompany the delegation to Jerusalem himself (16:4). Romans 15:25–26 indicates that he eventually did so.

Travel Plans for Paul, Timothy, and Apollos (16:5–12)

16:5–7. Paul has referred to his intention of visiting Corinth twice (4:19; 11:34). Since he deferred settling some issues about how the church should celebrate the Lord's Supper to that visit, its timing must have been of some concern. A sea route would have taken Paul directly from his current location in Asia Minor (Ephesus) to Corinth (Lloyd 1972). He plans a longer overland journey, however, so that he can visit the churches in Philippi and Thessalonica situated on the road across northern Greece, the *Via Egnatia*. He could have sailed from Troas to Neapolis, picking up the road at that point. Paul has chosen this route rather than heading directly to Corinth by sea because, he says, **I do not wish to see you now in passing because I hope to remain with you for some time** (16:7). Thus, after leaving Ephesus at about Pentecost, Paul will spend some part of the summer visiting the churches in Macedonia and will arrive overland in Corinth in time to **spend the winter** (of AD 54/55?) there (16:6a). The Corinthian church would provide the material assistance necessary for the next stage of his travels the following spring: **that you may send me off wherever I am going** (16:6b). That destination might be Jerusalem with the collection, in which case representatives from Corinth would accompany him, as eventually was the case (2 Cor. 1:16; Rom. 15:25).

16:8–9. Paul adds another reason for delay in his next visit to Corinth. He wishes to take advantage of opportunities for further evangelization at Ephesus: **A great and active door has been opened for me** (16:9a). At the same time, Paul admits that preaching the gospel has provoked opposition in the city, **and many oppose** him (16:9b). Acts 19:21–40 provides a dramatic account of such an incident.

16:10–11. Paul turns to the more immediate representative of his teaching in Corinth, his younger associate, Timothy (4:17; Phil. 2:19; 1 Tim. 1:1–4). Given the conflicts in Corinth, it could be difficult for Timothy to get a hearing in the church. Paul asks the Corinthians to extend the same reception to Timothy as they would to Paul himself, **for he works at the work of the Lord just as I do** (1 Cor. 16:10b). This visit will enable Paul to gain direct knowledge of how this letter has been received as well as of the situation in the church generally. After the visit Timothy will return to Paul: **You send him off in peace so that he comes to me** (16:11). It is not clear whether Timothy is part of the delegation bringing this letter to Corinth or is already en route, visiting the Macedonian churches overland (Acts 19:22).

16:12. Although Apollos built on the churches Paul had started during his founding visit to Corinth (3:5–17; 4:1–13), he is not part of Paul's missionary team as Timothy is. The partisan divisions in Corinth included some who apparently considered Apollos to be an apostle superior to the better-known figures Cephas and Paul (1:10–17; 3:4–7). Paul asserted his unique position in Corinth as its "only father" (4:15). He insists on the harmony between himself and Apollos in their ministry to the community. This note indicates ongoing communication between Paul and Apollos, who must be working in the vicinity of Ephesus. Paul denies any personal responsibility for Apollos's not returning to Corinth: **I have encouraged him to come to you with the brothers many times** (16:12a). Perhaps the Corinthians had instructed Stephanas and the others to raise that possibility. All Paul can report is that Apollos has no immediate plans to visit the city: **he will come whenever he thinks it appropriate** (16:12c).

Exhortation to Persevere in Love (16:13–14)

16:13–14. Paul breaks off to offer a brief word of encouragement, perhaps responding to the disappointment he anticipates in response to what he has just said. Paul exhorts the Corinthians in 16:13 to **remain alert** (1 Thess. 5:6), **stand firm in the faith** (1 Cor. 15:1), **act like men**, and **be strong** (Ps. 31:24). The list evokes the need for believers to stand up against opposition. That posture could be an echo of the combination of opportunity and hostility that Paul faces in Ephesus (1 Cor. 16:9), to which he earlier alluded as though he were sent into the arena as a gladiator confronting wild beasts (15:32a). In concluding, Paul then reminds his audience of the virtue that underlies all Christian activities: **Let everything you do be in love** (16:14; 13:1–13).

Recommendation for the Household of Stephanas (16:15–18)

16:15–16. Jewish synagogues and other private associations had officials charged with practical matters such as determining membership, maintaining order at worship or communal meals, and enforcing penalties. Partisan divisions among Christians may have contributed to Paul's reluctance to adopt a comparable solution in Corinth. This recommendation for the household of Stephanas edges, however, in that direction: **so that you be subject to such persons and to everyone who works together and labors** (16:16). Paul identifies this group as among his earliest converts in the province, **the firstfruits of Achaia** (16:15). He baptized them (1:16). But the basis for this recommendation is not personal ties to the apostle or the priority of being the first. It is their track record of **service to the saints**. This household could be held up as a prime example of using one's gifts, spiritual and otherwise, to build up the body of Christ (12:4–31; Zeller 2010, 541–42).

16:17–18. Stephanas and two others from Corinth are in Ephesus, having brought the letter that Paul received from Corinth. The names of the other two church members suggest slave origins, as they refer to attributes: **Fortunatus** ("Lucky") and **Achaicus** ("someone from Achaia"). Perhaps these two Roman freedmen belonged to the household of Stephanas (Fee 1987, 831). If the group had been traveling to Ephesus on commercial business, the church would have entrusted them with the letter. The expression **they refreshed my spirit and yours** (16:18a) is an indirect way of saying that they also provided

Paul with material resources necessary to his work in Ephesus. Compare the assistance Epaphroditus brought to the imprisoned apostle from Philippi (Phil. 2:30; 4:10–20; Zeller 2010, 542). The concluding exhortation **acknowledge such persons** (1 Cor. 16:18) is parallel to the earlier **be subordinate to such** (16:16). The verb **acknowledge** was invoked in referring to Paul's written instructions concerning prophecy and speaking in tongues (14:37; Schrage 2001, 459). Here it suggests that Stephanas and his associates should be accorded some form of authority in the church beyond the respect and social honor customarily given to benefactors.

Even though Paul himself is not planning to arrive in Corinth until some-time in the fall, he has established three substitute reference points for his absence. The letter itself is the most important. The visit by Timothy will serve to remind church members of how Paul conducts himself, but Timothy is to visit and then return to Ephesus. Finally, the household of Stephanas, founding members of the church, can provide permanent local leadership. Paul (and Apollos) may have thought it best to stay away from Corinth until the partisanship surrounding them (3:5–8) had died down (Mitchell 1993, 293).

Exchange of Greetings (16:19–20)

16:19–20. Greetings are common at the conclusion to letters. Paul formulates two parallel sentences that open with an expression that ties all the churches together, followed by a more specific greeting gesture:

> The churches of Asia greet you.
> Aquila and Prisca along with the church in their house
> greet you in many ways in the Lord.
> All the brothers greet you.
> Greet one another with a holy kiss.

Banished from Rome under Claudius (AD 49?), Aquila and Prisca had emigrated to Corinth, where they hosted Paul in their workshop (Acts 18:1–3). Now they host a house-church community in Ephesus as part of Paul's larger missionary effort. Sometime later, they returned to Rome, where they hosted another house-church (Rom. 16:3–5a).

Paul is employing the literary formula of "*x* sends you greetings" to make a point about unity among Corinth's fractious house-churches (Mitchell 1993, 294). **Greet one another with a holy kiss** (1 Cor. 16:20b) as a ritual gesture of fellowship requires that the elite Corinthians who were going ahead with their own meal wait for and acknowledge the presence of others, for example (11:17–22, 33). Justin Martyr indicates that the kiss had become a set ritual gesture by the mid-second century AD (*Apologia* 1.65.2). Combined with the earlier geographical references in the collection instructions and travel plans, this reference to **churches** (plural) in Asia also reminds the audience that their local church belongs to a much broader network. Both their conduct and welfare are of interest to other **brothers and sisters** whom they have never met (Fitzmyer 2008, 627).

Benediction in Paul's Own Hand (16:21–24)

16:21. Paul adds a personal greeting **in my hand, of Paul**. Scribes were employed to write letters. Romans 16:22 has a greeting from the person who wrote that letter, Tertius. Paul includes notes in his own hand at the end of several letters (Gal. 6:11; Col. 4:18; 2 Thess. 3:17; Philem. 19; Keith 2008). Within the competitive world of the Corinthians, Paul may have done so simply to remind readers that he too belonged to the literate minority (Keith 2008, 54–55).

16:22. Paul shifts back to liturgical expressions. The curse **let him be anathema** attached to **someone who does not love the Lord** could be aimed at any believers who continue the divisions that Paul has rejected ("who divide the church by their self-interests"; Mitchell 1993, 295). But it may have been a formula to exclude nonbelievers from some part of the communal meals. The man whose marriage to his stepmother violated ethical standards was excluded from the church altogether (5:5). An Aramaic phrase, *marana tha* ("come, O Lord"), follows the anathema. The same phrase in Greek occurs at the conclusion to Revelation (Rev. 22:20) and in the final liturgical prayer of *Didache* 10.5–6: "If anyone is holy, let him come. If one is not, let him repent. *Maranatha*. Amen!" (AT).

16:23–24. Paul concludes with a double blessing. The first, **the grace of our Lord Jesus be with you** (16:23), appears in other letters as well (1 Thess. 5:28; Rom. 16:20; 2 Thess. 3:18). The second he may have formulated for this occasion to reinforce his message to the community: **My love be with all of you in Christ Jesus** (1 Cor. 16:24). This last is the only place in his correspondence where Paul speaks of his love for the addressees (Fitzmyer 2008, 631). It both matches the general exhortation in 16:14 and recalls the encomium on love as the greatest spiritual gift in 1 Cor. 13.

If this chapter had a standard letter opening, it might stand on its own as a private letter. Separated from the addressees, an author must settle various affairs, provide others with the authority to act on his or her behalf, give instructions on how to regard such agents, describe his or her situation, indicate travel plans, and convey the greetings of others. The letter would provide useful information about organization and demographics of the Christian movement. Believers assemble in household groups hosted by prominent benefactors like Stephanas and the couple, Prisca and Aquila. The movement has spread from an Aramaic-speaking Jerusalem base through Greek-speaking communities from Asia Minor (northern Galatia) to its capital Ephesus into northern Greece (Macedonia) and down to the Isthmus of Corinth. Its membership was diverse and included former slaves. Believers retain liturgical phrases from the original group in praying for the return of the Lord Jesus.

All of the above underlines the considerable achievements of Paul's apostolic efforts. Since this chapter is not a private letter discovered by archeologists in some archive but the conclusion to a much longer work, we see echoes of earlier topics in these verses. How do these remarks shape one's understanding of the larger project, persuading the Corinthian church to accept Paul's theological and ethical corrections on a number of controversial issues and to adapt to norms at play in the other churches? Read from the perspective of the later tensions in Paul's relationship to the church at Corinth, the problems completing the collection and the disastrous visit (2 Cor. 1:12–2:11) found in 2 Corinthians, each item in the conclusion could suggest uncertainty about the reception of this letter. Paul is distancing himself from the collection for Jerusalem, hoping that the Corinthians will take charge of the project. He and Apollos will keep their distance. At the same time Paul needs to reinforce the authority of his associate, Timothy, and institute local leadership whose commitment to the gospel he trusts, Stephanas and his household. Paul hopes that a natural desire to be well thought of by members of this expansive network of churches will add weight to the changes in behavior and worship that Paul has recommended. But in the end Paul remains uncertain about whether his love for all members of the Corinthian church will be reciprocated.

Of course Paul may not have the foresight of an oracle. Those events in 2 Corinthians are months in the future, and outsiders then exacerbated tensions between the church and the apostle. On the face of it, the final chapter in 1 Corinthians could be read as a sign that Paul is confident in the success of his discourse. If Stephanas, Fortunatus, and Achaicus remained in Ephesus, perhaps to take Paul's letter back to Corinth, Paul may have communicated some or all of his arguments to them. Paul's delays in traveling to Corinth suggest that he is not operating in crisis mode. The substitutes for his own presence will be effective. He expects the Jerusalem collection to be completed before his return. Finally, the Corinthians are not distant relatives. Paul's love for them is reciprocated by those named and unnamed members of the church who are present with him in Ephesus.

Theological Issues

The concrete details of collecting for the poor in Jerusalem, travel plans, and mutual greetings may not rise to the level of theological reflection. But they do illustrate how these scattered and diverse house-churches came to understand themselves as one church. Simply having a single God and Lord Jesus Christ would not create that sense. The many nations, ethnic tribes, and petty kingdoms ruled by Rome continued to be fiercely loyal to their local communities. The many regional variations on the cult of a popular deity like Isis or Asclepius indicate that whatever the common features a cult possessed, devotees in one city or cult association felt no obligation toward worshipers from another city or a different ethnic group. Jewish Christians retained their ethnic and religious ties to fellow Jews even as they acknowledged Jesus as God's anointed. The extent to which the Jewish-Christian community in Jerusalem felt bound to the non-Jewish churches of the Pauline mission remains unclear. The anxieties that Paul expresses in Rom. 15:25–32 concerning the visit to Jerusalem, coupled with the ambivalence he expresses in 1 Cor. 16:3–4 about his own participation in the delivery of the collection, could indicate ongoing tensions between Jerusalem leaders and the Pauline mission. As Sanders (1997, 81) puts it, "For Paul, the definition of who Christians were was *not* the same as the definition given by other Christian leaders . . . Gal. 3.28, 'neither Jew nor Greek.' That is the definition that lies at the heart of formative Pauline Christianity."

The diverse cultural assumptions that have distorted the faith and practice of Christians in Corinth involve behavior that is considered normal in their social context. Paul replies by insisting on such Jewish boundary markers as "no participation in idol cults" and restricting male sexuality to marriage. He has to explain the "not Greek" side of the formula (Sanders 1997, 81). Having broken the profound social bond to their civic or ancestral community by withdrawing from the rituals of sacrifice to the gods, Paul's converts may have been anxious to forge new ones with believers in Jerusalem.

Paul frequently reminds the Corinthians that they are part of a network of churches. The handing on of traditional formulas and some conformity in conduct and belief are part of that unity, but so are the personal ties created by the apostles and their associates, as well as by individuals from a church in one area carrying a letter to another church. When they return to Corinth, Stephanas, Fortunatus, and Achaicus will not only bring the letter that Paul has written in reply; they will also convey information about Christians in the churches around Ephesus. These personal contacts also contributed to an important element of Paul's message that Hvalvik (2005, 126–27) refers to as an "ecumenical horizon." Paul never lets his churches forget that they belong to a larger group. Even in the instructions for the collection issued to Corinth, Paul will involve Galatia and Macedonia. Paul's instructions—whether practical, ethical, or concerning worship—are never just local (4:16–17; 7:17; Hvalvik 2005, 129). The situation of Aquila and Prisca is particularly intriguing. They had been living in Corinth and may have had Paul working alongside them in their common trade when the church at Corinth was founded. At the time 1 Corinthians is penned, they have a church meeting in their house in Ephesus. By the time Paul writes Romans they have returned to establish a house-church community in Rome.

Hvalvik points out that Paul's emphasis on this "ecumenical consciousness" among his churches—and between them and the original Jerusalem community—has important implications for reading his letters. However specific to a local group issues may be, Paul understands his teaching to be representative of what he teaches in all churches. What he teaches in 1 Corinthians, he teaches in the other churches as well (4:17; 7:17; 11:16; 14:33; 16:1; Hvalvik 2005, 136–37). Even 1 Cor. 16, which most resembles a private letter, breaks those boundaries. Paul expected his letters to be passed on beyond the specific church or individual to which they were addressed (Hvalvik 2005, 138).

Paul's own consciousness of being an apostle sent by God to the nations certainly contributed to this emphasis on creating and maintaining the web of relationships between churches scattered from Judea to Rome. Perhaps just as remarkable are all of the individual men and women who worked alongside the apostle to sustain the unity of the churches. They achieve this sense of unity without either a centralized authority or a particularized civic, social, or ethnic identity. The people of God is to be found "with all who call on the name of our Lord Jesus Christ in every place, theirs and ours" (1:2). Christians today must preserve a comparable global and ecumenical consciousness.

Bibliography

Aasgaard, Reidar. 2004. *"My Beloved Brothers and Sisters!" Christian Siblingship in Paul*. Journal for the Study of the New Testament Supplement 256. New York: T&T Clark.

———. 2007. "Paul as a Child: Children and Childhood in the Letters of Paul the Apostle." *Journal of Biblical Literature* 126:129–59.

Anderson, R. Dean, Jr. 1998. *Ancient Rhetorical Theory and Paul*. Rev. ed. Leuven: Peeters.

Arzt, Peter. 1994. "The 'Epistolary Introductory Thanksgiving' in the Papyri and in Paul." *Novum Testamentum* 36:24–46.

Arzt-Grabner, Peter, Ruth Elisabeth Kritzer, Papathomas Amphilochios, and Franz Winter. 2006. *1 Korinther: Papyrologische Kommentare zum Neuen Testament*, vol. 2. Göttingen: Vandenhoeck & Ruprecht.

Ascough, Richard S. 2003. *Paul's Macedonian Associations: The Social Context of Philippians and 1 Thessalonians*. Wissenschaftliche Untersuchungen zum Neuen Testament 2/161. Tübingen: Mohr Siebeck.

Bach, Alice, and Jennifer A. Glancy. 2003. "The Morning After in Corinth: Bread-and-Butter Notes, Part I." *Biblical Interpretation* 11:449–67.

Barclay, John M. G. 1995. "Matching Theory and Practice: Josephus's Constitutional Ideal and Paul's Strategy in Corinth." In *Paul beyond the Judaism/Hellenism Divide*, edited by Troels Engberg-Pedersen, 139–63. Louisville: Westminster John Knox.

———. 1996. *Jews in the Mediterranean Diaspora: From Alexander to Trajan (323 BCE–117 CE)*. Berkeley: University of California Press.

Barrett, C. K. 1998. *Acts*, vol. 2: *Acts xv–xxviii*. International Critical Commentary. Edinburgh: T&T Clark.

Bartchy, S. Scott. 2003. "Who Should Be Called Father? Paul of Tarsus between the Jesus Tradition and Patria Potestas." *Biblical Theology Bulletin* 33:135–47.

Barton, Stephen C. 1986. "Paul's Sense of Place: An Anthropological Approach to Community Formation in Corinth." *New Testament Studies* 32:225–46.

Beard, Mary. 2007. *The Roman Triumph*. Cambridge, MA: Harvard University Press.

———. 2008. *The Fires of Vesuvius: Pompeii Lost and Found*. Cambridge, MA: Harvard University Press.

Beard, Mary, John North, and Simon Price. 1998. *Religions of Rome*, vol. 1: *A History*; vol. 2: *A Sourcebook*. Cambridge: Cambridge University Press.

Betz, Hans Dieter. 1985. *2 Corinthians 8 and 9: A Commentary on Two Administrative Letters of the Apostle Paul*. Philadelphia: Fortress.

———. 2004. "The Gospel and the Wisdom of the Barbarians: The Corinthians' Question behind Their Questions." *Biblica* 85:585–94.

Bjerkelund, Carl J. 1967. *Parakalô: Form, Function und Sinn der parakalô-Sätze in den paulinischen Briefen*. Oslo: Universitetsforlaget.

Boer, Martinus C. de. 1988. *The Defeat of Death: Apocalyptic Eschatology in 1 Corinthians 15 and Romans 5*. Journal for the Study of the New Testament: Supplement Series 22. Sheffield: JSOT Press.

Bookidis, Nancy. 2005. "Religion in Corinth: 146 BCE to 100 CE." In *Urban Religion in Roman Corinth*, edited by Daniel N. Schowalter and Steven J. Friesen, 141–64. Harvard Theological Studies 53. Cambridge, MA: Harvard Theological Studies, Harvard Divinity School.

Bradley, Keith. 1994. *Slavery and Society at Rome*. Cambridge: Cambridge University Press.

Byrne, Brendan. 1983. "Sinning against One's Own Body: Paul's Understanding of the Sexual Relationship in 1 Corinthians 6:18." *Catholic Biblical Quarterly* 45:608–16.

———. 1997. "Christ's Pre-existence in Pauline Soteriology." *Theological Studies* 58:308–28.

Castelli, Elizabeth A. 1991. *Imitating Paul: A Discourse of Power*. Louisville: Westminster John Knox.

Chadwick, Henry, trans. 1998. *Saint Augustine: Confessions*. Oxford World's Classics. Oxford: Oxford University Press.

Champlin, Edward. 2003. *Nero*. Cambridge, MA: Harvard University Press.

Charlesworth, James H., ed. 1983. *The Old Testament Pseudepigrapha*, vol. 1: *Apocalyptic Literature and Testaments*. New York: Doubleday.

Chester, Stephen J. 2003. *Conversion at Corinth: Perspectives on Conversion in Paul's Theology and the Corinthian Church*. London: T&T Clark.

Clarke, A. D. 1993. *Secular and Christian Leadership in Corinth: A Socio-Historical and Exegetical Study of 1 Corinthians 1–6*. Arbeiten zur Geschichte des antiken Judentums und des Urchristentums 18. Leiden: Brill.

Collins, Raymond F. 1999. *1 Corinthians*. Sacra Pagina 7. Collegeville, MN: Liturgical Press.

Connelly, Joan Breton. 2007. *Portrait of a Priestess: Women and Ritual in Ancient Greece*. Princeton: Princeton University Press.

Conzelmann, Hans. 1975. *1 Corinthians: A Commentary on the First Epistle to the Corinthians*. Hermeneia. Philadelphia: Fortress.

Cook, John Granger. 2008. "1 Cor. 9,5: The Women of the Apostles." *Biblica* 89:352–68.

Cribiore, Raffaella. 2007. *The School of Libanius in Late Antique Antioch*. Princeton: Princeton University Press.

Crook, J. A. 1967. *Law and Life of Rome 90 B.C.–A.D. 212*. Ithaca, NY: Cornell University Press.

de Boer, Martinus C. *See* Boer, Martinus C. de.

DeMaris, R. E. 1995. "Corinthian Religion and Baptism for the Dead (1 Corinthians 15:29): Insights from Archaeology and Anthropology." *Journal of Biblical Literature* 114:661–82.

Deming, Will. 1996. "The Unity of 1 Corinthians 5–6." *Journal of Biblical Literature* 115:289–312:

————. 2004. *Paul on Marriage and Celibacy: The Hellenistic Background of 1 Corinthians 7*. 2nd ed. Grand Rapids: Eerdmans.

Dixon, Suzanne. 1992. *The Roman Family*. Baltimore: Johns Hopkins University Press.

Dodd, Brian J. 1995. "Paul's Paradigmatic 'I' and 1 Corinthians 6.12." *Journal for the Study of the New Testament* 59:39–58.

Dunkle, Roger. 2008. *Gladiators: Violence and Spectacle in Ancient Rome*. Harlow, UK: Pearson.

Dunn, James D. G. 1988. *Romans*. 2 vols. Word Biblical Commentary 38a–b. Dallas: Word.

————. 1996. *Christology in the Making: A New Testament Inquiry into the Origins of the Doctrine of the Incarnation*. 2nd edition. Grand Rapids: Eerdmans.

————. 1998. *The Theology of Paul the Apostle*. Grand Rapids: Eerdmans.

Du Toit, Andreas B. 1994. "Vilification as a Pragmatic Device in Early Christian Epistolography." *Biblica* 75:403–12.

Elliott, J. K., ed. 1993. *The Apocryphal New Testament: A Collection of Apocryphal Christian Literature in an English Translation Based on M. R. James*. Oxford: Oxford University Press.

Ellis, J. Edward. 2007. *Paul and Ancient Views of Sexual Desire: Paul's Sexual Ethics in 1 Thessalonians 4, 1 Corinthians 7 and Romans 1*. Library of New Testament Studies 354. New York: T&T Clark.

Engberg-Pedersen, Troels, ed. 1995. *Paul in His Hellenistic Context*. Minneapolis: Fortress.

————. 2000. *Paul and the Stoics*. Minneapolis: Fortress.

————. 2009. "The Material Spirit: Cosmology and Ethics in Paul." *New Testament Studies* 55:179–97.

————. 2010. *Cosmology and Self in the Apostle Paul: The Material Spirit*. Oxford: Oxford University Press.

Engels, Donald. 1990. *Roman Corinth: An Alternative Model for the Classical City*. Chicago: University of Chicago Press.

Fant, Clyde E., and Mitchell Glenn Reddish. 2003. *A Guide to Biblical Sites in Greece and Turkey*. New York: Oxford University Press.

Fee, Gordon D. 1987. *The First Epistle to the Corinthians*. New International Commentary on the New Testament. Grand Rapids: Eerdmans.

———. 1999. "Paul and the Trinity: The Experience of Christ and the Spirit for Paul's Understanding of God." In *The Trinity: An Interdisciplinary Symposium on the Trinity*, edited by S. T. Davis, D. Kendall, and G. O'Collins, 49–72. Oxford: Oxford University Press.

Feldman, Louis H. 1993. *Jew and Gentile in the Ancient World*. Princeton: Princeton University Press.

Fitzgerald, John T. 2003. "Paul and Friendship." In *Paul in the Greco-Roman World*, edited by J. Paul Sampley, 319–43. Harrisburg, PA: Trinity.

Fitzmyer, Joseph A. 2008. *First Corinthians*. Anchor Yale Bible 32. New Haven: Yale University Press.

Fotopoulos, John. 2006. "The Misidentification of Lerna Fountain at Corinth: Implications for Interpretations of the Corinthians Idol-Food Issue (1 Cor. 8:1–11:1)." In *The New Testament and Early Christian Literature in Greco-Roman Context: Studies in Honor of David E. Aune*, edited by John Fotopoulos, 39–50. Leiden: Brill.

Fredriksen, Paula. 2010. "Judaizing the Nations: The Ritual Demands of Paul's Gospel." *New Testament Studies* 56:232–52.

Friesen, Steven J. 2005. "Prospects for a Demography of the Pauline Mission: Corinth among the Churches." In *Urban Religion in Roman Corinth*, edited by Daniel Schowalter and Steven J. Friesen, 351–70. Harvard Theological Studies 53. Cambridge, MA: Harvard Theological Studies, Harvard Divinity School.

Furnish, Victor Paul. 1988. "Corinth in Paul's Time: What Can Archaeology Tell Us?" *Biblical Archaeology Review* 14 (May/June): 14–27.

Gaca, Kathy L. 2003. *The Making of Fornication*. Berkeley: University of California Press.

García Martínez, Florentino, and Eibert J. C. Tigchelaar. 1997. *The Dead Sea Scrolls Study Edition*, vol. 1: *1Q1–4Q273*. Leiden: Brill.

Georgi, Dieter. 1991. *Remembering the Poor: The History of Paul's Collection for Jerusalem*. Nashville: Abingdon.

Gerhardson, Birger. 2003. "Evidence for Christ's Resurrection according to Paul: 1 Cor. 15.1–11." In *Neotestamentica et Philonica: Studies in Honor of Peder Borgen*, edited by David E. Aune, Torrey Seland, and Harl Henning Ulrichsen, 73–91. Leiden: Brill.

Gill, Christopher. 2006. *The Structured Self in Hellenistic and Roman Thought*. Oxford: Oxford University Press.

Gill, D. W. J. 1990. "The Importance of Roman Portraiture for Head Coverings in 1 Corinthians 11.2–16." *Tyndale Bulletin* 41:245–60.

Gillihan, Yonder Moynihan. 2002. "Jewish Laws on Illicit Marriage, the Defilement of Offspring, and the Holiness of the Temple: A New Halakic Interpretation of 1 Corinthians 7:14." *Journal of Biblical Literature* 121:711–44.

Glad, Clarence E. 2003. "Paul and Adaptability." In *Paul in the Greco-Roman World*, edited by J. Paul Sampley, 17–41. Harrisburg, PA: Trinity.

Glancy, Jennifer A. 2002. *Slavery in Early Christianity*. New York: Oxford University Press.

Gleason, Maud. 1995. *Making Men: Sophists and Self-Presentation in Ancient Rome*. Princeton: Princeton University Press.

Gooch, Paul W. 1987. "'Conscience' in 1 Corinthians 8 and 10." *New Testament Studies* 33:244–54.

Gooch, Peter D. 1993. *Dangerous Food: 1 Corinthians 8–10 in Its Context*. Waterloo, ON: Wilfrid Laurier University Press.

Goodman, Martin. 2007. *Rome and Jerusalem: The Clash of Ancient Civilizations*. New York: Knopf.

Harrill, J. A. 1995. *The Manumission of Slaves in Early Christianity*. Tübingen: Mohr.

———. 2006. *Slaves in the New Testament*. Minneapolis: Fortress.

Hartog, Paul. 2006. "'Not Even among the Pagans' (1 Cor. 5:1): Paul and Seneca on Incest." In *The New Testament and Early Christian Literature in Greco-Roman Context: Studies in Honor of David E. Aune*, edited by John Fotopoulos, 51–64. Leiden: Brill.

Hays, Richard. 1996. *The Moral Vision of the New Testament*. New York: HarperCollins.

Henig, Robin Marantz. 2010. "When Does Life Belong to the Living?" *Scientific American* 303 (September): 50–55.

Hock, R. F. 1980. *The Social Context of Paul's Ministry: Tentmaking and Apostleship*. Philadelphia: Fortress.

Holladay, Carl R. 1990. "1 Corinthians 13: Paul as Apostolic Paradigm." In *Greeks, Romans, and Christians: Essays in Honor of Abraham J. Malherbe*, edited by David L. Balch, Everett Ferguson, and Wayne A. Meeks, 80–98. Minneapolis: Fortress.

Hollander, Harm W., and J. Holleman. 1993. "The Relationship of Death, Sin, and Law in 1 Cor. 15.56." *Novum Testamentum* 35:270–91.

Hollander, Harm W., and Gijsbert E. van der Hout. 1996. "The Apostle Paul Calling Himself an Abortion: 1 Cor. 15:8 within the Context of 1 Cor. 15:8–10." *Novum Testamentum* 38:224–36.

Holleman, Joost. 1996. *Resurrection and Parousia: A Traditio-Historical Study of Paul's Eschatology in 1 Corinthians 15*. Novum Testamentum Supplements 84. Leiden: Brill.

Holmberg, B. 1980. *Paul and Power: The Structure of Authority in the Primitive Church as Reflected in the Pauline Epistles*. Philadelphia: Fortress.

Horrell, David G. 1996. *The Social Ethos of the Corinthian Correspondence*. Edinburgh: T&T Clark.

———. 2006. "Domestic Space and Christian Meetings at Corinth: Imagining New Contexts and the Buildings East of the Theatre." *New Testament Studies* 50:349–69.

Horsley, Richard A. 1979. "Spiritual Marriage with Sophia." *Vigiliae christianae* 33:30–54.

Hubbard, Moyer V. 2005. "Urban Uprisings in the Roman World: The Social Setting of the Mobbing of Sosthenes." *New Testament Studies* 51:416–28.

Hurtado, Larry W. 2003. *Lord Jesus Christ: Devotion to Jesus in Earliest Christianity*. Grand Rapids: Eerdmans.

Hvalvik, Reidar. 2005. "All Those Who in Every Place Call on the Name of Our Lord Jesus Christ: The Unity of the Pauline Churches." In *The Formation of the Early Church*, edited by Jostein Adna, 123–43. Tübingen: Mohr Siebeck.

Instone-Brewer, D. 2001. "1 Corinthians 7 in the Light of the Jewish, Greek, and Aramaic Divorce Papyri." *Tyndale Bulletin* 52:225–43.

Jackson, Bernard S. 2005. "The Divorces of the Herodian Princesses: Jewish Law, Roman Law, or Palace Law?" In *Josephus and Jewish History in Flavian Rome and Beyond*, edited by Joseph Sievers and Gaia Lembi, 343–68. Journal for the Study of Judaism Supplements 104. Leiden: Brill.

Jewett, Robert. 2007. *Romans*. Hermeneia. Minneapolis: Fortress.

Johnston, Mark. 2010. *Surviving Death*. Princeton: Princeton University Press.

Keith, Chris. 2008. "'In My Own Hand': Grapho-Literacy and the Apostle Paul." *Biblica* 89:39–58.

Klauck, Hans-Josef. 2000. *The Religious Context of Early Christianity: A Guide to Graeco-Roman Religions*. Studies of the New Testament and Its World. Edinburgh: T&T Clark.

———. 2006. *Ancient Letters and the New Testament*. Waco: Baylor University Press.

Kleiner, Diana E. E. 2005. *Cleopatra and Rome*. Cambridge, MA: Harvard University Press.

Kloppenborg, John S. 2006. "Associations in the Ancient World." In *The Historical Jesus in Context*, edited by Amy-Jill Levine, Dale C. Allison Jr., and John Dominic Crossan, 323–38. Princeton: Princeton University Press.

Klutz, Todd E. 2003. "Re-reading 1 Corinthians after *Rethinking Gnosticism*." *Journal for the Study of the New Testament* 26:193–216.

Knox, Ronald. 1950. *Enthusiasm: A Chapter in the History of Religion with Special Reference to the XVII and XVIII Century*. New York: Oxford University Press.

Konstan, David. 1997. *Friendship in the Classical World*. Cambridge: Cambridge University Press.

Krentz, Edgar. 2003. "Logos or Sophia: The Pauline Use of the Ancient Dispute between Rhetoric and Philosophy." In *Early Christianity and Classical Culture: Comparative Studies in Honor of Abraham J. Malherbe*, edited by John T. Fitzgerald, Thomas H. Olbricht, and L. Michael White, 277–90. Novum Testamentum Supplements 110. Leiden: Brill.

Kyle, D. G. 1998. *Spectacles of Death in Ancient Rome*. London: Routledge.

Lambrecht, Jan. 1990. "Structure and Line of Thought in 1 Cor. 15:23–28." *Novum Testamentum* 32:143–51.

Lampe, Peter. 2003. *From Paul to Valentinus: Christians at Rome in the First Two Centuries*. Minneapolis: Fortress.

Lefkowitz, Mary R., and Maureen B. Fant. 2005. *Women's Life in Greece and Rome: A Source Book in Translation*. 3rd ed. Baltimore: Johns Hopkins University Press.

Levenson, Jon D. 2006. *Resurrection and the Restoration of Israel: The Ultimate Victory of the God of Life*. New Haven: Yale University Press.

Lloyd, Seton. 1972. "Paul in Asia Minor." *Asian Affairs* 59:182–90.

Loader, William. 2005. *Sexuality and the Jesus Tradition*. Grand Rapids: Eerdmans.

———. 2007. *Enoch, Levi, and Jubilees on Sexuality*. Grand Rapids: Eerdmans.

Lombardo, Stanley, and Karen Bell, trans. 1997. "Protagoras." In *Plato: Complete Works*, edited by John M. Cooper, 746–90. Indianapolis: Hackett.

MacDonald, Dennis R. 1980. "A Conjectural Emendation of 1 Cor. 15:31–32; or, The Case of the Misplaced Lion Fight." *Harvard Theological Review* 73:265–76.

MacDonald, Margaret Y. 2000. *Colossians and Ephesians*. Sacra Pagina 17. Collegeville, MN: Liturgical Press.

———. 2007. "Slavery, Sexuality and House Churches: A Reassessment of Col. 3.18–4.1 in Light of New Research on the Roman Family." *New Testament Studies* 53:94–113.

Malherbe, Abraham. 1995. "Determinism and Free Will in Paul: The Argument of 1 Corinthians 8 and 9." In *Paul in His Hellenistic Context*, edited by T. Engberg-Pedersen, 231–55. Minneapolis: Fortress.

———. 2000. *The Letters to the Thessalonians*. Anchor Bible 32a. New York: Doubleday.

Marcus, Joel. 2006. "Crucifixion as Parodic Exaltation." *Journal of Biblical Literature* 125:73–87.

Marshall, Paul. 1987. *Enmity in Corinth: Social Convention in Paul's Relations with the Corinthians*. Wissenschaftliche Untersuchungen zum Neuen Testament 2/23. Tübingen: Mohr Siebeck.

Martin, Dale B. 1991. "Tongues of Angels and Other Status Indicators at Corinth." *Journal of the American Academy of Religion* 59:547–89.

———. 1995. *The Corinthian Body*. New Haven: Yale University Press.

———. 2007. "Paul without Passion: On Paul's Rejection of Desire in Sex and Marriage." In *The Writings of Paul: Annotated Texts, Reception and Criticism*, edited by Wayne A. Meeks and John T. Fitzgerald, 678–88. 2nd ed. New York: Norton.

Martin, Troy W. 2006. "Paul's Pneumatological Statements and Ancient Medical Texts." In *The New Testament and Early Christian Literature in Greco-Roman Context: Studies in Honor of David E. Aune*, edited by John Fotopoulos, 105–26. Leiden: Brill.

Martyn, J. Louis. 1997. *Galatians*. Anchor Bible 33a. New York: Doubleday.

———. 2007. "Paul's Opponents in Galatia." In *The Writings of Saint Paul*, edited by Wayne A. Meeks and John T. Fitzgerald, 235–41. New York: Norton.

Massey, Preston T. 2007. "The Meaning of κατακαλυπτω and κατα κεφαλης εχων in 1 Corinthians 11.2–16." *New Testament Studies* 53:502–23.

Matson, John. 2010. "Laying Odds on the Apocalypse." *Scientific American* 303 (September): 82–83.

McGowan, Andrew. 1999. "'Is There a Liturgical Text in This Gospel?' The Institution Narratives and Their Early Interpretive Communities." *Journal of Biblical Literature* 118:73–87.

Mee, Christopher, and Antony Spawforth. 2001. *Greece*. Oxford Archaeological Guides. Oxford: Oxford University Press.

Meeks, Wayne A. 1974. "The Image of the Androgyne: Some Uses of a Symbol in Earliest Christianity." *History of Religions* 13:189–208.

———. 2002. "The Polyphonic Ethics of the Apostle Paul." In *In Search of the Early Christians*, edited by Allen R. Hilton and H. Gregory Snyder, 196–209. New Haven: Yale University Press.

Meilaender, Gilbert. 1997. "The Venture of Marriage." In *The Two Cities of God: The Church's Responsibility for the Earthly City*, edited by C. E. Braaten and R. W. Jenson, 117–32. Grand Rapids: Eerdmans.

Mitchell, Margaret M. 1992. "New Testament Envoys in the Context of Greco-Roman Diplomatic and Epistolary Conventions: The Example of Timothy and Titus." *Journal of Biblical Literature* 111:641–62.

———. 1993. *Paul and the Rhetoric of Reconciliation: An Exegetical Investigation of the Language and Composition of 1 Corinthians*. Louisville: Westminster John Knox.

———. 2001. "Pauline Accommodation and 'Condescension' (συγκατάβασις): 1 Cor 9:19–23 and the History of Influence." In *Paul beyond the Judaism/Hellenism Divide*, edited by Troels Engberg-Pedersen, 197–214. Louisville: Westminster John Knox.

———. 2005. "Paul's Letters to Corinth: The Interpretive Intertwining of Literary and Historical Reconstruction." In *Urban Religion in Roman Corinth*, edited by Daniel N. Schowalter and Steven J. Friesen, 307–38. Harvard Theological Studies 53. Cambridge, MA: Harvard Theological Studies, Harvard Divinity School.

Murphy-O'Connor, Jerome. 1981. "'Baptized for the Dead' (1 Cor. xv,29): A Corinthian Slogan?" *Biblica* 88:532–43.

———. 1996. *Paul: A Critical Life*. Oxford: Oxford University Press.

———. 2009. *Keys to First Corinthians*. Oxford: Oxford University Press.

Nasrallah, Laura. 2003. *An Ecstasy of Folly: Prophecy and Authority in Early Christianity*. Harvard Theological Studies 52. Cambridge, MA: Harvard University Press.

Nehamas, Alexander, and Paul Woodruff, trans. 1989. *Plato: Symposium*. Indianapolis: Hackett.

Newton, Derek. 1998. *Deity and Diet: The Dilemma of Sacrificial Food at Corinth*. Journal for the Study of the New Testament: Supplement Series 169. Sheffield: Sheffield Academic Press.

Nguyen, V. Henry T. 2007. "The Identification of Paul's Spectacle of Death Metaphor in 1 Corinthians 4.9." *New Testament Studies* 53:489–501.

———. 2008. "God's Execution of His Condemned Apostles: Paul's Imagery of the Roman Arena in 1 Cor. 4,9." *Zeitschrift für die neutestamentliche Wissenschaft* 99:33–48.

Niehoff, Maren. 2001. *Philo on Jewish Identity and Culture*. Texte und Studien zum antiken Judentum 86. Tübingen: Mohr Siebeck.

Oropeza, B. J. 1998. "Situational Immorality: Paul's 'Vice Lists' at Corinth." *Expository Times* 110:9–10.

Osiek, Carolyn, and Margaret MacDonald, with Janet Tulloch. 2006. *A Woman's Place: House Churches in Earliest Christianity.* Minneapolis: Fortress.

Oster, Richard E., Jr. 1988. "When Men Wore Veils to Worship: The Historical Context of 1 Corinthians 11:4." *New Testament Studies* 34:481–505.

———. 1992. "Use, Misuse and Neglect of Archaeological Evidence in Some Modern Works on 1 Corinthians (1 Cor. 7,1–5; 8,10; 11,2–16; 12,14–26)." *New Testament Studies* 83:52–73.

Patterson, Stephen J. 2009. "A Rhetorical Gem in a Rhetorical Treasure: The Origin and Significance of 1 Corinthians 13:4–7." *Biblical Theology Bulletin* 39:87–94.

Pearson, Birger. 1973. *The Pneumatikos-Psychikos Terminology in 1 Corinthians.* Society of Biblical Literature Dissertation Series 12. Missoula, MT: Scholars Press.

Pervo, Richard. 2009. *Acts.* Hermeneia. Minneapolis: Fortress.

Phua, Richard Liong-Seng. 2005. *Idolatry and Authority: A Study of 1 Corinthians 8.1–11.1 in Light of the Jewish Diaspora.* Library of New Testament Studies 299. London: T&T Clark.

Porter, S. E., and T. H. Olbricht. 1993. *Rhetoric and the New Testament.* Journal for the Study of the New Testament: Supplement Series 90. Sheffield: Sheffield Academic Press.

Reed, Jeffrey T. 1996. "Are Paul's Thanksgivings 'Epistolary'?" *Journal for the Study of the New Testament* 61:87–99.

Reumann, John. 2008. *Philippians: A New Translation with Introduction and Commentary.* Anchor Yale Bible 33b. New Haven: Yale University Press.

Rowlandson, Jane, ed. 1998. *Women and Society in Greek and Roman Egypt.* Cambridge: Cambridge University Press.

Sampley, J. Paul. 2002. "The First Letter to the Corinthians." In *The New Interpreter's Bible,* edited by Leander E. Keck, 10:773–1003. Nashville: Abingdon.

———, ed. 2003. *Paul in the Greco-Roman World: A Handbook.* Harrisburg, PA: Trinity.

Sanders, Jack T. 1997. "Paul between Jews and Gentiles in Corinth." *Journal for the Study of the New Testament* 65:67–83.

Satlow, Michael L. 2001. *Jewish Marriage in Antiquity.* Princeton: Princeton University Press.

Schrage, Wolfgang. 1991. *Der Erste Brief an die Korinther,* vol. 1: *1 Kor 1,1–6,11.* Evangelisch-katholischer Kommentar zum Neuen Testament 7/1. Neukirchen-Vluyn: Neukirchener Verlag.

———. 1995. *Der Erste Brief an die Korinther,* vol. 2: *1 Kor 6,12–11,16.* Evangelisch-katholischer Kommentar zum Neuen Testament 7/2. Neukirchen-Vluyn: Neukirchener Verlag.

———. 1999. *Der Erste Brief an die Korinther,* vol. 3: *1 Kor 11,17–14,40.* Evangelisch-katholischer Kommentar zum Neuen Testament 7/3. Neukirchen-Vluyn: Neukirchener Verlag.

———. 2001. *Der Erste Brief an die Korinther,* vol. 4: *1 Kor 15,1–16,24.* Evangelisch-katholischer Kommentar zum Neuen Testament 7/4. Neukirchen-Vluyn: Neukirchener Verlag.

Schütz, John H. 1975. *Paul and the Anatomy of Apostolic Authority*. Cambridge: Cambridge University Press.

Segal, Alan. 2004. *Life after Death: A History of the Afterlife in the Religions of the West*. New York: Doubleday.

Smit, Joop F. M. 1994. "Tongues and Prophecy: Deciphering 1 Cor. 14,22." *Biblica* 75:175–90.

Smith, Dennis E. 2002. *From Symposium to Eucharist*. Minneapolis: Fortress.

Sterling, Gregory E. 1995. "'Wisdom among the Perfect': Creation Traditions in Alexandrian Judaism and Corinthian Christianity." *Novum Testamentum* 37:355–84.

Theissen, Gerd. 1982. *The Social Setting of Pauline Christianity: Essays on Corinth*. Philadelphia: Fortress.

Thiselton, Anthony C. 2000. *The First Epistle to the Corinthians*. New International Greek Testament Commentary. Grand Rapids: Eerdmans.

Thomas, Christine M. 2005. "Placing the Dead: Funerary Practice and Social Stratification in the Early Roman Period at Corinth and Ephesos." In *Urban Religion in Roman Corinth*, edited by Daniel N. Schowalter and Steven J. Friesen, 281–304. Harvard Theological Studies 53. Cambridge, MA: Harvard Theological Studies, Harvard Divinity School.

Thompson, James W. 2003. "Creation, Shame and Nature in 1 Cor. 11:2–16: The Background and Coherence of Paul's Argument." In *Early Christianity and Classical Culture: Comparative Studies in Honor of Abraham J. Malherbe*, edited by John T. Fitzgerald, Thomas H. Olbricht, and L. Michael White, 237–57. Leiden: Brill.

Thompson, Michael B. 1998. "The Holy Internet: Communication between Churches in the First Christian Generation." In *The Gospels for All Christians: Rethinking the Gospel Audiences*, edited by Richard Bauckham, 49–70. Grand Rapids: Eerdmans.

Tibbs, Clint. 2008. "The Spirit (World) and the (Holy) Spirits among the Earliest Christians: 1 Corinthians 12 and 14 as a Test Case." *Catholic Biblical Quarterly* 70:313–30.

Tippett, Krista. 2010. *Einstein's God: Conversations about Science and the Human Spirit*. New York: Penguin.

Tobin, Thomas H. 1983. *The Creation of Man: Philo and the History of Interpretation*. Catholic Biblical Quarterly Monograph Series 14. Washington, DC: Catholic Biblical Association.

Toner, Jerry P. 2009. *Popular Culture in Ancient Rome*. Cambridge: Polity.

Trapp, Michael, ed. 2003. *Greek and Latin Letters*. Cambridge: Cambridge University Press.

Trobisch, D. 1994. *Paul's Letter Collection: Tracing the Origins*. Minneapolis: Fortress.

Turcan, Robert T. 2000. *The Gods of Ancient Rome*. New York: Routledge.

Tyldesley, Joyce A. 2008. *Cleopatra: Last Queen of Egypt*. New York: Basic Books.

Unnik, Willem C. van. 1993. "The Meaning of 1 Corinthians 12:31." *Novum Testamentum* 35:142–60.

Vass, Arpad A. 2010. "Dust to Dust." *Scientific American* 303 (September): 56–59.

Vos, Johan S. 1993. "Das Rätsel von I Kor. 12:1–3." *Novum Testamentum* 35:251–69.

———. 2002. *Die Kunst der Argumentation bei Paulus*. Wissenschaftliche Untersuchungen zum Neuen Testament 149. Tübingen: Mohr Siebeck.

Walbank, Mary E. Hoskins. 2005. "Unquiet Graves: Burial Practices of Roman Corinthians." In *Urban Religion in Roman Corinth*, edited by David N. Schowalter and Steven J. Friesen, 249–80. Harvard Theological Studies 53. Cambridge, MA: Harvard Theological Studies, Harvard Divinity School.

Walker, William O. 1989. "The Vocabulary of 1 Cor. 11:3–16: Pauline or Non-Pauline?" *Journal for the Study of the New Testament* 35:75–88.

Wanamaker, Charles A. 2007. "The Power of the Absent Father: A Socio-Rhetorical Analysis of 1 Corinthians 4:14–5:13." In *The New Testament Interpreted: Essays in Honour of Bernard C. Lategan*, edited by Cilliers Breytenback, Johan C. Thom, and Jeremy Punt, 339–64. Novum Testamentum Supplements 124. Leiden: Brill.

Wedderburn, A. J. M. 1981. "The Problem of the Denial of the Resurrection in 1 Corinthians xv." *Novum Testamentum* 23:229–41.

Welborn, L. L. 1987. "On Discord in Corinth: 1 Corinthians 1–4 and Ancient Politics." *Journal of Biblical Literature* 106:85–111.

———. 2005. *Paul, the Fool of Christ: A Study of 1 Corinthians 1–4 in the Comic-Philosophic Tradition*. Journal for the Study of the New Testament: Supplement Series 293. London: T&T Clark.

White, John L. 1986. *Light from Ancient Letters*. Philadelphia: Fortress.

White, L. Michael. 1990. *The Social Origins of Christian Architecture*, vol. 1: *Building God's House in the Roman World*. Valley Forge, PA: Trinity.

———. 2005. "Favorinus' 'Corinthian Oration': A Piqued Panorama of the Hadrianic Forum." In *Urban Religion in Roman Corinth*, edited by Daniel N. Schowalter and Steven J. Friesen, 61–110. Harvard Theological Studies 53. Cambridge, MA: Harvard Theological Studies, Harvard Divinity School.

White, Robert J., trans. 1975. *The Interpretation of Dreams = Oneirocritica*. By Artemidorus Daldianus. Noyes Classical Studies. Park Ridge, NJ: Noyes.

Williams, Guy. 2006. "An Apocalyptic and Magical Interpretation of Paul's 'Beast Fight' in Ephesus (1 Corinthians 15:32)." *Journal of Theological Studies*, n.s., 57:42–56.

Wimbush, Vincent L. 1987. *Paul, the Worldly Ascetic: Response to the World and Self-Understanding according to 1 Corinthians 7*. Macon, GA: Mercer University Press.

Winter, Bruce W. 1991. "Civil Litigation in Secular Corinth and the Church: The Forensic Background to 1 Corinthians 6.1–8." *New Testament Studies* 37:559–72.

———. 2002. *Philo and Paul among the Sophists: Alexandrian and Corinthian Responses to a Julio-Claudian Movement*. 2nd ed. Grand Rapids: Eerdmans.

———. 2003. "The Toppling of Favorinus and Paul by the Corinthians." In *Early Christianity and Classical Culture: Comparative Studies in Honor of Abraham J. Malherbe*, edited by John T. Fitzgerald, Thomas H. Olbricht, and L. Michael White, 291–306. Novum Testamentum Supplements 110. Leiden: Brill.

Wire, Antoinette G. 1990. *The Corinthian Women Prophets*. Minneapolis: Fortress.

Wright, N. T. 2003. *The Resurrection of the Son of God*, vol. 3 of *Christian Origins and the Question of God*. Minneapolis: Fortress.

Yarbrough, O. Larry. 1985. *Not like the Gentiles: Marriage Rules in the Letters of Paul*. Society of Biblical Literature Dissertation Series 80. Atlanta: Scholars Press.

Zeller, Dieter. 2010. *Der erste Brief an die Korinther*. Meyers Kommentar 5. Göttingen: Vandenhoeck & Ruprecht.

Index of Subjects

Index of Modern Authors

223

Index of Scripture and Ancient Sources

233